Junctures
in Women's Leadership

M000073687

⟨ # Health Care
and Public Health ⟩

JUNCTURES

Case Studies in Women's Leadership
Mary K. Trigg, Series Editor

The books in this series explore decisions women leaders make in a variety of fields. Using the case study method, the editors of each volume focus on strategies employed by the women profiled as they face important leadership challenges in business, various social movements, the arts, public health and health care, and other sectors. The goal of the series is to broaden our conceptions of what constitutes successful leadership in these changing times.

Junctures in Women's Leadership: Social Movements, edited by Mary K. Trigg and Alison R. Bernstein

Junctures in Women's Leadership: Business, edited by Lisa Hetfield and Dana M. Britton

Junctures in Women's Leadership: Women in the Arts, by Judith K. Brodsky and Ferris Olin

Junctures in Women's Leadership: Higher Education, edited by Carmen Twillie Ambar, Carol T. Christ, and Michele Ozumba

Junctures in Women's Leadership: Health Care and Public Health, edited by Mary E. O'Dowd and Ruth Charbonneau

Junctures
in Women's Leadership

$\langle$ **Health Care
and Public Health** $\rangle$

Edited by Mary E. O'Dowd and Ruth Charbonneau

RUTGERS UNIVERSITY PRESS
NEW BRUNSWICK, CAMDEN, AND NEWARK, NEW JERSEY, AND LONDON

Library of Congress Cataloging-in-Publication Data

Names: O'Dowd, Mary E., editor. | Charbonneau, Ruth, editor.
Title: Junctures in women's leadership: health care and public health /
    edited by Mary E. O'Dowd and Ruth Charbonneau.
Description: New Brunswick: Rutgers University Press, 2021. |
Series: Junctures: case studies in women's leadership | Includes
    bibliographical references and index.
Identifiers: LCCN 2020051585 | ISBN 9781978803688 (paperback) |
    ISBN 9781978803695 (hardcover) | ISBN 9781978803701 (epub) |
    ISBN 9781978803718 (mobi) | ISBN 9781978803725 (pdf)
Subjects: LCSH: Health services administration. | Leadership in women.
Classification: LCC RA564.85 .J86 2021 | DDC 362.1082—dc23
LC record available at https://lccn.loc.gov/2020051585

A British Cataloging-in-Publication record for this book is available from the
British Library.

This collection copyright © 2021 by Rutgers, The State University of
New Jersey
Individual chapters copyright © 2021 in the names of their authors
All rights reserved
No part of this book may be reproduced or utilized in any form or by any
means, electronic or mechanical, or by any information storage and retrieval
system, without written permission from the publisher. Please contact Rutgers
University Press, 106 Somerset Street, New Brunswick, NJ 08901. The only
exception to this prohibition is "fair use" as defined by U.S. copyright law.

⊖ The paper used in this publication meets the requirements of the American
National Standard for Information Sciences—Permanence of Paper for Printed
Library Materials, ANSI Z39.48-1992.

www.rutgersuniversitypress.org

Manufactured in the United States of America

Contents

〈   v   〉

Foreword to the Series
Junctures: Case Studies in Women's Leadership

Throughout history, women have always been leaders in their societies and communities. Whether the leadership role was up front
such as hereditary Queens and Clan Mothers, as elected officials, or
as business executives and founders of organizations, women have
participated at the highest levels of decision-making. Yet, up through
most of the twentieth century, we seldom associated the word *leader*
with women. I might even argue that the noun *leader* is one of the
most masculinized words in the English language. When we thought
of leaders, our minds seldom conjured up a woman.

Fortunately, there has been a recent shift in our thinking, our
images, and our imaginations. In the United States, credit may go
to those women in the public eye like Gloria Steinem, Oprah Win-
frey, Cecile Richards, and even Eleanor Roosevelt, who have blazed
new trails in politics, media, and statecraft. Now leadership is beginning to look more gender-neutral. That said, it's important to
remember that, in many parts of the world, women leaders, including prominent feminists, have risen to power more rapidly than
seems to be the case here. I think of Gro Bundtland in Norway, Helen
Clarke in New Zealand, Michelle Bachelet in Chile, and others. These
leaders certainly raise new and interesting questions about linking
feminism with powerful political leadership. We in the United States
also have Sheryl Sandberg to thank for using the word *feminist* in
the same sentence as *leadership*.

Despite progress in the past few decades, women have not reached any kind of rough parity with men in terms of positional leadership— i.e., the form of leadership which is appointed or elected and recognized as powerful and influential in coeducational public life. Women continue to be dramatically underrepresented in all major domains of leadership from politics to Fortune 500 companies, to labor unions, to academic administration, and even in fields where they are the majority like health-care professionals, teaching, or in the arts. Scholars like Deborah Rhode and Nannerl O. Keohane note that, at the rate the United States is going, there will not be a "convergence toward parity" for an additional three centuries. Given the need for outstanding leadership at all levels and sectors of society, and given the huge waste of talent that exists when so many capable women are not encouraged to move into senior leadership positions, we cannot afford to wait for parity even three decades, let alone three centuries!

If we wish to accelerate the process of gender parity in producing leaders in the twenty-first century, what steps might we take and what role can academia play in helping to increase the pool and percentage of women leaders? Historically, women's colleges, according to pioneering research by Elizabeth Tidball and others, graduated disproportionate numbers of women leaders up through the 1970s. More recently, business schools, which were largely male bastions, have educated a share of women leaders.

Today, in interdisciplinary fields such as women's and gender studies, examining the concept of *leadership* and teaching women students to be more effective leaders in a given profession or context is highly contested. For example, *Ms.* magazine noted that, in 2011, "only a handful of the more than 650 women's studies programs at colleges and universities provide practical and theoretical knowledge necessary for the next generation to make a significant impact on their communities and world" as leaders. Many feminists and women scholars have negative associations with traditional ideas of leadership, arguing that the concept is elitist, individualistic, hierarchical, and justifies putting work ahead of family and parenting. Moreover, traditional leadership studies often have failed to take account of structural and contextual frameworks of unequal power and privilege, especially around gender and race. And yet, approaching the study of leadership with a gender-sensitive lens is crucial if we are to make more progress toward a fairer and more just distribution of power and opportunity for women and men alike.

Which brings us to the genesis of this series, Junctures in Women's Leadership. The volumes in the series are designed to provide insights into the decision-making process undertaken by women leaders, both well-known and deserving to be better known. The case studies run the gamut from current affairs to past history. The Rutgers Institute for Women's Leadership (IWL) consortium, a group of nine separate units at the university including Douglass Residential College, the Department of Women's and Gender Studies, and the Center for American Women in Politics, is sponsoring this series as a way to provide new pedagogical tools for understanding leadership which has been exercised by women. Each volume will consist of a dozen or so case studies of leaders in a specific field of endeavor. The focus is not on the woman leader per se, but rather on the context that surrounded her decision, the factors she considered in making the decision, and the aftermath of the decision. Also, even though the series is focused on decision making by women leaders, it is not designed to demonstrate that all decisions were good ones or yielded the results expected.

The series does not promote the notion that there are biologically determined differences between women's and men's decision-making practices. There is no such thing as a "women's" approach to leadership. Nothing universally characterizes women's approaches to leadership as opposed to men's. Neither gender is genetically wired to be one kind of leader as opposed to another. That kind of biologically determined, reductionist thinking has no place in this series. Nor does the series suggest that women make decisions according to a single set of "women's values or issues," though there is some evidence to suggest that once women reach a critical mass of decision makers, they tend to elevate issues of family and human welfare more than men. This evidence, collected by Rutgers University's Center for American Women in Politics, also suggests that women are more likely to seek compromise across rigid ideologies than are men in the same position.

Our series of case studies on women in leadership is not designed to prove that simply electing or appointing women to leadership positions will miraculously improve the standard of living outcomes for all people. Few of us believe that. On the other hand, it is important to examine some questions that are fundamental to understanding the values and practices of women leaders who, against the odds, have risen to shape the worlds in which we all live. The series employs the "case study" method because it provides a concrete, real-life example of a woman leader in action. We hope the case studies will prompt many questions, not the least of which is: what fresh perspectives and expanded insights do women bring to leadership decisions? And, more theoretical and controversial, is there a feminist model of leadership?

In conclusion, the IWL is delighted to bring these studies to the attention of faculty, students, and leaders across a wide range of disciplines and professional fields. We believe it will contribute to accelerating the progress of women toward a more genuinely gender-equal power structure in which both men and women share the responsibility for forging a better and more just world for generations to come.

Alison R. Bernstein (1947–2016)
Director, Institute for Women's Leadership (IWL) Consortium
Professor of History and Women's and Gender Studies
Rutgers University–New Brunswick
April 2015

New Foreword to the Series
Junctures: Case Studies in Women's Leadership

The last time I saw Alison Bernstein—director of the Institute for Women's Leadership (IWL), professor of history and women's and gender studies at Rutgers University, and original editor of the Junctures series, which is sponsored by the IWL—was at a launch party for the first two volumes in the Junctures series in the late spring of 2016. Sadly, on June 30 of that year, Alison died. The first volume, *Junctures in Women's Leadership: Social Movements*, which she and I coedited, was published one month before Alison's death. (The second volume, which focuses on women's leadership in business, was published simultaneously.) The day before Alison died, I was visiting the progressive, independent City Lights Bookstore in San Francisco and saw our newly published Junctures volume on the shelf. I texted Alison a photograph of the book because I knew it would please her. Margaret Hempel, one of her former colleagues at the Ford Foundation—where she served first as a program officer, later as director of the Education and Culture Program, and then as vice president for Knowledge, Creativity and Freedom and its successor program Education, Creativity, and Free Expression—described Alison as "a powerful voice for justice" and "a ferocious defender of and advocate for the rights of women and girls."[1] In its illumination of women who led change across a range of contexts, including social movements, business, the arts, higher education, public health, politics, the media, and scholarship, the Junctures in Women's Leadership series carries these feminist and egalitarian impulses forward. It carries them forward as well in its advocacy of gender parity and its message that for women to take their full place as leaders, our expectations and stereotypes about leadership must change.

The Junctures series seeks to redress the underrepresentation of women in leadership positions and to suggest a different kind of future. Although quick to denounce a "women's" approach to leadership, Alison did note that research indicates that once women reach a critical mass of decision makers, they tend to elevate issues of family and human welfare more than men do. In addition, the Junctures series suggests that when women wield power and hold decision-making positions, they transform organizations, ideas, industries, institutions, culture, and leadership itself.[2] Women's lived experiences are distinct from men's, and women's lives collide with history in unique ways. Moreover, the diversity of experience among women further enriches their perspectives. This influences how they lead. For example, women broaden art and museum collections to include more work by women and by artists from diverse backgrounds. This is not insignificant. The arts volume in the series makes a persuasive case for the necessity of women artists and arts professionals in leadership positions to advance gender parity in the arts. "Women leaders make a difference," its editors conclude.[3] Similarly the editors of the business volume determine: "From their [women leading change in business] experiences come unique business ideas and the passion to address women's needs and interests."[4] Each volume, in its way, illustrates this central point.

The Junctures series aims to capture women's leadership in action and at pivotal junctures or moments of decision making. Its goal is to broaden our conceptions of what constitutes successful leadership in these changing times. Our approach is intersectional: we consider gender, race, class, ethnicity, physical and social location, and how they influence access to and the practice of leadership. We wander through time and historical context and consider multiple ways of leading. The authors and editors of each volume conducted multiple interviews with the living subjects, which make this series a contribution to academic scholarship on women's leadership. Collectively, the volumes contemplate the ways that gender conventions influenced how some women have practiced leadership, the pain and impetus of gender and/or racial discrimination and exclusion, and the challenges some women leaders have faced as mothers and primary caretakers of home and children.

We use the format of the case study broadly. Each essay or case study is organized into a background section, which describes the protagonist's rise to leadership and lays out a decision-making juncture or problem, and a resolution section, which traces both the ways the leader resolved the problem or juncture and her legacy. Each volume considers what prepared these particular women for leadership; highlights personal strategies and qualities; and investigates the ways that family members, education, mentors, personal experience with injustice, interaction with social movements, and pivotal moments in history shaped these protagonists' approaches and contributions as leaders in varied contexts. We have sought to cast a wide net and gather examples from the United States as well as around the world (the first three volumes include case studies from Kenya, Nicaragua, South Africa, the United Kingdom, and Laos). Volume editors have had to make difficult decisions about which women to include. Our goal is to offer a rich abundance of diverse examples of women's leadership and the difference it makes, rather than a comprehensive theory about women's leadership or even what feminist leadership might entail. We seek to prompt questions as well as provide answers.

Alison and I stated in the preface to the social movements volume that some of the qualities that fuel leadership include "courage, creativity, passion and perseverance."[5] Alison Bernstein exemplified all of these qualities. "She was wild, clear, and shameless," Ken Wilson, Alison's former colleague at the Ford Foundation, wrote of her.[6] The same could be said of many of the audacious and brave change makers in this series. The IWL sends their stories out into the world to document and preserve them and to educate and inspire faculty, students, and leaders across a range of fields and disciplines. We hope these volumes will inform those who aspire to leadership and apprise those who practice it. Leadership has the potential to forge gender and racial equity, bring about innovative solutions, and advance social justice.

Mary K. Trigg
Faculty Director of Leadership Programs and Research,
Institute for Women's Leadership (IWL) Consortium
Associate Professor, Department of
Women's and Gender Studies
Rutgers University–New Brunswick
February 2021

Notes

1 Margaret Hempel, "Remembering Alison Bernstein," July 11, 2016, https://www.fordfoundation.org/ideas/equals-change-blog/posts/remembering-alison-bernstein/.
2 Lisa Hetfield and Dana M. Britton, eds., preface to *Junctures in Women's Leadership: Business* (New Brunswick, NJ: Rutgers University Press, 2016), xi.
3 Judith K. Brodsky and Ferris Olin, preface to *Junctures in Women's Leadership: Women in the Arts*, ed. Judith K. Brodsky and Ferris Olin (New Brunswick, NJ: Rutgers University Press, 2018), xv.
4 Hetfield and Britton, preface, xiii.
5 Mary K. Trigg and Alison R. Bernstein, eds., preface to *Junctures in Women's Leadership: Social Movements* (New Brunswick, NJ: Rutgers University Press, 2016), xii. This insight is drawn from Linda Gordon, "Social Movements, Leadership, and Democracy: Toward More Utopian Mistakes," *Journal of Women's History* 14, no. 2 (2002): 104.
6 Quoted in Hempel, "Remembering Alison Bernstein."

Preface

Suerie Moon of the Global Health Centre at the Graduate Institute of International and Development Studies in Geneva, Switzerland (the subject of this volume's last case study), has observed: "The power to change the world can often occur when groups of interested players come together around powerful ideas to unite in a common voice for a greater good."[1] Leaders who work as agents for change are required to bring individuals and groups together effectively and move them toward a common goal. This is the kind of leadership that we admire and what binds together the women in these case studies. Several of the women describe themselves as servant leaders focused primarily on the growth and well-being of people and the communities to which they belong.[2] The women present a broad range of individual leadership styles and backgrounds: some are quiet, collaborative, and powerful, while others are outspoken, controversial, and bold; some were privileged at birth, while others were poor. However, they all shared a vision and the determination to use their expertise and experiences to affect change in their immediate community or professional field and then expand their influence to change culture, policy, health systems, and the world.

Our intention is that the case studies in this volume will achieve two concurrent goals. The first goal is to contribute to the Junctures in Women's Leadership series by highlighting interesting and transformational women leaders in the field of health care and public health while illustrating the impact these women have had on individual lives, communities, and social norms. The second goal is to demonstrate a broad definition of population health as an integrated application or practice between the traditionally understood disciplines of health care and public health. The impact of these leaders is best understood through a population health orientation as it encompasses the broader view of what affects the health of a community and how the context of where we live, work, learn, and play can promote or reduce health.

As background for these concepts, the World Health Organization defines health as "a state of complete physical, mental and social well-being and not merely the absence of disease or infirmity."[3] The Centers for Disease Control and Prevention (CDC) Foundation defines public health as "the science of protecting and improving the health of people and their communities," work that "is achieved by promoting healthy lifestyles, researching disease and injury prevention, and detecting, preventing and responding to infectious diseases."[4] According to a growing understanding of the relative impact of major influences on health outcomes, while social, neighborhood, and environmental factors (or the social determinants of health)[5] play the predominant role in predicting outcomes, far more public funding in the United States is dedicated to the health care delivery system, which plays a less influential role.[6] Just as the social determinants of health have a greater presence and impact on health outcomes, public health offers the ability to engage in "almost every aspect of life"[7] but often is underfunded and considered secondary to services offered through health care systems.

We endorse a broad definition of the public health workforce to include everyone engaged in work that creates the conditions within which people can be healthy.[8] These case studies illustrate this perspective on the influential spheres of public health and health care on the workforce and population health. The women profiled in the volume have each worked to improve population health on the local, national, or global level. We purposely engaged women with experience in academia, health care systems or the health care industry, and/or public health to serve as case study authors, for two reasons. First, we wanted authors who could apply their experience to understanding the junctures that these women faced and the impact they made. And second, we wanted authors who could be the subject of a case study themselves.

The case studies span nearly 150 years, from 1872 until the present. The women profiled were educated in an assortment of disciplines, including biology, chemistry, journalism, medicine, midwifery, nursing, and public health. Several of the women in this volume promoted interdisciplinary teams' "venturing beyond one's formal discipline" to improve care or solve a problem.[9] This willingness to draw on ideas in different disciplines is found in feminist research as well.[10] Each woman followed a different path that provided an opportunity for leadership, innovation, and change. Many of the women had executive roles, while others demonstrated leadership through exercising influence in the community; using the media to stimulate public discussion; or engaging in scientific development as a researcher, inventor, or philanthropist. Some of the women served in dual capacities and roles. Consistent with the broad view of what constitutes, contributes to, and affects our health is an understanding of the way in which women influence our health. In terms of numbers, but not necessarily in traditional leadership roles, women often dominate the organizations and environments that create and support health. The women in this volume worked in different settings where they were able to influence social change, including nonprofits, advocacy organizations, communities, hospitals, newspapers, philanthropy, private industry, schools or universities, state or federal government, and as independent consultants. Many of the women faced personal and professional obstacles in the time and culture in which they lived and worked. Race and gender dynamics permeate their stories, and many of the women were engaged in and influenced by American social justice movements such as women's suffrage and civil rights. Therefore, it is not surprising that many of these women were dedicated to the elimination of health disparities, which can be caused by the effects of social determinants of health on particular populations and can stem from sexism and racism within a culture.

At the beginning of this project, we did not anticipate a global public health crisis that would raise awareness of public health professionals and the scientific process. The current global pandemic of COVID-19 has no boundaries and has brought to the fore the challenges facing our country and other nations around the world regarding disparities in health outcomes and the disparate societal impact on subsets of national populations. The authors of a 2020 report on women working in corporate America noted that "women—especially women of color—are more likely to have been laid off or furloughed during the COVID-19 crisis, stalling their careers and jeopardizing their financial security. . . . [M]any mothers are considering downshifting their career or leaving the workforce, and mothers are significantly more likely to be thinking about taking these steps than fathers."[11] Furthermore, the impact of the pandemic—including the shutdown of many structural aspects of society as a strategy to slow or stop the spread of the disease—is also affecting the mental health of women more than that of men. As families continue to experience the closure of schools and child care centers and have to provide the additional support required for children learning virtually at home, data have shown that women, particularly mothers, are reporting negative impacts on their mental health (such as stress, anxiety, and depression) more frequently than men.[12] Additionally, certain racial and ethnic groups across America have been more severely affected by the disease and are experiencing higher rates of hospitalizations and deaths. Public health leaders, researchers, and health care providers continue to grapple with how to better understand and address this disproportionate impact. The causes seem to be a complex array of issues ranging from the social determinants of health (including housing, work environments, and education level), as well as preexisting higher burdens of chronic diseases such as diabetes, among racial and ethnic minorities in addition to other factors such as access to health care and the effects of implicit bias.[13] This reiterates the importance of a multifaceted approach in acknowledging, understanding, and addressing the issues and impacts of gender and race in society.

This volume presents a range of approaches to addressing health problems. Several themes emerge throughout the case studies. The studies are not presented chronologically, but in an order that allows

Timeline of Significant Events

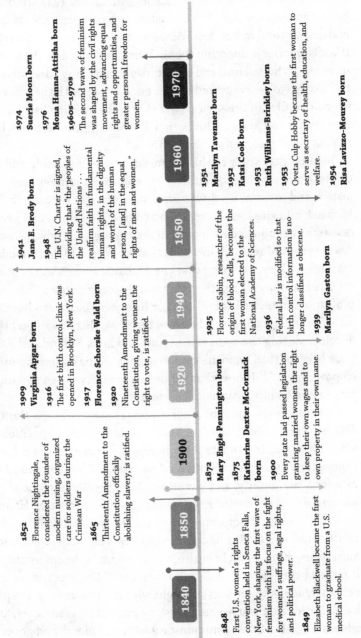

1840

1848
First U.S. women's rights convention held in Seneca Falls, New York, shaping the first wave of feminism with its focus on the fight for women's suffrage, legal rights, and political power.

1849
Elizabeth Blackwell became the first woman to graduate from a U.S. medical school.

1850

1852
Florence Nightingale, considered the founder of modern nursing, organized care for soldiers during the Crimean War

1865
Thirteenth Amendment to the Constitution, officially abolishing slavery, is ratified.

1872
Mary Engle Pennington born

1875
Katharine Dexter McCormick born

1900

1900
Every state had passed legislation granting married women the right to keep their own wages and to own property in their own name.

1909
Virginia Apgar born

1916
The first birth control clinic was opened in Brooklyn, New York.

1917
Florence Schorske Wald born

1920

1920
Nineteenth Amendment to the Constitution, giving women the right to vote, is ratified.

1925
Florence Sabin, researcher of the origin of blood cells, becomes the first woman elected to the National Academy of Sciences.

1936
Federal law is modified so that birth control information is no longer classified as obscene.

1939
Marilyn Gaston born

1940

1941
Jane E. Brody born

1948
The U.N. Charter is signed, providing that "the peoples of the United Nations . . . reaffirm faith in fundamental human rights, in the dignity and worth of the human person, [and] in the equal rights of men and women."

1950

1951
Marilyn Tavenner born

1952
Katsi Cook born

1953
Ruth Williams-Brinkley born

1953
Oveta Culp Hobby became the first woman to serve as secretary of health, education, and welfare.

1954
Risa Lavizzo-Mourey born

1960

1970

1974
Suerie Moon born

1976
Mona Hanna-Attisha born

1960s–1970s
The second wave of feminism was shaped by the civil rights movement, advancing equal rights and opportunities, and greater personal freedom for women.

connections between various themes and allows case studies to build upon one another. It is important to be cognizant of the societal and cultural mores, historical events, legal reforms, and scientific discoveries influencing the circumstances faced by the women included in this volume, and more broadly impacting all women, for the nearly 150 years covered by this book. Along with the years the women profiled in this volume were born, the timeline lists significant events and firsts in this period. Despite these milestones, barriers of class, race, and gender continued.

The first case study in this volume discusses leadership and the connection between women's health, environmental reproductive justice, and community-driven environmental health research. The Mohawk midwife Katsi Cook impacted how environmental health research is conducted in communities through the advocacy and development of research methods that partnered Mohawk women with researchers, ensuring that the Mohawk women were equally included in studying health impacts on their community. This work is akin to feminist observational or interview-based studies that include a strong connection between the researcher and subject that develops during the course of a study and lasts beyond it.[14] Katsi Cook believes that "women's empowerment begins with community empowerment."[15] Her work redefined community-based participatory research with Indigenous communities.

Continuing the topic of environmental justice, Mona Hanna-Attisha, a pediatrician in Flint, Michigan, leveraged her position to assemble a team to validate the community's concerns and publicly expose the city's water pollution crisis. She used her voice to advocate for a community, and her efforts have greatly influenced the national discussion on the negative impacts of lead in water. Hanna-Attisha's parents, Iraqi immigrants, taught her that "challenging injustice meant standing up for the weak, the vulnerable, the abused, and the forgotten—be it in health, employment, or the environment. It means being vigilant on behalf of people."[16] She sees herself as a servant leader and took on this fight with a sense of duty. Despite harsh criticism, she used her skills as a physician, researcher, and advocate to effectively communicate with the media and government officials until action was taken.

Born in 1875, Katharine Dexter McCormick leveraged her privilege and wealth to advocate for women's suffrage and reproductive rights. Ignoring the Comstock Act of 1873, which prohibited the distribution of contraceptives, McCormick smuggled vaginal diaphragms obtained in Europe into the United States for distribution in newly established birth control clinics. This laid the foundation for her philanthropic work more than twenty years later, when she acted as what is now called an "angel investor" in the development of the first hormonal birth control pill available to American women. The availability of affordable birth control was a transformative health care achievement: it was also a critical social determinant of health that held the potential, if available, to impact all aspects of a woman's life. This case study also confronts complicated questions concerning research and vulnerable populations and the relationship between cultural inequities and science.

Continuing with the impact of research, our fourth case study is of Mary Engle Pennington, who earned a PhD in chemistry from the University of Pennsylvania in 1895 without the support of the Board of Trustees—whose members did not accept the idea of a woman being accepted to the university. Her leadership transformed food safety through science, public health, and education. Pennington was persuasive, methodical, and collaborative. It was not unusual for farmers, vendors, and manufacturers who had heard Pennington present her evidence to voluntarily adopt practices to improve food safety. Building on the home economics movement, Pennington promoted the central role of homemakers in maintaining the nutrition and health of the family. She employed women to educate other women about the importance of home refrigeration. Her leadership skills translate to today's environment, as "successful people in nearly every profession have become those capable of convincing others to take action on their ideas."[17]

The research and advocacy work of Katsi Cook and Mary Engle Pennington is separated by more than a century, and the women had dramatically different family and cultural experiences. However, despite this distance there are remarkable similarities in the leadership approach that both took, as they engaged mothers as collaborators and advocated for them as paid colleagues.

Florence Schorske Wald, the subject of our fifth case study, believed that collaboration was a strategy that could transform the model of health care delivery for those at the end of life. Born in 1917 and raised by activist parents, Wald was a highly educated nurse who rose to the position of dean at the Yale School of Nursing. Her belief in social justice guided her to a new path of challenging the way health care professionals delivered medical care at the end of life. Wald envisioned equality among various professionals and insisted upon teamwork and collaboration. In the 1960s, nurses were treated as subordinate to physicians, a fact that was compounded by the gender dynamics of the era. During this time, Wald was introducing a new model of care called hospice, in which the physician was seen not as the leader but rather as a member of an interdisciplinary team of equals, focused on improving care for the dying. In this context, Wald was revolutionary, pushing for health care professionals to collaborate as equal partners as she advocated for cultural and systemic changes in health care.

Our sixth case study is of another woman leader who advocated for changes in health care delivery. In 1949, Virginia Apgar was the first woman to be named a full professor at the College of Physicians and Surgeons at Columbia University, where she laid the groundwork for improvements in maternal and child health as an anesthesiologist through her emphasis on research and evidence-based medicine. Apgar identified the lack of improvement in anesthesia care given to women and newborns as a problem and challenged her colleagues by writing that anesthesiologists had neglected the field of obstetrics. She argued that this contributed to high rates of maternal and infant mortality. She then used her skills and influence as a physician, educator, and researcher to better understand the causes of death and developed the now widely known Apgar scoring system as a prevention tool. Like Wald, Apgar advocated for a multispecialty team approach to caring for patients—in this case, during childbirth—and similar standards in medical and nursing student education. Perhaps partly because of her experience with gender inequities in medicine, she was uniquely qualified to succeed in this effort. Not content to stop there, Apgar leveraged the reputation she had gained from this work into a new role at the March of Dimes, where she focused on the development of a national public health system to track and research birth defects with the goal of prevention. Similar to Pennington, Apgar developed educational campaigns aimed directly at parents to help them understand how to participate in preventing or managing birth defects in their children. The infrastructure that Apgar advocated for remains in place in the United States today. Just as women physicians claimed preventive medicine as their province well before it became fashionable in the years after 1900,[18] several of the women in these case studies focused on prevention to achieve healthier lifestyles.

Prevention is a key element to the work of Marilyn Gaston, the subject of our seventh case study, who created change from within the U.S. government. In 1986, Gaston was the deputy branch chief and deputy director of the Sickle Cell Disease Branch at the National Institutes of Health. She would be the lead author of a study that significantly impacted the management of children with sickle cell disease. Growing up in Ohio, she had faced outright racism and remembered participating in civil rights protests with her godmother to integrate a public swimming pool. Gaston brought this perspective to her work as she initiated the Bureau of Primary Health Care's campaign One Hundred Percent Access and Zero Health Disparities. She was the first Black woman to direct a public health service bureau. Her efforts to expand and improve the network of health centers around the country were aimed at eliminating health disparities due to race, ethnicity, income, health status, or access to care. She believes in a servant leadership philosophy, one that is centered on people and their best interests. Gaston's leadership and personality have been described as joyful, collaborative, and humble. Like Pennington and Apgar, Gaston transitioned her career toward consumer education, and she worked directly with Black women to address preventable health disparities. After writing a book as a practical guide about prevention and health improvement, she created Sister Circles to provide midlife Black women with opportunities to come together in short-term support groups as a strategy to promote wellness and improve the outcomes of chronic disease.

Our eighth case study, Jane Brody, advances the themes of education and prevention through her use of a popular newspaper column.

In 1976, Brody, having changed her focus from research science to journalism, became the first personal health columnist for the *New York Times*. Brody's column covers a wide range of health-related topics intended to educate the public on health and prevention. It created a bridge between physicians and their patients, empowering patients to participate in conversations about health. Her leadership through writing and public speaking combines her boldness, competence, and love for science with femininity and warmth. She broke ground in her *New York Times* column by sharing her personal experiences as a mother and grandmother to be relatable to her readers. Brody's life and work transcends traditional gender character traits and roles. Brody's husband stayed at home to care for their twins in the mid-1960s, which was very unusual then and remains uncommon today: only 7 percent of fathers stay home, versus 27 percent of mothers.[19] Brody writes on a broad range of subjects, producing relevant and timely columns on healthy eating and exercise, flu shots, youth suicide, and the safety of genetically modified foods, among others. Her columns are not without controversy, but she continues to make her case. Brody's gender may have played a role in her interest in prevention and consumer education. A 2013 survey found that "female and minority journalists were more likely than white males to use a variety of sources, and to say it is important to develop the health and scientific literacy of audiences and influence public health behaviors."[20]

Our ninth case study explores how a leader can impact an organization and its role in policy, cultural change, and society. Risa Lavizzo-Mourey, the first woman and the first Black person to serve as the president and CEO of the nation's largest health philanthropy organization, the Robert Wood Johnson Foundation (RWJF), used her role to reshape the American understanding of the intersection of culture and health. Lavizzo-Mourey's parents were both physicians and close friends of Martin Luther King Jr. This gave her an early and intimate exposure to the civil rights movement and the health-care system. Lavizzo-Mourey saw how her mother approached caring for the uninsured in her work as a pediatrician. She knew each of her patients and explained to her daughter that if a patient received a bill but could not pay it because the person did not have health insurance or was out of work, then that patient would not return for needed care. This educated Lavizzo-Mourey early in her life about the factors that could impact health. Leading the RWJF during the passage of the Affordable Care Act (ACA) and its implementation gave her the opportunity to address the issue of the uninsured by providing technical support to states during implementation of the health reform law. But she saw that insurance alone would not achieve better health outcomes.

As the American perspective on health was beginning to shift away from health systems and to communities as the source of health, Lavizzo-Mourey led the RWJF to consider a new strategic plan to reframe the focus for future funding. Her work culminated in a new vision of a culture of health, which emphasizes well-being and the links between health, access, and social justice. She used her quiet but powerful leadership to build a social movement outside the RWJF and guide an internal reorganization fostering multisectoral collaboration. She redirected the power and influence of an organization that funds work in the academic, governmental public health, and private health care sectors.

The successful implementation of the ACA relied on the calm and steady leadership of Marilyn Tavenner, the subject of our tenth case study. Tavenner also had a vision for improved health for Americans through this new governmental program, which she and Howard Koh described as "an unprecedented opportunity to overcome fragmentation and integrate primary care and public health."[21] The ACA was intended to be a comprehensive health insurance reform and was designed to expand coverage while investing in public health and prevention programs. However, it became a political lightning rod. In the context of a highly charged political debate, poor implementation of the program could destabilize its future. Two hours after the launch of the enrollment website, it crashed. Only six people out of the millions of users who visited the site were able to register. Tavenner, who had started her career as a critical care nurse, had her leadership tested when she was tapped to run the Centers for Medicare and Medicaid Services during President Barack Obama's rollout of the ACA and in the aftermath of the website's difficult launch. Tavenner was able to use her leadership skills and history of building respectful working relationships with people on both sides of the aisle to turn the program around. According to reported studies, the ACA's impact has resulted in positive results in terms of both individual and population health outcomes.[22] In addition, the ACA included provisions to fund preventive services and has aided efforts to combat socioeconomic and racial disparities in access to health care. Tavenner's perseverance helped implement one of the health policy initiatives with the greatest impact in recent U.S. history.

National policy can be a powerful lever to create change. Governance, the composition of leadership teams, and how organizations cultivate leaders are other important influences. Our eleventh case study explores how Ruth Williams-Brinkley brought her leadership and experience to that effort. Williams-Brinkley grew up on a farm in rural Georgia during segregation. Early in her career as a nurse she understood the relationship between health care and the community, knowledge she carried with her into a career in health care administration. During dramatic transformation of the health care industry and the ACA's implementation, Williams-Brinkley was willing to relocate to take on challenging positions and advance her career. She cites her grandmother as a model for the leadership traits of strength, courage, and independence. Through her professional journey, Williams-Brinkley saw women fail to advance in their careers due to a lack of opportunities, mentors, and role models, and she observed the gender gap among CEOs. When the opportunity presented itself, she chose to advance her career goals at Kaiser Permanente. Williams-Brinkley took the opportunity to combine her personal and professional experience in a leadership role at Kaiser, where she advocated for diversity at all levels of leadership and worked to advance women through mentoring.

Interestingly, the gender dynamics that Williams-Brinkley is working to change in the United States are also seen internationally. Recent studies on women's global leadership and gender equality show that women are underrepresented in leadership positions, decision-making structures, and in influential policy discussions. The studies make the case that "increasing women's leadership within global health is an opportunity to further health system resilience and system responsiveness."[23] Our final case study is of a woman leading an international discussion on how to make our world more resilient in the face of global health crises such as the current COVID-19 pandemic. Suerie Moon has combined her experience on the front lines of providing international humanitarian aid working for Doctors without Borders with her academic research to promote a global approach to addressing health disparities and emergencies. As codirector of the Global Health Centre in Geneva, she has become a leading force in the global health governance arena. Moon grew up near Chicago, and her life's work brought her through the halls of Yale, Princeton, and Harvard Universities (she holds a PhD in health policy) as well as to Africa, China, and Switzerland. Her academic work has influenced complex health issues such as access to medicines in developing countries, the West African Ebola crisis, and the international debate on health care as a human right. She is now in the middle of the international discourse on how to structure global cooperation to effectively and fairly curb the devastation brought about by COVID-19. Moon has become a fierce advocate for addressing the multifaceted economic, social, and political dynamics that impact global health—dynamics that often create inequities and disparate health outcomes. Moon believes that an equitable and integrated global governance structure supported by informal networks, financial incentives targeting the best outcomes for the most people, and countries setting an example are key. Amid this international crisis, she is advocating for equitable access to the scientific advances developed with COVID-19 funding, including vaccines and treatments. She is also calling for governments to empower the World Health Organization with additional tools, authority, and funding.

One of the important themes that cuts through many of these case studies is the influence and importance of role models in the lives of these women. Mothers, fathers, grandmothers, teachers, and siblings supported and encouraged the women to pursue education despite gender and racial barriers and other discrimination. They were taught to challenge authority when doing so was necessary. In the 1890s, Pennington was blocked from acquiring a science degree by university governance, yet her mother's Pennsylvania Quaker family promoted gender equity, including access to education. Williams-Brinkley's grandmother not only encouraged her to attend college and pursue a career in nursing, but also "taught [Williams-Brinkley her] worth as a woman and as a woman leader."[24] Hanna-Attisha had a high school librarian as a leadership mentor, whom she described as a "badass woman" who "defied the status quo and did what was right."[25] Many of these women, in fact, became mentors themselves. Williams-Brinkley recognizes the value of mentorship and works to develop and support diverse leadership teams in health care while others serve as professional educators like Apgar who taught, "do what is right and . . . do it now."[26]

Facing both gender and racial discrimination, Black women needed to overcome significant barriers to pursue medical education.[27] Once they became doctors, these women of color made important contributions by bringing better standards of care to their own communities and serving as role models for all women. Growing up in Ohio in the 1940s and 1950s, Gaston faced outright racism and had teachers tell her she could not study medicine because she was a "Negro," a girl, a Catholic, and poor. However, Gaston's mother urged her to persist, claiming that "every *no* you hear in life is just a *yes* waiting to happen!"[28] Lavizzo-Mourey's mother was her principal life mentor[29] and, as the first Black woman pediatrician in Washington State, presented a model for her daughter to follow into medicine. When Lavizzo-Mourey attended medical school, she was one of only four women in her class. Ultimately, many of the women in this volume served as predecessors and instigators of change[30] in normalizing opportunities for education.

Another theme that ties many of these stories together is a shared focus on prevention and working directly with individuals as collaborators and agents for change in improving health. As a journalist, Brody broke ground with her focus on prevention and was often a lone voice in the public domain educating readers on how to prevent health problems before they occurred. She wanted to communicate directly with the public and share health information and her understanding of the causes of diseases and strategies on how to prevent them. In the 1920s, Pennington used her scientific acumen and leadership role in the refrigeration industry to focus on teaching homemakers the benefits of refrigeration to prevent foodborne disease in their own homes. In the 1960s and 1970s, Apgar was a national leader in the prevention of birth defects and led the March of Dimes to advocate prevention to Congress, as well as directly to providers and the public. She used these skills to campaign for widespread immunization of children with the rubella vaccine to prevent birth defects—a campaign that ultimately led to the elimination of the disease in the United States in 2004. Apgar also coauthored a book (titled *Is My Baby All Right?*) that provided direct consumer education on the causes of birth defects and prevention strategies and that was endorsed by Brody on the back cover of the book. These women used their education and positions to develop innovative research or approaches coupled with their unique styles to persuade others of the value of prevention. Their work changed systems of public health, health care, and knowledge in communities, empowering individuals to make better informed choices for themselves and their families.

Perhaps the leadership philosophy of many of the women profiled in this book originates from a shared vision with two components: within individuals, particularly women, there is a power to create change; and acquiring a diversity of thought and elevating the voices of those heard less often promotes positive change. Katsi Cook insisted that Mohawk women be employed as fieldworkers so that they could directly engage in the research being conducted in their communities. Williams-Brinkley advocates for women in leadership positions and works to develop an equitable, inclusive, and diverse workforce. Wald advocated for the most vulnerable in our society, those at the end of life. Her desire to help others consider the body, mind, spirit, and emotions when providing care led her to see that the medical model of practice that put dying patients out of sight and limited family involvement was counter to the goal of meeting the patient's needs. She advocated for a holistic approach to caring for the sick and dying through the collaboration of an equitable team of providers. Tavenner's leadership approach to building diverse teams served her well in a time of crisis. When the ACA website failed, rather than look for someone to blame, she worked to cultivate and support a cohesive team and a culture of problem solving and critical thinking. Moon takes this thinking to the global scale and believes that we need a plurality of views to generate innovative ideas with the ability to transcend national boundaries and secure the right to health care. However, even though her work has international impact, she has a very practical and humble approach to who can create change in the world. She shares with her students that "there are lots of examples that are surprising in the sense that organizations or actors who would not assume they had the power to change things, do, in fact, end up doing that."[31]

These case studies reflect the variety of ways in which women interact with their community, their workplace, and the world. Remarkably, the influence of their work remains relevant today in many meaningful ways. Their professional experiences can inform work at the bedside; in organizations; and more broadly in the fields of public health, policy, social and environmental change, health care systems, and population health at the national and global level.

This project was a new and challenging endeavor, and we are most appreciative to Alison Bernstein and Mary Trigg for making this opportunity possible. For us, this project was beyond the scope of anything we had done in the past and an effort to emulate the leadership of many of the women we have included in the volume. We have learned much from the examples and stories of these women leaders. Their experiences, unique or shared, are inspiring.

Notes

1 Suerie Moon, interview by Alexander M. Bartke and Ann Marie Hill, May 16, 2019.
2 For more on servant leadership, see "What Is Servant Leadership?," Robert K. Greenleaf Center for Servant Leadership, accessed October 6, 2020, https://www.greenleaf.org/what-is-servant-leadership/.
3 World Health Organization, "Constitution," accessed February 4, 2021, http://who.int/about/mission/en.
4 CDC Foundation, "What Is Public Health?," accessed February 4, 2021, https://www.cdcfoundation.org/what-public-health.
5 The World Health Organization states that the "social determinants of health (SDH) are the non-medical factors that influence health outcomes. They are the conditions in which people are born, grow, work, live, and age, and the wider set of forces and systems shaping the conditions of daily life. These forces and systems include economic policies and systems, develop-

ment agendas, social norms, social policies, and political systems." See "Social Determinants of Health," Health Topics, World Health Organization at https://www.who.int/health-topics/social-determinants-of-health#tab =tab_1.

6 Linda Diem Tran, Frederick J. Zimmerman, and Jonathan E. Fielding, "Public Health and the Economy Could Be Served by Reallocating Medical Expenditures to Social Programs," *SSM–Population Health* 3 (December 2017): 185–191, doi:10.1016/j.ssmph.2017.01.004.

7 Paul Starr, *The Social Transformation of American Medicine* (New York: Basic Books, 1982), 180.

8 Hugh Tilson and Kristine M. Gebbie, "The Public Health Workforce," *Annual Review of Public Health* 25 (2004): 341–356, https://doi.org/10.1146/annurev .publhealth.25.102802.124357.

9 Shulamit Reinharz, *Feminist Methods in Social Research* (New York: Oxford University Press, 1992), 250.

10 Reinharz, *Feminist Methods in Social Research*, 250.

11 Sarah Coury et al., "Women in the Workplace 2020," McKinsey and Company, September 30, 2020, https://www.mckinsey.com/featured-insights /diversity-and-inclusion/women-in-the-workplace.

12 The shares of women with children under the age of eighteen who reported negative mental health impacts of the coronavirus outbreak due to worry and stress were 57 percent in Liz Hamel and Alina Salganicoff's, "Is There a Widening Gender Gap in Coronavirus Stress?," Kaiser Family Foundation Policy Watch, April 6, 2020, https://www.kff.org/policy-watch/is-there -widening-gender-gap-in-coronavirus-stress/; 53 percent in May 13–18, 2020; and 59 percent in July 14–19, 2020 (see kff.org, respectively). See also Nirmita Panchal et al., "The Implications of COVID-19 for Mental Health and Substance Use," Kaiser Family Foundation Issue Brief, August 21, 2020, https://www.kff.org/coronavirus-covid-19/issue-brief/the-implications-of -covid-19-for-mental-health-and-substance-use/view/footnotes/.

13 Marie E. Killerby, et al., "Characteristics Associated with Hospitalization among Patients with COVID-19—Metropolitan Atlanta, Georgia, March–April 2020," *Morbidity and Mortality Weekly Report* 69, no. 25 (June 26, 2020): 790–794, DOI: http://dx.doi.org/10.15585/mmwr.mm6925e1; Jazmyn T. Moore et al., "Disparities in Incidence of COVID-19 among Underrepresented Racial/Ethnic Groups in Counties Identified as Hotspots during June 5–18, 2020—22 States, February–June 2020," *Morbidity and Mortality Weekly Report* 69, no. 33 (August 21,2020): 1122–1126, https://www .cdc.gov/mmwr/volumes/69/wr/mm6933e1.htm.; William J. Hall, et al., "Implicit Racial/Ethnic Bias Among Health Care Professionals and Its Influence on Health Care Outcomes: A Systematic Review," *American Journal of Public Health* 105, no.12 (2015): e60–76. doi:10.2105/AJPH.2015.302903.

14 Reinharz, *Feminist Methods in Social Research*, 263.

15 Katsi Cook, interview by Joyce Follet, Voices of Feminism Oral History Project, Sophia Smith Collection, Smith College, Northampton, MA,

October 26–27, 2005, https://www.smith.edu/libraries/libs/ssc/vof
/transcripts/Cook.pdf.

16 Mona Hanna-Attisha, *What the Eyes Don't See: A Story of Crisis, Resistance,
and Hope in an American City* (New York: Random House, 2018), 219–220.

17 Carmine Gallo, "The Art of Persuasion Hasn't Changed in 2,000 Years,"
Harvard Business Review, July 15, 2019, https://hbr.org/2019/07/the-art-of
-persuasion-hasnt-changed-in-2000-years.

18 Regina Morantz-Sachez, *Sympathy and Science: Women Physicians in American
Medicine* (Chapel Hill: University of North Carolina Press, 2000).

19 Gretchen Livingston, "Stay-at-Home Moms and Dads Account for about
One-in-Five U.S. Parents," Pew Research Center, September 24, 2018,
https://www.pewresearch.org/fact-tank/2018/09/24/stay-at-home-moms
-and-dads-account-for-about-one-in-five-u-s-parents/.

20 M. P. McCauley et al., "The Social Group Influences of US Health Journalists
and Their Impact on the Newsmaking Process," *Health Education Research* 28,
no. 2 (April 2013), 339, https://www.ncbi.nlm.nih.gov/pmc/articles
/PMC3594925/.

21 Howard K. Koh and Marilyn Tavenner, "Connecting Care through the Clinic
and Community for a Healthier America," *American Journal of Public Health*
102, supplement 3 (June 2012): S305, https://doi.org/10.2105/AJPH.2012
.300760.

22 Madeline Guth, Rachel Garfield, and Robin Rudowitz, "The Effects of
Medicaid Expansion under the ACA: Updated Findings from a Literature
Review," Kaiser Family Foundation, March 17, 2020, https://www.kff.org
/medicaid/report/the-effects-of-medicaid-expansion-under-the-aca
-updated-findings-from-a-literature-review/.

23 R. Dhatt et al., "The Role of Women's Leadership and Gender Equity in
Leadership and Health System Strengthening," in *Global Health, Epidemiology
and Genomics* 2, e8 (2017), published online by Cambridge University Press,
https://www.cambridge.org/core/journals/global-health-epidemiology-and
-genomics/article/role-of-womens-leadership-and-gender-equity-in
-leadership-and-health-system-strengthening/A6AEB63AFE17295E0EF9E40
741A2EC5B.

24 Furst Group, "What Healthcare Leaders Need to Know Now," C-Suite
Conversations, September 29, 2017, https://www.furstgroup.com/blog/2017
/09/ruth-brinkley.

25 Mona Hanna-Attisha, interview by Mary E. O'Dowd and Colleen Blake,
April 24, 2019.

26 Quoted in L. Stanley James, "Fond Memories of Virginia Apgar," *American
Academy of Pediatrics* 55, no. 1 (1975): 2.

27 Patia Braithwaite, "Why Are There So Few Black Women Doctors?," Vice,
February 8, 2017, https://www.vice.com/en/article/xy5edz/why-are-there-so
-few-black-women-doctors.

28 County Cable Montgomery, "Marilyn Gaston," June 6, 2019, video, 5:06,
https://archive.org/details/Marilyn_Gaston.

29 Risa Lavizzo-Mourey, "Lessons I've Learned about Improving Health in America," lifetime achievement award speech, National Network of Public Health Institutes Annual Conference and Public Health Workforce Forum, New Orleans, LA, May 23, 2018.

30 Helen S. Astin and Carole Leland, *Women of Influence, Women of Vision: A Cross-Generational Study of Leaders and Social Change* (San Francisco: Jossey-Bass, 1991), 160.

31 Moon, interview.

Junctures
in Women's Leadership

⟨ # Health Care
and Public Health ⟩

Katsi Cook. Photo by Elizabeth Hoover.

Katsi Cook

"Research and Ceremonies and Healing Are an Empowerment Process"—a Mohawk Midwife Brings the Needs of Women into Environmental Health Research

Elizabeth Hoover

Background

Katsi Cook (a midwife whose full Mohawk name is Tekatsitsiakwa, meaning "she's picking up flowers") comes from a community that traces its roots to a long line of strong women. The Mohawk Nation of the Haudenosaunee Confederacy (also known as the Iroquois or Six Nations) traces its members' clanship through their mothers' lines. Clan mothers select chiefs and leaders, name the children, and traditionally owned the homes. In the Mohawk creation story, life on Earth began with a woman on the back of a turtle. The story of environmental health research and health reclamation in the Mohawk community of Akwesasne, located at the intersection of New York, Ontario, and Quebec, begins with Katsi and the women she collaborated with to reclaim sovereignty over their bodies, their birthing practices, and the health of their communities.[1]

Katsi was delivered at home by her grandmother, another midwife, and raised in Akwesasne. As she prepared for the birth of her first child, Wahiahawi, in 1975, Katsi sought out traditional birthing methods and Native midwives among her own people and other Native communities, both to assert herself as an Indigenous woman and as a means of avoiding the sterile white institution of the hospital. Throughout the 1970s, as she became more involved in Native American activism and helped found Women of All Red Nations (WARN), she identified control over reproduction as one of the essential elements of Native sovereignty.[2] She decided to take up midwifery, a profession practiced by women in her family for several generations. In 1978, Katsi completed an apprenticeship in midwifery at The Farm in Tennessee, followed by clinical training at the University of New Mexico's Women's Health Training Program. Through this program, she worked with Navajo and Pueblo women who, like women in other Native cultures, had been discouraged from incorporating their traditional birthing methods. She also completed a clinical placement in St. Paul, Minnesota, at the Red Schoolhouse Clinic, a WARN project in the Twin Cities. There she trained a birthing crew of Anishinaabe women in conducting home births and created the Women's Dance Health Program[3] through a grant administered by the Youth Project in Minneapolis.

In 1980 Katsi returned to Akwesasne, where she gave birth at home to her second son, Anontaks.[4] She then became involved in the standoff between the community's traditional government—the Mohawk Nation Council of Chiefs and New York State—over jurisdictional issues on the Raquette Point portion of the community.[5] Katsi began providing health care for families impacted by the standoff, delivering babies in women's homes and providing complete prenatal care; labor and delivery assistance at home and in the hospital; postpartum care; family planning; family counseling; and general obstetrical, gynecological, and infant care.[6]

In addition to jurisdictional issues with the state, the most significant challenge faced by Akwesasne has been environmental contamination. Akwesasne is an environmental justice community—disproportionately affected by environmental contamination leaching from industrial plants sited just upriver from the community and powered by a hydroelectric dam built on land taken unscrupulously from the tribe (Barnhart Island), for which it was never compensated. In 1954 the Saint Lawrence River, which bisects Akwesasne and had served as a major source of food, transportation, and recreation, was converted through a billion-dollar infrastructure project into the Saint Lawrence Seaway so that ships could travel from the Atlantic Ocean to the Great Lakes.[7] The project also included the construction of the Moses Saunders Power Dam, which offered cheap hydroelectricity to draw industry to the region. General Motors (GM), Alcoa, and Reynolds[8] all built plants upstream, upwind, and upgradient from Akwesasne.

In the late 1970s, Cornell University researchers confirmed that fluoride emitted by the Reynolds aluminum smelting foundry located about a mile from Akwesasne was the source of illness that had decimated the dairy cattle herds on the Cornwall Island portion of the community.[9] The Mount Sinai School of Medicine conducted a study in Akwesasne, prompted by an interest in how the contamination might be impacting human health. Mohawks found out about the inconclusive results of the study through a newspaper article and felt that the time they had invested as participants had not proven useful to them.[10] Katsi, who had been following the studies in the hope of learning about any potential health impacts on her community, expressed the people's frustration: "How do we badger Mount Sinai to get that data back to the community?"[11] The community felt as though any useful information had vanished with the researchers.

In 1981, two dormant sludge pits filled with polychlorinated biphenyls (PCBs) were discovered behind the GM plant, located directly adjacent to the Raquette Point portion of Akwesasne. GM had periodically flushed PCB-laced hydraulic fluids from the machinery in the plant and disposed of them in reclamation lagoons. They were then drained, and the sludge was buried in an unlined landfill on the site. The lagoons were found to have flooded several times, contaminating the beds of the Saint Lawrence River, Raquette River, and Turtle Creek, as well as the groundwater.[12] The U.S. Environmental Protection Agency (EPA) placed the entire 270-acre site on the National Priorities List as a Superfund site in 1984. Katsi described how the children from the Akwesasne Freedom School had swum in Turtle Cove, where they played "mudmen," covering their bodies with the thick, PCB-laced mud. A few years later, this

cove was renamed "Contaminant Cove" by the workers who exca-
vated the toxic sediment.

While regulators as well as tribal organizations were working to
understand the extent of the contamination, Katsi was developing
concerns about its potential health impact. As someone who was
intimately connected to the women in the community through her
midwifery practice, Katsi began hearing about miscarriages among
young mothers around the same time the contamination was being
discovered. She also saw an unusual number of birth defects, especially of the intestines. One child was born with no intestines. A different child had a torsion of the intestines that had to be surgically
corrected, and another was born with the stomach and intestines
on the outside of the abdomen. Searching the literature, Katsi found
that female beagles exposed to PCBs produced puppies with intestinal abnormalities. She became concerned about the babies in her
community who were being exposed to the same contaminant. She
recognized the importance of her position in the community for
bringing women's issues to the fore, noting, "I don't have an environmental engineering degree, I don't have anything like that, but
what I do have as a midwife and as a Mohawk woman moving
through the small world webs of the community, I would hear this
one had a miscarriage, that one over here is sick with this."[13] This
"situated knowledge," as Donna Haraway describes it, gave Katsi
insight into a portion of the community whose members felt as
though they had been overlooked by previous studies and health
professionals.[14]

In January 1984, thirty-two-year-old Katsi began an undergraduate program in biology and society in the School of Human Ecology
at Cornell University. There she met a medical sociologist named
Lin Nelson, who assisted her with further literature searches about
PCB contamination. She researched articles written by Ward Stone,
a wildlife pathologist with the New York State Department of Environmental Conservation. He reported on samples of owls and turtles
with high levels of PCBs in their livers and brains that he had found
convulsing or already dead along the Saint Lawrence River. Katsi
also discovered papers by Brian Bush, a chemist with the New York

State Department of Health, about breast milk studies he had done in Oswego, a town about 150 miles southwest of Akwesasne, on the shores of Lake Ontario.[15]

As women in Akwesasne learned more about environmental contamination, they became especially concerned about its effects at the top of the food chain—specifically, the breast milk they were feeding their infants. Previous health studies had collected various samples across Akwesasne, leading to a heightened consciousness in the community about contamination. However, Katsi and the mothers she worked with were frustrated that researchers had not sampled breast milk. Katsi recalled how staff members from the Mohawk Council of Akwesasne's Department of Environment and from Mount Sinai gave presentations at the office of a local newspaper, *Akwesasne Notes*, and at the Akwesasne Freedom School detailing how and why people should sign up to take part in the study. At one meeting, Katsi asked if they would include breast milk, to which researchers responded that this would not be necessary since they would be doing fat biopsies. She recognized that the researchers had not necessarily considered breast milk and would have had a difficult time collecting milk samples from women in the community, because most of the researchers were men. But as a midwife promoting breastfeeding, Katsi was faced with concerns about the safety of this practice as more was being discovered about the extent of the contamination.

> Mothers in my care who also lived in some of these geographic areas of our communities that were under special focus of the Mt. Sinai study because they were practicing traditional subsistence lifestyles—raising their own food, raising their own animals—and so the scientists were taking samples of ducks, of cattle, of vegetables, and the mother, who's ready to have her baby at home, is saying, Gee, Katsi, these scientists are coming to my home taking samples of everything but me. Is it safe to breastfeed? And I said, "You know what? I don't really know. I wish I did." And so, the Akwesasne Mother's Milk Project began as an effort to find that out.[16]

Resolution

To try to address the gaps between what people in Akwesasne needed to know and what authorities and past studies were willing or able to tell them, in April 1984 Katsi, Lin Nelson, Janet Rith-Najarian, and Doug Brown from Cornell met with Brian Bush about constructing a breast milk study at Akwesasne.

With that work under way, Katsi also met with Ward Stone at his office that fall and invited him to come to Akwesasne and test the wildlife there. He did, and he began announcing his startling results in the summer of 1985: a snapping turtle taken from Raquette Point registered 835 parts per million (ppm) of PCBs, which is 7–28 times higher than levels found in turtles taken from the upstream Thousand Islands region in the previous year. Chicken containing more than 3 ppm of PCBs is considered unfit for human consumption and anything with over 50 ppm qualifies as toxic waste.[17] High levels were also found in other animals in the area, including 190 ppm in a duck, 11 ppm in a sturgeon, and 3,067 ppm in a male snapping turtle.[18] The results, which Stone shared directly with the community, had immediate resonance, due not only to the concern about food sources but also to the painful connection between the contaminated turtles and the Mohawk creation story.[19] In the creation story, Sky Woman fell through a hole in the Sky World and was saved from the watery world below by the turtle, who offered his back for her resting place and the birthplace of humanity. Turtle is also one of the three clans of the Mohawk Nation, further demonstrating the animal's cultural significance.

Finding contamination in the food chain highlighted the urgency of determining the contamination of breast milk. One woman who lived on Raquette Point at that time described to me conversations she had had with Katsi, who delivered four of her children in her home. She recalled asking Katsi: "Well, if everything is so bad around here, what about our milk, the mother's milk? I mean, if I'm drinking the water here, what's happening to our milk?" In 1985, with a small grant from the Need More Foundation, the Mother's Milk Project began. Katsi presented a proposal to the two health services departments supported by the federally recognized tribal governments at Akwesasne (St. Regis Mohawk Health Services and the Mohawk Council of Akwesasne's Department of Health), and after it was approved, she began collecting samples of breast milk: "The first 30 or so samples I collected myself, beginning with clients, women that I had delivered their babies, and then extended out into the broader base of Mohawk women who were nursing. And it was fun. I'd go to their homes and hold their babies, visit with them, talk about their birth stories. They'd go take a warm shower, their milk would let down, and the next thing I knew, we had a milk sample of 500 mills [ml]. You know, piece of cake (laughter). And those would get frozen and shipped, and attached with it a legal document, chain of custody, so that we could be assured that nobody in between was messing with those samples."[20] Katsi has described this work as "barefoot epidemiology,"[21] with Indigenous women developing their own research projects based on community concerns and then collecting their own data. This initial "street science"[22] study led to a health risk assessment[23] and then two Superfund Basic Research Program (SBRP) grants[24] that supported several research studies designed and carried out jointly by the State University of New York (SUNY) at Albany and the grassroots organization Akwesasne Task Force on the Environment (ATFE), the first such community-based participatory research (CBPR) project of its kind to involve an Indigenous community in every step of the research process.[25]

The Mother's Milk Project founded by Katsi morphed into the First Environment Research Project (FERP), so named in recognition of the fact that the mother is the first environment experienced by each human and in support of Katsi's deeply held belief that "community empowerment, beginning with women's empowerment, that's a given."[26] Mohawk fieldworkers and their director were paid by SUNY through the SBRP grant but worked together under the FERP. The First Environment Communications Project was an offshoot of the FERP and worked to educate the community about environmental health issues through health fairs, workshops, a radio show in the Mohawk language, and a publication. As described by ATFE members Alice Tarbell and Mary Arquette, the Communications Project "helps provide the community with information on how to cope with contaminants by using culturally relevant strategies. For example, a workshop provided information and training on how to prepare meals using alternative sources of proteins."[27] This came in the form of the publication and a series of videos on preparing protein-rich PCB-free foods like tofu. Not content to just collect samples, the FERP and the Communications Project worked to deliver strategies to avoid exposure to PCBs.

Part of what made the research conducted at Akwesasne an important CBPR project was the Mohawk community's insistence that SUNY Albany hire and train local people for the project, as opposed to using professional researchers or graduate students. This was an important means of promoting equity and empowerment, as laid out by the "Good Mind Research Protocol" (the community's Institutional Review Board's guiding document), and it was also seen as necessary for recruiting study participants.[28] Katsi explained:

> At the very outset, I demanded that the only way we're going to work with Mohawk women in the precious intimacy of Mohawk mothers' milk and our relationship to our young is to assure the mothers that they are co-investigators in this study. There's not going to be any one of you researchers that stand taller than the Mohawk mothers. We're all of the same height, which is a traditional principle in our Longhouse. That we're not going to be guinea pigs. You're not going to run back to your funding agency with our analyses before you tell us. Those are our tissues. That's our data. It doesn't belong to your funding agency first. We want control over how this happens.
>
> And so, in fact, in the generations of research that followed from that, we were able to position fluent Mohawk women speakers to do the fieldwork, to go collect the samples.[29]

Katsi began the FERP as a means of organizing Mohawk women fieldworkers and coordinating the data for the health studies. She collected most of the samples for the pilot study in 1986. She also recruited women whose babies she had delivered at home, like Trudy Lauzon—who is fluent in Mohawk and has an extensive network of relatives, which was helpful in identifying who was going to give birth and could be recruited into the study. When Katsi became pregnant with twins, she suggested that the scientists hire Trudy to take her place. The initial response from the scientists was, "She doesn't have a degree." To which Katsi replied:

> Why does she need a degree?! Train her in venipuncture, train her in the protocols, you don't have to be—this is not rocket science, this is human interaction to get a milk sample. The women have got to know you, got to trust you. You've got to know what it feels like to nurse a baby, what it means when—to know how to recognize when your milk lets down. How to problem solve in that visit. 'I can't get a sample.' Well, you know what, let's take it easy, let's make tea, go have a hot shower. I will watch the baby. Don't you know, they've got to trust that you are not going to be doing something weird to their baby while they are in the shower. You know, it has got to be complete trust and who are you going to have that for, except someone you have known all your life?[30]

Trudy, whose milk Katsi had collected in the pilot study, ended up working on all the SUNY SBRP human health studies in the following years, in what she describes as a rewarding eleven-year job.

The FERP staff had an office in Akwesasne, but its members were hired through the Epi-Core, the epidemiological core of the SBRP at Albany.[31] Fieldworkers were trained in the necessary methods, including collecting blood and breast milk samples and, for some studies, conducting cognitive assessments, body measurements, and nutritional surveys. Staff members might visit a participant's home three or four times, once to secure participation and set up future visits; then a return visit to collect biological samples and, for some participants, a psychological evaluation or dietary survey (or for some studies several interviews); and then often a repeat visit to see if there were any differences. The data these women collected was sent to Albany for analysis, and eventually a letter was sent back to the participant explaining her individual results.[32] The SUNY researchers also hosted retreats at Akwesasne, where they presented the progress of the studies to the broader community.

The studies conducted by SUNY Albany and the Akwesasne Mohawk community to determine the health impacts of exposure to PCBs represented the first large-scale CBPR project in the nation with a Native community. The results of the first round of studies connected levels of PCBs in participants' breast milk and blood to fish consumption,[33] which decreased as community members began heeding fish advisories published by the tribal government.[34] Decreasing fish consumption proved a complex trade-off, as community members and scientists would later report that the substitution of affordable foods for fish has contributed to other health problems[35] as well as culture loss. As a midwife, Katsi's first concern had been for community members at the top of the food chain: breastfed infants. The contamination of this environment is a significant human transgression, impacting the sacred relationship between mother and child and the ability of a nation to reproduce itself. The second major round of studies began to document specific health impacts in community members with relatively higher PCB body burdens. These impacts include a greater likelihood of having diabetes;[36] higher levels of total serum lipids, which contribute to heart disease;[37] abnormal thyroid functioning in adolescents;[38] and effects on cognitive function in adolescents[39] and older adults.[40] Additional studies eventually corroborated local concerns that the PCB contamination could be impacting reproductive abilities, through effects on sex hormones in both adolescents and adults.[41] Among adult men, testosterone concentrations were found to be inversely correlated with total PCB concentrations, and especially with the types of PCB congeners found in fish.[42] Similarly, among adolescent boys, researchers found that exposure to the more highly persistent congeners of PCBs, in particular, were associated with lower testosterone levels.[43] Researchers also found that higher levels of certain estrogenic PCB congeners found in Mohawk girls led to menarche among those girls that was earlier by about half a year than that of the median predicted age for the total sample.[44] In addition, preliminary results of a more recent study of the impact of PCBs on reproductive hormones in adult women show that higher levels of PCBs decrease the likelihood that a woman will have the type of regular cycle necessary to conceive and maintain a pregnancy.[45]

Katsi's insistence on community partnership in research studies, especially the inclusion of Mohawk women, ensured that women received the most accurate and useful information about the contaminants in their bodies. Due to her work, first women and then other community members who participated in studies received their results. For the FERP employees who received training to work on these studies, the ATFE members who consulted on them, and the study participants and community members who learned from the study process and results, this built capacity to research issues that continue to impact Akwesasne and other Native nations.[46]

The work of Katsi and other Mohawks has also impacted science more broadly. In addition to community members' gaining greater capacity to take part in and conduct future scientific research, the SUNY researchers' experience of working with the Akwesasne Mohawk community has increased their ability to conduct future community-based research. Lawrence Schell, who led the adolescent thyroid studies in the Mohawk Adolescent Well-Being Study portion of the second SBRP project (as well as the follow-up Young Adult Well-Being Study), went on to conduct an additional study in 2009–2013 with the Mohawk community centered on reproductive health in women. Describing the progression of their research from conventional health studies to CBPR work with the Mohawks, he and his colleagues noted that this was the trend for future research: "In the future, it seems likely that community willingness to participate in research may not be assumed. Many communities and populations that human biologists want to work with . . . are politically galvanized and expect more from research that is conducted in their backyards."[47] David Carpenter, who worked on both phases of the SBRP grants, went on to conduct CBPR research with the Yupik on St. Lawrence Island in Alaska.[48] At a conference organized by Katsi that brought together environmental health scientists and members of Indigenous communities impacted by environmental contamination, the Yupik women thanked the Mohawk women for "training David so well" on how to work with Native communities.[49] This experience has positioned both scientists and their colleagues to conduct future CBPR work with Indigenous people.

Even after the completion of the health studies, Katsi continued to advocate for environmental and reproductive health promoting policies and practices, and for strengthening the capacity of Native communities to find health and well-being through empowering Indigenous women. She served as a fellow in the Reach the Decision Makers Program on Reproductive Health and the Environment at the University of California, San Francisco, working to develop policy for the EPA on chlorpyrifos, an organophosphate insecticide that is sprayed on food crops and that can have neurodevelopmental effects on fetuses and small children.[50] In addition, Katsi served as a member of the Indigenous People's Working Group of the EPA's National Environmental Justice Advisory Council (NEJAC), working to ensure that the interests of Indigenous women and children were considered in federal policy related to health and the environment.

Katsi currently lives in Akwesasne with her husband, Jose, and near her five children and ten grandchildren. While she is no longer delivering babies, Katsi continues to advocate in support of reproductive health, midwifery, and Indigenous community–based birthing practices across the United States and Canada, serving as what she describes as "an ambassador to the landscape of Indigenous women and girls' leadership circles" and creating for communities "a web of resilience through women."[51] Katsi serves as the Maternal and Child Health consultant for the United South and Eastern Tribes (USET) Tribal Epidemiology Center, a consortium of thirty-three federally recognized tribal nations from the Northeast Woodlands to the Everglades and across the Gulf of Mexico. Katsi is just as busy in Canada, where she is the founding aboriginal midwife of the Six Nations Birthing Centre, near Hamilton, Ontario. She is also an elder midwife of the National Aboriginal Council of Midwives of Canada, where she monitors Indigenous rights and ensures that the wisdom of elders is involved in regulating midwifery. Although she does not have a PhD, she has sat on several PhD dissertation committees for projects involving the health of Indigenous women, and she was integral in getting universities like Carleton University in Ottawa to shift their policies about accepting Indigenous scholars on such committees.[52] From her home community, situated at the confluence of international, state, and tribal borders and jurisdictions, Katsi's work has crossed a variety of spatial and bureaucratic boundaries.

This work has also included advising donors on how to fund Indigenous women's work on environmental health and birthing. Currently, Katsi is the director of the Spirit Aligned Leadership Program, which exists to elevate the lives, voices, and dreams of North American Indigenous women elders who are working to heal, strengthen, and restore the balance within Indigenous communities. Legacy Leader Fellowship Awards support Indigenous women elder leaders to re-imagine their relationships to themselves grounded within their ancestral knowledge, tribal histories and the challenges of their contemporary communities.[53] Legacy leaders are brought together in cohorts of eight for a three-year fellowship. With support from Katsi and other staff members, as well as development funds, the women develop and curate a dream project for their community. They receive funds for self-care and wellness (to increase health-span, not just life-span), as well as the types of training they identify as necessary to carry out their work. One of the most rewarding parts of the fellowship for women is the relationship building and connection forming among their circle of peers, as well as support for identifying and developing their dream project. Katsi notes that "Legacy Leaders are supported by a team of thoughtful and committed helpers so that the Leaders may impact a larger, more public audience across interrelated focus areas: violence against women, girls and the Earth, leadership of Indigenous girls and women, cultural expression, healing from historic trauma and oppression, and advancing Indigenous education through the applications of cultural superlatives. Everywhere we hear people exclaim: 'This has never been done before!'"[54]

Katsi continues to work to address women's reproductive health issues in her community of Akwesasne. She and Beverly Cook, one of her cousins, began a Centering Pregnancy model at the St. Regis Mohawk Health Services clinic in 2010, while Beverly was the director there. Rather than having each woman go through her pregnancy as an individual, this model brought together a cohort of women to support each other through their pregnancies. Women came in 14–16 weeks into their gestation and attended ten prenatal sessions as part of a cohort of six expecting mothers. At the beginning of each two-hour session, the women had the opportunity to see a health-care provider. In the sessions, the women charted their own vital statistics and then took part in group discussions. These meetings gave women the opportunity to network and support each other through relationship difficulties, health issues, and challenges like breastfeeding. Older mothers were able to give advice for those experiencing pregnancy for the first time, and in a way that might replace some of the close kinship network that some of these women no longer had access to. This is a model that can also be applied to other health conditions, as Katsi noted: "Whether it's cardiovascular disease, pregnancy, aging, diabetes, centering health care can be applied to all of these different contexts," and she is working to make that happen.[55] She is also an active member of the Kanonkwe Council—a council of Mohawk women that works to develop women- and family-centered tribal policies and works with clan mothers to assess and develop curricula related to the Ohero:kon Rites of Passage ceremonies.

Katsi's life work has been based on an intersectional philosophy that she has dubbed environmental reproductive justice. To fully understand the impact of environmental contamination in an Indigenous community like Akwesasne and the many others that she has worked in, issues of environmental justice have to be considered alongside issues relating to the physical reproduction of Indigenous people, as well as the reproduction of culture. In reflecting on the process by which her community tackled these issues, Katsi says: "Our story and unique context as a designated environmental justice community coevolved our struggle for reproductive justice. The restoration of culture sustaining practitioners such as midwives and doulas (who provide woman-centered, continuous childbearing and child birthing support) were always included with strategies for the restoration of the holism of our environment in the protection of women's health over the life span. We understood that many other aspects of women's health were at risk from exposure to industrial chemicals in our environment."[56]

Environmental reproductive justice, a concept developed through work by Katsi and others in Akwesasne and by people in other Indigenous communities, brings together the concepts of reproductive justice and environmental justice to ensure that a community's reproductive capabilities are not inhibited by environmental contamination. This entails considering the impact of environmental contamination on both the physical reproduction of humans (and nonhuman relatives) and the reproduction of knowledge and culturally informed tribal citizens.[57]

Katsi's aunt, grandmother, and great-grandmother were all midwives, and she has spent her life trying to help Indigenous women reclaim this birth process. When she took up that mantle four decades ago, no one could have guessed that her insistence on the assurance of reproductive justice for the women she worked with would end up reshaping the field of environmental health research. In addition to carrying on the legacy of these earlier midwives, she has extended it through reforming how environmental health research is done, insisting that the research be centered on women in communities. This has also meant that across the nation, Indigenous study participants can expect to be considered equal partners in the processes of developing research and gathering data and to have access to their study results. Katsi has continued this work of empowering women through the development of midwifery programs, the promotion of better environmental health policy, and directing programs that work to empower Indigenous women's work in their own communities. As Katsi noted as part of an interview for the Voices of Feminism Oral History Project, "Research, like healing, is a process. It's not just one night and one ceremony that's going to do it. It's a lifetime commitment. And research and ceremonies and healing are an empowerment process. It's a process and it's an outcome. And so, empowerment entails mastery, control, the ability to do education, communications, outreach, networking."[58]

The empowerment of Indigenous women, as both a process and an outcome, has been the noted goal and outcome of Katsi Cook's work.

Notes

1 Katsi's story has been pieced together through several conversations I had with her in 2007, a formal interview in 2008, and ongoing conversations; a folder of papers she loaned to me containing grant applications and articles written by her, as well as letters to her from personnel at the State University of New York at Albany; the collection of Katsi Cook Papers (1976–2005) in

the Sophia Smith Collection, Smith College, Northampton, MA; the transcript of an interview conducted with her in 2005 by Joyce Follet of Smith College; her published articles and book chapters; and a follow-up conversation I had with her in May 2019. While there are many Cooks in Akwesasne, there is only one Katsi, and this is how she is known in her community. To refer to her by her last name would be more reflective of the conventions of academia than those of the community, so to make this chapter more reflective of Katsi's work, I have referred to her by her first name. Portions of this chapter are drawn from Elizabeth Hoover, *The River Is in Us; Fighting Toxics in a Mohawk Community* (Minneapolis: University of Minnesota Press, 2017).

2 WARN is an organization of American Indian women initially formed in South Dakota in the 1970s. It was affiliated with the American Indian Movement but provided a female complement to the largely male-dominated movement. WARN supported improved educational opportunities, health care, and reproductive rights for American Indian women and pushed to combat violence against women, end the stereotyping and exploitation of American Indians, uphold treaties related to Indian lands, and fight against the contamination of American Indian lands and environments.

3 The women's dance is a traditional Haudenosaunee dance in which the women's feet never leave the ground, performed to remind women of their connection to the earth. In the creation story, Sky Woman made the earth larger through a dance done on the back of the turtle, and women carry on this reminder of creation through a traditional, shuffling dance.

4 She describes that experience in Katsi Cook, "The Coming of Anontaks," in *Reinventing the Enemy's Language: Contemporary Native Women's Writings of North America*, ed. Joy Harjo and Gloria Bird (New York: Norton, 1997), 45–51.

5 Doug George-Kanentiio, *Iroquois on Fire: A Voice from the Mohawk Nation* (Lincoln: University of Nebraska Press, 2006); Peter Matthiessen, *Indian Country* (New York: Viking, 1984); Raynald Harvey Lemelin, "Social Movements and the Great Law of Peace in Akwesasne" (master's thesis, University of Ottawa, 1996); Louellyn White, *Free to Be Mohawk: Indigenous Education at the Akwesasne Freedom School* (Norman: University of Oklahoma Press, 2015).

6 Katsi Cook, "Akwesasne Community Health Project," grant application submitted by the Women's Dance Health Program to the John H. Whitney Foundation, New York, NY, in 1981. Katsi gave me the document from her personal files, 6.

7 According to the historian Laurence Hauptman, the construction of the Saint Lawrence Seaway cost a billion dollars and led to the relocation of nine thousand individuals and the condemnation of a hundred square miles (*Seven Generations of Iroquois Leadership* [Syracuse, NY: Syracuse University Press, 2008], 133).

8 Alcoa acquired Reynolds in 2000, renaming the site Alcoa East.

9   Lennart Krook and George A. Maylin, "Industrial Fluoride Pollution: Chronic Fluoride Poisoning in Cornwall Island Cattle," *Cornell Veterinarian* 69 & supplement 8 (1979): 1–70. https://pubmed.ncbi.nlm.nih.gov/467082/

10 Elizabeth Hoover, "Environmental Reproductive Justice: Intersections in an American Indian Community Impacted by Environmental Contamination," *Environmental Sociology* 4, no. 2 (September 30, 2017): 8–21, doi: 10.1080/23251042.2017.1381898

11 Katsi Cook, interview by Elizabeth Hoover, March 17, 2008.

12 Donald Grinde and Bruce Johansen, *Ecocide of Native America: Environmental Destruction of Indian Lands and Peoples* (Santa Fe, NM: Clear Light, 1995).

13 Katsi Cook, interview by Hoover.

14 Donna Haraway, "Situated Knowledge: The Science Question in Feminism and the Privilege of Partial Perspective," *Feminist Studies* 1, no. 3 (1988): 575–599.

15 Brian Bush et al., "Polychlorinated biphenyl congeners (PCBs) p,p'-DDE and Hexachlorobenzene in Human Milk in Three Areas of Upstate New York," *Archives of Environmental Contamination and Toxicology* 14, no. 4 (July 1985): 443–450.

16 Katsi Cook, interview by Joyce Follet, Voices of Feminism Oral History Project, Sophia Smith Collection, Smith College, Northampton, MA, October 26–27, 2005, https://www.smith.edu/libraries/libs/ssc/vof/transcripts/Cook.pdf.

17 Joanne Skoog, "Stone Finds GM Contaminating Animals," *Massena (NY) Observer*, August 1, 1985.

18 Robert Andrews, "Ruin on the Reservation," *Post Standard* (Syracuse, NY), October 16, 1989.

19 Reporting the test results directly back to the community was not standard procedure and was considered to run counter to the protocols put in place by the state's Department of Environmental Conservation. Stone was warned and then punished by his supervisors for directly releasing data to the public rather than going through the necessary bureaucratic channels. See, for example, "Ward Stone, Once Clipped, Now Bound, Gagged," *Post Standard* (Syracuse, NY), May 23, 1989.

20 Katsi Cook, interview by Follet.

21 Hoover, *The River Is in Us*.

22 Jason Coburn, *Street Science: Community Knowledge and Environmental Health Justice* (Cambridge, MA: MIT Press, 2005), 217.

23 Edward F. Fitzgerald et al., "Chemical Contaminants in the Milk of Mohawk Women from Akwesasne," *Report for the Health Risk Assessment of the General Motors Central Foundry Division Superfund Waste* (Albany: New York State Department of Health, 1992).

24 The National Institute of Environmental Health Sciences's Superfund Research Program (prior to a name change in 2009, the program was called the Superfund Basic Research Program) funds university-based multidisciplinary teams to conduct research on human health and environmental

issues related to hazardous substances. See National Institute of Environmental Health Sciences, n.d. https://www.niehs.nih.gov/research/supported/centers/srp/index.cfm

25 CBPR projects are jointly created by community members and professional scientists, power is shared between both sides in all aspects of the research process, and study outcomes benefit the community via interventions and policy change. In structure, a CBPR project begins with a topic of importance to the community and works to combine knowledge with action for social change to improve community health. CBPR projects represents a shift from the top-down science that has traditionally been performed by Western scientific institutions, in which research subjects have little control over the content or structure of a study and most often are not informed of the final results. See Monica D. Ramirez-Andreotta et al., "Environmental Research Translation: Enhancing Interactions with Communities at Contaminated Sites," *Science of the Total Environment* 497–498 (November 1, 2014): 651–664, doi: 10.1016/j.scitotenv.2014.08.021; Meredith Minkler and Nina Wallerstein, eds. *Community-Based Participatory Research for Health: From Process to Outcomes*, 2nd ed. (San Francisco: Jossey-Bass, 2008), 544; Phil Brown et al., "Measuring the Success of Community Science: The Northern California Household Exposure Study," *Environmental Health Perspectives* 120, no. 3 (2012): 326–331, doi: 10.1289/ehp.1103734; Elizabeth Hoover, "'We're Not Going to Be Guinea Pigs': Citizen Science and Environmental Health in a Native American Community," *Journal of Science Communication* 15, no. 1 (January 21, 2016), http://jcom.sissa.it/archive/15/01/JCOM_1501_2016_A05.

26 Katsi Cook, interview by Follet.

27 Alice Tarbell and Mary Arquette, "Akwesasne: A Native American Community's Resistance to Cultural and Environmental Damage," in *Reclaiming the Environmental Debate: The Politics of Health in a Toxic Culture*, ed. Richard Hofrichter (Cambridge, MA: MIT Press, 2000), 107.

28 The "Good Mind Research Protocol" is an Institutional Review Board document created by the ATFE Research Advisory Committee that must be adhered to by researchers working in Akwesasne. Based on Mohawk cultural teachings, this agreement stipulates that both parties must receive respect, equity, and empowerment—a process that includes practicing cultural sensitivity, sharing resources, returning information to the community, and including community members as coauthors on publications. See Akwesasne Task Force on the Environment Research Advisory Committee, "Akwesasne Good Mind Research Protocol," *Akwesasne Notes* 2, no. 1 (1996): 94–99.

29 Katsi Cook, interview by Follet.

30 Katsi Cook, interview by Hoover.

31 The Epi-Core is charged with managing the collection of data, as well as conducting studies on the adult (over 35) population.

32 Lawrence M. Schell et al., "Advancing Biocultural Models by Working with Communities: A Partnership Approach," *American Journal of Human Biology* 19, no. 4 (2007): 511–524.

33 Edward F. Fitzgerald et al., "Fish Consumption and Breast Milk PCB Concentrations among Mohawk Women at Akwesasne," *American Journal of Epidemiology* 148, no. 2 (1998): 164–172.

34 Tarbell and Arquette. "Akwesasne"; Elizabeth Hoover, "Cultural and Health Implications of Fish Advisories in a Native American Community," *Ecological Processes* 2, no. 4 (2013):1–42. doi:10.1186/2192-1709-2-4.

35 Lawrence M. Schell, Mia V. Gallo, and Katsi Cook, "What's NOT to Eat—Food Adulteration in the Context of Human Biology," *American Journal of Human Biology* 24, no. 2 (2012): 139–148.

36 Neculai Codru et al., "Diabetes in Relation to Serum Levels of Polychlorinated Biphenyls and Chlorinated Pesticides in Adult Native Americans," *Environmental Health Perspectives* 115, no. 10 (2007): 1442–1447.

37 Alexey Goncharov et al., "High Serum PCBs Are Associated with Elevation of Serum Lipids and Cardiovascular Disease in a Native American Population," *Environmental Research* 106, no. 2 (2008): 226–239.

38 Lawrence M. Schell et al., "Thyroid Function in Relation to Burden of PCBs, p,p'-DDE, HCB, Mirex and Lead among Akwesasne Mohawk Youth: A Preliminary Study," *Environmental Toxicology and Pharmacology* 18, no. 2 (October 31, 2004): 91–99; Lawrence M. Schell and Mia V. Gallo, "Relationships of Putative Endocrine Disruptors to Human Sexual Maturation and Thyroid Activity in Youth," *Physiology and Behavior* 99, no. 2 (February 9, 2010): 246–253.

39 Joan Newman et al., "PCBs and Cognitive Functioning of Mohawk Adolescents," *Neurotoxicology and Teratology* 28, no. 4 (July–August 2006): 429–445.

40 Richard F. Haase et al., "Evidence of an Age-Related Threshold Effect of Polychlorinated Biphenyls (PCBs) on Neuropsychological Functioning in a Native American Population," *Environmental Research* 109, no. 1 (January 2009): 73–85.

41 Hoover, "Environmental Reproductive Justice."

42 Alexey Goncharov et al., "Lower Serum Testosterone Associated with Elevated Polychlorinated Biphenyl Concentrations in Native American Men," *Environmental Health Perspectives* 117, no. 9 (September 1, 2009): 1454–1460.

43 Lawrence M. Schell et al., "Relationship of Polychlorinated Biphenyls, Dichlorodiphenyldichloroethylene (p,p'-DDE) with Testosterone Levels in Adolescent Males," *Environmental Health Perspectives* 122, no. 3 (March 1, 2014): 304–309, doi: 10.1289/ehp.1205984.

44 Melinda Denham et al., "Relationship of Lead, Mercury, Mirex, Dichlorodiphenyldichloroethylene, Hexachlorobenzene and Polychlorinated Biphenyls to Timing of Menarche among Akwesasne Mohawk Girls," *Pediatrics* 115, no. 2 (January 13, 2005): e127–e134.

45 Mia V. Gallo et al., "Endocrine Disrupting Chemicals and Ovulation: Is There a Relationship?," *Environmental Research* 151 (November 2016), 410–418: doi: 10.1016/j.envres.2016.08.007.

46 Hoover, "'We're Not Going to Be Guinea Pigs.'"

47 Schell et al., "Advancing Biocultural Models by Working with Communities," 513.

48 David O. Carpenter, "Polychlorintaed Biphenyls (PCBs): Routes of Exposure and Effects on Human Health," *Reviews on Environmental Health* 21, no. 1 (January–March 2006): 1–23; David O. Carpenter and Pamela K. Miller, "Environmental Contamination of the Yupik People of St. Lawrence Island, Alaska," *Journal of Indigenous Research* 1, no. 1 (2011): article 1, http://digitalcommons.usu.edu/kicjir/vol1/iss1/1; Pamela Miller et al., "Community-Based Participatory Research Projects and Policy Engagement to Protect Environmental Health on St Lawrence Island, Alaska," *International Journal of Circumpolar Health* 72, supplement 1 (published online August 5, 2013), http://dx.doi.org/10.3402/ijch.v72i0.21656.

49 For a description of the conference and outcomes, see Elizabeth Hoover et al., "Indigenous Peoples of North America: Environmental Exposures and Reproductive Justice," *Environmental Health Perspectives* 120, no. 12 (December 2012): 1645–1649, https://doi.org/10.1289/ehp.1205422; Hoover, "'We're Not Going to Be Guinea Pigs.'"

50 United States Environmental Protection Agency, "Chlorpyrifos Revised Human Health Risk Assessment," November 17, 2016, https://www.regulations.gov/document/EPA-HQ-OPP-2015-0653-0454.

51 Katsi Cook, telephone conversation with Elizabeth Hoover, May 21, 2019.

52 Ibid.

53 Spirit Aligned Leadership Program, "Intergenerational Indigenous Women's Fellowship: Circle Three," March 25, 2021, https://spiritaligned.org/the-fellowship-circle-three/

54 Telephone conversation with Elizabeth Hoover, May 21, 2019.

55 Katsi Cook, "Critical Contexts: Research to Support Community Environmental Reproductive Health," keynote speech at the Social Science Environmental Health Research Institute conference at Northeastern University, Boston, MA, May 21, 2015.

56 Katis Cook, "Environmental Justice: Woman is the First Environment," in *Reproductive Justice Briefing Book: A Primer on Reproductive Justice and Social Change*, (developed by Sistersong Women of Color Reproductive Justice and Pro-Choice Education Project in collaboration with many others for the United States Social Forum, 2007); 62–63, https://www.law.berkeley.edu/php-programs/courses/fileDL.php?fID=4051.

57 Hoover, "Environmental Reproductive Justice"; Hoover et al., "Indigenous Peoples of North America."

58 Katsi Cook, interview by Follet.

Mona Hanna-Attisha. Photo courtesy of Greg L. Kohuth, Michigan
State University.

Mona Hanna-Attisha

Using Her Voice to Advocate for Environmental Justice in the City of Flint

Colleen Blake and Mary E. O'Dowd

Background

In 2015, Mona Hanna-Attisha, a pediatrician in Flint, Michigan, used data and research to validate the concerns raised by the people of Flint and exposed the city's water crisis. Her efforts empowered a community, changed the national discussion on the impact of lead in water, and laid the groundwork for a recovery plan for the children of Flint that focused on public health. Lead exposure in children can be devastating, impacting brain development and resulting in life-long consequences. Exposure caused by environmental contamination can lead to lower IQs, slowed growth, learning difficulties, and other physical and cognitive health challenges.[1] Although the exposure is preventable, the Centers for Disease Control and Prevention (CDC) reported in 2019 that exposure to high levels of lead impacted at least four million households with children, and exposure is frequently unrecognized because there are no obvious immediate symptoms.[2] According to the American Academy of Pediatrics, "Pediatricians play a key role in preventing exposure, identifying and treating lead poisoning in patients, and advocating for public health measures to address the problem."[3] Hanna-Attisha worked as a physician advocate with a dynamic group of community members, public officials, and scientists to provide scientific evidence of the lead exposure in children in Flint. She built upon the work of others and served as the tipping point that drove a governmental response in Michigan and beyond.

Hanna-Attisha's story starts with her parents, M. David and Talia Hanna, and their decision to emigrate. During the 1970s, Hanna-Attisha's parents left Iraq to further their education and find better opportunities for their future. The family settled in Sheffield, England, where David Hanna entered a doctoral program in metallurgical science and where Hanna-Attisha was born in December 1976. As Hanna-Attisha recalls, she was "born a bossy, confident kid."[4] In 1980, the family intended to return to Iraq, but at the time Saddam Hussein was gaining power.[5] As tyranny and oppression spread throughout Iraq, Hanna-Attisha's parents knew they could not return and emigrated to the Upper Peninsula of Michigan. They lived close to Michigan Tech University, where her father completed his postdoctoral research.[6]

The family spent several years in the Upper Peninsula, traveling to Detroit to visit relatives. During one winter drive back from Detroit, Hanna-Attisha and her family were in a car accident that badly injured the five-year-old girl. She woke up in the hospital with a broken neck and jaw, but she vividly remembered a young woman doctor with brown skin and dark hair who told her she was going to be OK.[7] From that moment on, Hanna-Attisha was interested in medicine.[8] She and her family moved to Royal Oak, Michigan, where her father started his career with General Motors (GM).[9] Her mother continued her education, earning a master's degree in chemistry and a teaching certificate. With both parents being scientists, Hanna-Attisha and her older brother were raised to love math, biology, chemistry, "and the majestic order of the natural sciences."[10]

Hanna-Attisha retained her love of science in high school, as she joined the environmental club with her friend Elin Warn (later Betanzo). Hanna-Attisha and Betanzo met at the start of high school and soon realized that their fathers both worked for GM. The two grew up side by side, sharing many interests—especially the environment. One of Hanna-Attisha's early leadership mentors was the high school librarian who led the environmental club. She was a "badass woman" who "defied the status quo and did what was right."[11] She not only educated the students about the environment, but she also taught the club members how to strategize and create change through direct action.[12] Hanna-Attisha and her peers studied activism by becoming activists themselves and exploring how policy and politics could help a cause. Hanna-Attisha, Betanzo, and a few other classmates advocated on behalf of the community when an incinerator was proposed for a site next to the local elementary school. They argued that an incinerator would pollute the air and soil of the surrounding area and cause harm. The group protested, canvassed door-to-door, wrote letters, and campaigned to elect an environmentalist to the state legislature (who won the election).[13] From this moment on, Hanna-Attisha and Betanzo shared a deep love for environmental activism that drove their careers and cemented their friendship.

Hanna-Attisha's community activism and her desire to fight for her beliefs were consistent with her family's history and values, which were instilled in her by her father—whom she recognizes as one of her first leadership role models.[14] Before the start of the Iran-Iraq War, her father had moved the family to the United States from England. During the war, the United States provided classified intelligence and food credit to Iraq, which inadvertently supported Saddam Hussein's regime.[15] While the U.S. government looked the other way as Iraq's allies in the Middle East (such as Jordan, Saudi Arabia, Egypt, and Kuwait) channeled American-made arms into Baghdad, Hanna-Attisha's father took it upon himself to spread the word of the regime's horrendous actions.[16] He involved his children and made sure they understood the horrors that Iraqis faced. When Hanna-Attisha was around twelve years old, her father showed her a picture of an infant who had been poisoned in a chemical weapons attack in the city of Halabja. Traumatized and haunted by the image, Hanna-Attisha felt lucky to be growing up in the United States. Her parents taught her that "challenging injustice meant standing up for the weak, the vulnerable, the abused, and the forgotten—be it in health, employment, or the environment. It means being vigilant on behalf of people . . . [and] fighting oppression at every opportunity."[17] Hanna-Attisha's early exposure to science, medicine, and environmental activism shaped her decision to become a doctor and pursue a degree in public health. Furthermore, her exposure to political activism through her father's work shaped her values. She strived to use her education, skills, and values to make her community a better place.[18]

After high school, Hanna-Attisha attended the University of Michigan. Her formative experiences as an environmental activist led her to study environmental health, and she earned a bachelor of science degree in 1998.[19] She went on to medical school at Michigan State University and then had a pediatric residency at the Children's Hospital of Michigan, in Detroit.[20] During this time, Hanna-Attisha met Elliott Attisha, another aspiring pediatrician, and they married in 2004. The couple had two daughters, Nina and Layla.[21] After completing her residency, Hanna-Attisha returned to the University of Michigan in 2006, where she earned a master's degree in public health. By 2015, she was living a full life as a mother, practicing pediatrician, assistant professor of pediatrics and human development at Michigan State University, and director of the Hurley Medical Center's Pediatric Residency Program.[22]

Throughout Hanna-Attisha's educational and professional experiences, environmental justice has been a consistent theme. The Environmental Protection Agency (EPA) defines environmental justice as "the fair treatment and meaningful involvement of all people regardless of race, color, national origin, or income, with respect to the development, implementation, and enforcement of environmental laws, regulations, and policies."[23] If environmental justice is achieved, all people in a population receive the same degree of protection from environmental and health hazards and have equal access to the decision-making process that influences a healthy environment in which they live, learn, and work.[24]

Located approximately seventy miles north of Detroit, Flint was the birthplace of GM. Housing close to 200,000 residents at its peak, Flint flourished and was considered one of the most prosperous cities in the United States during the mid-twentieth century. The city started to decline during the 1980s as auto plants closed, workers were laid off, and residents relocated.[25] In 1989, Michael Moore's film *Roger & Me* depicted the deterioration of the city.[26] The city's population fell to approximately 100,000 by the early 2000s, of whom 54 percent were Black and 39 percent white, with 39 percent having incomes below the federal poverty line.[27] By 2011, the city reached an all-time low, having accumulated over $25 million in debt. During the years of decline, Governor Rick Snyder of Michigan appointed a series of emergency managers to oversee Flint's budget, and the city's financial decision making fell under state control.[28] To cut costs in 2013, the emergency manager at the time announced that a new pipeline would be constructed to deliver water to the city directly from Lake Huron, rather than channeling pretreated water through Detroit's pipeline. In April 2014, with the new pipeline under construction, the emergency manager temporarily switched Flint's main water supply to the nearby Flint River to save money.[29] This was when the Flint water crisis began. At the time, officials described the switch as "a historic moment for the city of Flint to return to its roots," and assured residents that there would be no difference in their water.[30] However, soon after the change, members of the Flint community began to see negative consequences.

Individuals from across the city complained of discolored, foul-smelling water; mysterious rashes; and unknown illnesses. For more than a century, the Flint River had served as an unofficial waste disposal site for many of the companies located in the city. Raw sewage from the city's waste treatment plant, agricultural and urban runoff, and toxins from leaching landfills had found their way into the river.[31] Unbeknown to the public, the water now being used from the Flint River had not been adequately tested or treated for pollutants, resulting in significant water quality and health issues for Flint residents. While the city corrected some of these new water quality issues by treating the polluted river for coliform bacteria and chemical by-products, officials neglected to use corrosion controlling agents in the water. Corrosion in water systems can cause metal in the piping system to be transferred into the water.[32] In Flint, the uncontrolled, corrosive water eroded lead and other metals out of old pipes and into the taps that flowed into homes, schools, and businesses.

Lead in water is undetectable to the eye, and it has no color, odor, or taste. Lead poisoning can be difficult to detect, as most symptoms do not occur until dangerous amounts have accumulated in the body. Hazardous levels of lead are associated with developmental delays, learning disabilities, weight loss, irritability, and fatigue.

Extreme lead levels may cause seizures, unconsciousness, and death.[33] When exposed to lead before birth, infants are born prematurely and have lower birth weight and slowed development. Even at low levels, exposure over time can cause irreversible damage, especially in growing children. Children exposed to lead are at risk for damage to the brain, kidneys, and central nervous system.[34] There is no known safe concentration of lead in the blood, and research shows that as exposure increases, the range and severity of symptoms intensify.[35] While children from all social and economic backgrounds can be affected, children who live in older housing containing lead-based paint and who are living in poverty are at greatest risk of lead exposure.[36] High lead levels in water can be considered an environmental injustice issue because some racial and ethnic groups (such as Black communities) and the poor are at higher risk for exposure.[37]

For months, the untreated and corrosive water flowing from the Flint River caused the city's infrastructure to deteriorate and exposed residents to lead. Lead concentrations in Flint's tap water during the first eighteen months after the switch and later often exceeded the EPA action level, which is 15 parts per billion (ppb). (The action level is the concentration of lead in water that triggers a requirement for the government to take action, including efforts to control corrosion, inform the public, and potentially replace service lines.)[38] In some cases, lead concentrations were greater than 5,000 ppb.[39] Other metal and chemical by-products also remained uncontrolled in the water. In October 2014, six months after the water switch, GM announced that it would no longer use the water from Flint River for fear that high levels of chlorine were corroding engine parts.[40] After months of worsening conditions, community members began directly contacting officials at the EPA and asking that they test Flint's water. In February 2015, LeeAnne Walters, a mother of four, insisted that the city test the water in her home.[41] When the city finally tested the water at Walters's home, the results showed lead levels of over 104 ppb. Walters sent the findings to the EPA.[42]

Seeking help, Walters turned to Marc Edwards, a civil and environmental engineering professor at Virginia Polytechnic Institute and State University (Virginia Tech) and an expert on water quality. Edwards had gained national attention for his work testing water quality in Washington, D.C., during the early 2000s. Residents had reported levels of lead in their water that were six to eight times higher than the EPA action level.[43] Local officials attributed the lead to old service lines and planned to replace pipes until lead levels decreased. In 2003, Washington's Water and Sewer Authority (WASA) asked Edwards to investigate why pinhole-size leaks were occurring in copper pipes throughout the area.[44] He began testing the water and ultimately found that the leaks were due to the corrosion of pipes. In 2001, the EPA had switched the regulatory water-disinfectant agent from chlorine to chloramine, which unintentionally increased corrosiveness in the water.[45] The layers of mineral deposits that protected the pipes and service lines corroded away, causing lead to leach out of pipes and into the water supply. When Edwards reported his findings, the EPA discontinued his funding and access to data, and his subcontract was terminated.[46] At the time, Betanzo, Hanna-Attisha's friend, was an environmental engineer at the EPA serving the Washington area. She attended several agency meetings to address how to reduce the elevated lead levels. After she asked questions about how the issue would be corrected, Betanzo was removed from the project and promoted to a position in another department within the agency.[47] The EPA and the CDC published a study that perpetuated the belief within the public health community that water was not a contributing factor in lead exposure.[48] In 2010, the CDC acknowledged that its original statement was "misleading because it referred only to data from the cross-sectional study and did not reflect findings of concern from the separate longitudinal study that showed that children living in homes serviced by lead water pipes were more than twice as likely as other DC children" to have elevated blood-lead levels.[49]

Concerned that history might have been repeating itself, Edwards responded to Walters's plea. In March 2015, Edwards began testing the water in the Walters's home and found extremely high lead levels. He assembled and funded a team of Virginia Tech researchers and traveled to Flint to continue testing the water.[50] Despite the fact that Edwards's test results, made public via his website, identified widespread problems with elevated lead levels in Flint's water,[51] the

Michigan Department of Environmental Quality (MDEQ) repeatedly attempted to discredit the findings and downplay the public health impact.[52] During the same period, Miguel Del Toral, a regional groundwater regulations manager for the EPA, became aware of Flint's water issues after Walters called the EPA to report the lead in her home. In April 2015, Del Toral conducted his own tests in Walters's home and drafted a memo to the EPA on June 24, 2015, titled "High Lead Levels in Flint." The memo warned that Flint was not providing proper corrosion control treatment to water from the river and referred to the test results from the Virginia Tech scientists.[53] Before Del Toral drafted his memo, he and other EPA representatives met with state environmental regulators and insisted that corrosion control treatment was required. Despite the warning, state officials disagreed with the EPA recommendation and stated that they needed time to assess Flint's water source.[54] Del Toral gave a copy of his memo to Walters, and his conclusions were reported in July 2015 by Michigan Radio and national news stations. A month after the EPA memo became public, Hanna-Attisha learned of the lead in Flint's water.

On August 26, 2015, Hanna-Attisha and her family hosted a barbeque for their close friends. Among the piles of food and children playing, Hanna-Attisha found herself seated with Betanzo, who asked, "What are you hearing about the Flint water?"[55] The simple question turned into an unsettling conversation about Betanzo's former colleague, Del Toral; his now-public EPA memo; the lack of corrosion control in Flint's water; and the high possibility of lead in the water. Questions and recent encounters with her pediatric patients flooded Hanna-Attisha's mind.[56] How could this situation be ignored? How could money be more important than clean water or the safety of Flint's kids? Had she unknowingly perpetuated lead exposure in her patients by telling them the water was safe? Betanzo went on to explain that the MDEQ was likely using testing methods that would result in lower lead levels and could be underestimating the amount of potential lead exposure.

Betanzo recounted her experiences at the EPA during Washington's water crisis. At that time, scientists and activists had tried to prove that children were harmed by lead in the water, but they could not get the necessary health data to effectively demonstrate the impact of exposure.[57] Nothing happened until the story was broadcast three years later. Despite a federal investigation, the EPA and WASA took almost no action, because researchers could not establish the link between the lead levels in the water and the health impact on children—Betanzo felt this type of evidence would be needed to bring about change.[58] Concerned that Flint could be headed down the same path, Hanna-Attisha's next thought was: What could she do? Her patients, mostly children on Medicaid, had their blood-lead levels checked at one and two years of age, as mandated by the state. She began thinking about how to obtain the blood-level data to see if there had been a rise in the levels. Betanzo finished their conversation by urging her, "You can do this."[59] With reality setting in, Hanna-Attisha knew what she needed to do. She recalled the moment as being "a choice-less choice. So, there was no option that I could ignore this information—that I could press rewind and go back. The only, only, only option was going forward, so there was no choice. So there was a juncture, but there wasn't even the possibility of taking the other road."[60]

Resolution

That evening, after the guests had left the barbeque, Hanna-Attisha received an email from Betanzo with links to reports and news articles about the Washington crisis and Flint's water. Hanna-Attisha started her research by reading every major news article and report written between April 2014 and August 2015 that related to Flint and the problems with the city's water quality. The next day, she and three of her residents had a previously scheduled meeting with an employee from the Genesee County Health Department to discuss a program to educate families about lead abatement. Seeing an opportunity, Hanna-Attisha asked what the department knew about lead in the water. The department staff member told Hanna-Attisha that their branch of the department dealt with lead only in dust or paint, and that no one in their branch looked at the lead levels in water. From the general perspective of the public health community, the threat of lead exposure was connected primarily to lead paint and paint dust, which were thought to be the gravest and most common pathways for exposure. Unfortunately, the actions of the CDC during the Washington water crisis had misled many people in public health.[61] Frustrated by this response, Hanna-Attisha reached out to the county health officer and medical director, expressing her concern about lead in the water. When representatives of the County Health Department replied, they suggested that a study could be initiated to investigate the issue, but that it could not start for at least six months.

Unsatisfied, Hanna-Attisha spent the next few days reaching out to state officials, her public health mentors, physicians, and staff members at the Hurley Medical Center, asking for guidance and blood-level data. She also began to research Edwards and his water testing in Flint, keeping in mind Betanzo's warnings about Edwards's prior experience with the MDEQ and its attempts to discredit his data. Hanna-Attisha tried contacting the state health department directly by calling a nurse, Karen Lishinski, who had given a presentation at a lead poisoning prevention program. In their conversation, Lishinski said, "Yes, we looked at the lead levels over the summer, and we did see a spike."[62] Despite attempts to continue their discussion, Hanna-Attisha never heard back from the state department.

Hanna-Attisha attained the blood-lead levels of her clinic patients from the hospital's electronic record system and contacted the director of the hospital's research department requesting help to conduct a study. The director assigned a research coordinator, Jenny LaChance, to Hanna-Attisha and her team of residents. The team analyzed the data and compared blood-lead levels from before and after the water switch. By September 10, 2015, Hanna-Attisha and LaChance realized that to conduct an adequate study, they required additional data. The team submitted a proposal to the medical center's institutional review board (IRB) for approval to access data for all of the children served by the hospital.

While waiting for IRB approval, Hanna-Attisha continued to build her group of supporters. Sensitive to the racial dynamics of the community she was studying, she called Lawrence Reynolds, a

Black pediatrician and the CEO of Mott Children's Health Center, a nearby facility located in Flint. Hanna-Attisha knew that if she wanted to successfully navigate the political and community dynamics within Flint, gaining the support of a well-respected pediatrician who was engaged in health policy on the state level and known for advocacy on behalf of underserved pediatric populations was vital.[63] Reynolds provided support and collaboration, which included an introduction that led to Hanna-Attisha's presenting her initial findings at a Michigan Academy of American Pediatricians meeting with approximately a hundred physician participants. This presentation and subsequent discussion helped build a coalition of support within the pediatric community.[64]

Given the complexity of the research study she was designing and her lack of expertise in the area, Hanna-Attisha knew that she needed to recruit a water expert as a collaborator. Despite her reservations, she recognized Edwards's expertise and ongoing involvement in Flint and asked Betanzo to contact Edwards on her behalf. As a result of Betanzo's introduction Hanna-Attisha learned that Edwards had requested the same state data set she needed, and they agreed to meet and discuss their concerns. By the end of their meeting, Hanna-Attisha believed that she had made a new friend and ally—all of her doubts about Edwards's participation were gone.

For two weeks, Hanna-Attisha worked to determine if the water in Flint was affecting the blood-lead levels of Hurley's pediatric patients. This task consumed all of her time. Her husband, Elliott, and her mother, Talia, were able to tend to the household and child care needs. Under normal circumstances, her mother helped take care of her granddaughters, Nina and Layla. Living only ten minutes away, she spent time with the girls after school, taught them to cook, recounted family stories from Iraq, and even worked out the logistics of school activities. Hanna-Attisha noted that Talia does not just help take care of the girls, "she helps us raise them."[65] During this extremely stressful time, her husband and mother did everything they could at home to help. Hanna-Attisha not only built a team of supporters at work, but she also relied on a team at home. Without them, she might not have been able to fully dedicate herself to the Flint water crisis.

On September 16, just one day after submitting their IRB proposal, Hanna-Attisha and LaChance received approval to access all necessary Hurley lab work for their study. Within minutes, Hanna-Attisha's sample size went from 350 to nearly 2,000.[66] While analyzing the data, she realized she needed advice. In addition to Edwards, who provided scientific expertise, she brought together experts in health care, nonprofits, policy making, community advocacy, and local and state governments. By September 21, Hanna-Attisha had completed her study. After receiving emails from members of her team voicing their concerns, Dayne Walling, Flint's mayor, reached out to arrange a meeting. Hanna-Attisha; Reynolds; Kirk Smith, CEO of the Greater Flint Health Coalition; state Senator Jim Ananich; and Melany Gavulic, the CEO of the Hurley Medical Center, met with the mayor; Natasha Henderson, Flint's city manager; and Howard Croft, the public works department head, to present the study results and give the office a deadline for responding. When the mayor's office did not respond in time, Hanna-Attisha's team moved forward to release the data.[67]

On September 24, Hanna-Attisha presented her findings at a press conference. To demonstrate community support, she chose to stand at the front of the room with Reynolds; Smith; Pete Levine, executive director of the Genesee County Medical Society; Jaime Gaskin from United Way; Clarence Pierce, CEO of the Hamilton Health Network; and Mark Valacak, director of the Genessee County Health Department.[68] Combining science and research data with the personal stories of her patients, Hanna-Attisha spent forty minutes presenting her findings. One communication tactic she used was showing a baby bottle filled with Flint tap water, which demonstrated that lead in water was not visible. Due to the urgency of the situation, Hanna-Attisha released the study findings before they could be peer-reviewed and published. This strategy later earned Hanna-Attisha an award for professional disobedience from the Massachusetts Institute of Technology, which Hanna-Attisha admitted was her "favorite accolade" throughout this journey.[69] Knowing that without peer review, the scientific community could dispute her findings, Hanna-Attisha completed a subsequent study that demonstrated the impact of lead exposure through water on the children of Flint in a sample of approximately 8,000 children. The study was published by the *American Journal of Public Health* in January 2016, which contributed to scientific understanding of contaminated water as a source of lead exposure.[70]

Following the press conference, Hanna-Attisha faced immediate backlash from the state, MDEQ, Michigan Department of Health and Human Services, and media. The MDEQ's spokesman, Brad Wurfel, called Hanna-Attisha "an unfortunate researcher . . . causing near hysteria . . . [and] splicing and dicing numbers" and said that the state maintained its stance that the water was safe.[71] In their coverage of the press conference, the media referred to Hanna-Attisha as a "local pediatrician,"[72] not recognizing the scientific process or scientists and experts involved in the study. Hanna-Attisha recounted feeling "defeated and unbelievably small."[73] Despite the harsh criticism and attempts to discredit her, she persisted and continued to share her data. Taking at least one interview per day, she presented her findings until the state conceded on October 2, 2015. The state held a press conference to announce that its data showed an increased percentage of children with elevated blood levels and that it planned to evaluate how many children were affected. On January 11, 2016, Governor Snyder announced to the media that the findings of the state health department had identified about forty cases of lead poisoning. During that press conference, Hanna-Attisha, who stood with the governor and his staff members, very publicly shook her head no and continued to shake her head because she felt that the comments were inaccurate and minimized the damage caused by lead poisoning in Flint.[74] After reports of her display of disapproval circulated in the media, the state began to use the same numbers as Hanna-Attisha's study and take more aggressive action. Snyder wrote to President Barack Obama to expedite the declaration of a state of emergency.[75] Hanna-Attisha and her team developed a comprehensive plan for recovery, designed with a public health approach to promote resilience and improve health outcomes. She continues to advocate for the children of Flint by telling the story.

At times, Hanna-Attisha felt as though she was straddling the communities where she was working to generate change. Knowing she was not fully within the Flint community or the scientific community, Hanna-Attisha built her team in a way that provided external validity to her work. In turn, her work validated the work of Edwards and the community's concerns that had been raised but ignored. Consistent with that strategy, Hanna-Attisha routinely referred to GM's 2014 decision to stop using the water because it corroded engine parts. She intentionally engaged members of the local, public health, and medical communities that she was part of to enhance her work and influence. Her partnerships and public appearances were intentionally executed, using her "toolbox of communication strategies."[76] Her tools included her flair for storytelling, and they allowed her to convey her research to scientists, government officials, the community, and media outlets with ease and clarity.

Hanna-Attisha firmly believes that leadership is a privilege. When discussing her leadership, she describes herself as being lucky to "have the opportunity to serve [her] community and elevate these issues."[77] She considers great leaders to be effective listeners who successfully bring people together and build passion and excitement in their work. Hanna-Attisha believes that one of the main ways to achieve success is by taking advantage of being different. She quickly recognized that she was often the only woman in the room throughout the Flint crisis, and this set her apart from her peers. Being a mother, she felt emotionally connected to the children, and that changed how she talked about the crisis.[78] Hanna-Attisha could easily put herself in the shoes of the mother activists who started the fight, "amazing moms who not only fight for their kids, but are fighting for the entire city's kids. And who become like absolute experts. Like LeeAnne Walters, who was this incredible, incredible mom."[79] She believes that, women "tackle problems differently" and that "at a fundamental gut level . . . there is a difference in terms of how women lead. I think maybe from listening, and being humble . . . and bringing those different perspectives to the table."[80] Passionate and driven in her work, Hanna-Attisha strives to demonstrate the qualities of a leader that she admires most.

Through her work to expose the lead in the Flint water supply, Hanna-Attisha demonstrated tremendous leadership throughout the Flint water crisis. She says the experience is, "like I have this amazing microphone now," and she is "going to hold onto that microphone for as long as I have to," so that she can "make a larger impact on the lives of children."[81] Her continued advocacy, along with the collective actions of the community, has changed the national discussion of lead exposure in children. The American Public Health Association directly cites the Flint water crisis in the context of how to design public health systems: "Everyone deserves access to safe drinking water. Yet in Flint, Michigan, lead in the water supply caused many in the community to be exposed and, ultimately, resulted in lead poisoning in many children. This case has brought about concerns of inequities and environmental injustice. As a public health priority, systems must be in place that reduce and respond to environments that are harmful to the public's health. This requires more resources to communities facing the greatest threats."[82] Cities and states across the country have passed new laws and policies regarding lead testing in water in response to the story of Flint. This impact would not have been possible without Hanna-Attisha's tactical decision making and combined experience in primary care, public health, academic medicine, and media engagement. She used multiple approaches to create change and have a lasting impact on the city of Flint. Viewing herself as a servant leader and change agent, Hanna-Attisha believed that helping the children of Flint was her professional, civic, and human duty.[83] She feels as though "doctors have become so silent . . . [and] they forgot that they have this incredible voice in their community that they need to use."[84] Reflecting upon her experience in the Flint water crisis, Hanna-Attisha believes that she was an effective leader because she used the following strategies: creating a team, building credibility, being a good communicator, and always being prepared. She intentionally transformed characteristics traditionally perceived as weaknesses to her advantage. Being a short Arabic woman physician and mother became a defining strength in her advocacy for the children of Flint.[85]

Notes

1   American Public Health Association, "Lead," accessed February 6, 2021, https://www.apha.org/topics-and-issues/environmental-health/lead.

2   Centers for Disease Control and Prevention, "Childhood Lead Poisoning Prevention Program," accessed February 6, 2021, https://www.cdc.gov/nceh /lead/default.htm.

3   American Academy of Pediatrics, "Lead Exposure in Children," 2016, https://www.aap.org/en-us/advocacy-and-policy/aap-health-initiatives/lead -exposure/Pages/Lead-Exposure-in-Children.aspx.

4   Mona Hanna-Attisha, interview by Mary E. O'Dowd and Colleen Blake, April 24, 2019.

5   Mona Hanna-Attisha, "Pediatrician Who Exposed Flint Water Crisis Shares Her 'Story of Resistance,'" interview by Terry Gross, National Public Radio, June 25, 2018, https://www.npr.org/transcripts/623126968#:~:text =Mona%20Hanna%2DAttisha.,lead%20in%20the%20tap%20water.

6   Ibid.

7   Mona Hanna-Attisha, *What the Eyes Don't See: A Story of Crisis, Resistance, and Hope in an American City* (New York: Random House, 2018), 11.

8   Hanna-Attisha, "Pediatrician Who Exposed Flint Water Crisis Shares Her 'Story of Resistance.'"

9   Hanna-Attisha, *What the Eyes Don't See*, 74.

10 Ibid., 19.

11 Hanna-Attisha, interview.

12 Hanna-Attisha, *What the Eyes Don't See*, 44.

13 Ibid., 45.

14 Hanna-Attisha, interview.

15 Noah Adams, "U.S. Links to Saddam during Iran-Iraq War," National Public Radio, September 22, 2005, https://www.npr.org/templates/story/story.php ?storyId=4859238.

16 Seymour M. Hersh, "U.S. Secretly Gave Aid to Iraq Early in Its War against Iran," *New York Times*, January 26, 1992, https://www.nytimes.com/1992/01 /26/world/us-secretly-gave-aid-to-iraq-early-in-its-war-against-iran.html; Howard Teicher, "The Teicher Affidavit: Iraqgate," January 31, 1995, www .realhistoryarchives.com/collections/hidden/teicher.htm; Hanna-Attisha, *What the Eyes Don't See*, 218.

17 Hanna-Attisha, *What the Eyes Don't See*, 219–220.

18 Hanna-Attisha, "Pediatrician Who Exposed Flint Water Crisis Shares Her 'Story of Resistance.'"

19 Hanna-Attisha, *What the Eyes Don't See*, 19.

20 Michigan State University–Hurley Children's Hospital Pediatric Public Health Initiative, "About Dr. Mona Hanna-Attisha," accessed February 6, 2021, https://msuhurleypphi.org/about/about-mona.html.

21 Hanna-Attisha, *What the Eyes Don't See*, 247.

22 Hurley Medical Center, "Mona Hanna-Attisha, MD," accessed February 6, 2021, https://education.hurleymc.com/people/mona-hanna-attisha.

23 United States Environmental Protection Agency, "Environmental Justice," accessed February 6, 2021, https://www.epa.gov/environmentaljustice.

24 Ibid.

25 Melissa Denchak, "Flint Water Crisis: Everything You Need to Know," Natural Resources Defense Council, November 8, 2018, https://www.nrdc.org/stories/flint-water-crisis-everything-you-need-know.

26 Michael Moore, dir., "Roger & Me" (Burbank, CA: Warner Home Video, 1989).

27 United States Census Bureau, "QuickFacts Flint City, Michigan," accessed March 23, 2021, https://www.census.gov/quickfacts/fact/table/flintcitymichigan/PST045218#.

28 Denchak, "Flint Water Crisis."

29 CNN, "Flint Water Crisis Fast Facts," Updated January 14, 2021, https://www.cnn.com/2016/03/04/us/flint-water-crisis-fast-facts/index.html.

30 Quoted in Dominic Adams, "Closing the Valve on History: Flint Cuts Water Flow from Detroit after Nearly 50 Years," MLive, Updated January 20, 2019, https://www.mlive.com/news/flint/2014/04/closing_the_valve_on_history_f.html.

31 Denchak, "Flint Water Crisis."

32 United States Environmental Protection Agency, "Optimal Corrosion Control Treatment Evaluation Technical Recommendations for Primacy Agencies and Public Water Systems," March 2016, https://www.epa.gov/sites/production/files/2016-03/documents/occtmarch2016.pdf.

33 Mayo Clinic, "Lead Poisoning: Symptoms and Causes," accessed February 6, 2021, https://www.mayoclinic.org/diseases-conditions/lead-poisoning/symptoms-causes/syc-20354717.

34 Ibid.

35 World Health Organization, "Lead Poisoning and Health," August 23, 2019, https://www.who.int/news-room/fact-sheets/detail/lead-poisoning-and-health.

36 Centers for Disease Control and Prevention, "Childhood Lead Poisoning Prevention: Children," July 30, 2019, https://www.cdc.gov/nceh/lead/prevention/children.htm.

37 Centers for Disease Control and Prevention, "Childhood Lead Poisoning Prevention: Populations at Higher Risk," November 2, 2020, https://www.cdc.gov/nceh/lead/prevention/populations.htm.

38 United States Environmental Protection Agency, "Drinking Water Requirements for States and Public Water Systems: Lead and Copper Rule," accessed February 6, 2021, https://www.epa.gov/dwreginfo/lead-and-copper-rule.

39 Terese M. Olson et al., "Forensic Estimates of Lead Release from Lead Service Lines during the Water Crisis in Flint, Michigan," *Environmental Science and Technology Letters* 4, no. 9 (2017), 356–361, https://pubs.acs.org/doi/pdf/10.1021/acs.estlett.7b00226.

40 CNN, "Flint Water Crisis Fast Facts."

41 Sofia Lotto Persio, "Who Is LeeAnne Walters? Activist Who Helped Expose Flint Water Crisis Wins Top Prize," *Newsweek*, April 23, 2018, https://www.newsweek.com/who-leeanne-walters-activist-who-helped-expose-flint-water-crisis-wins-top-897326.

42 Perry Stein, "Aqua Man," *Washington Post Magazine*, January 16, 2019, https://www.washingtonpost.com/news/magazine/wp/2019/01/16/feature/they-helped-expose-unsafe-lead-levels-in-flints-and-in-d-c-s-water-then-they-turned-on-each-other/?utm_term=.4bd447da59e7.

43 Josh Levin, "Plumbing the Depths," *Washington City Paper*, October 18, 2002, https://www.washingtoncitypaper.com/news/article/13025198/plumbing-the-depths.

44 Hanna-Attisha, *What the Eyes Don't See*, 63–65.

45 Tee L. Guidotti et al., "Elevated Lead in Drinking Water in Washington, DC, 2003–2004: The Public Health Response," *Environmental Health Perspectives* 115, no. 5 (May 2007): 695–701, https://www.ncbi.nlm.nih.gov/pmc/articles/PMC1868000/.

46 Pierre Home-Douglas, "The Water Guy," *Prism* American Society for Engineering Education 14, no.3 (Fall 2004), https://web.archive.org/web/20110915195413/http://www.prism-magazine.org/nov04/feature_water.cfm.

47 Hanna-Attisha, *What the Eyes Don't See*, 63–65.

48 Centers for Disease Control and Prevention, "Blood Lead Levels in Residents of Homes with Elevated Lead in Tap Water—District of Columbia, 2004," *Morbidity and Mortality Weekly Report* 53, no. 12 (April 2, 2004): 268–270, https://pubmed.ncbi/nlm/nih/gov/15057194.

49 Centers for Disease Control and Prevention, "Notice to Readers: Examining the Effect of Previously Missing Blood Lead Surveillance Data on Results Reported in *MMWR*," *Morbidity and Mortality Weekly Report* 59, no. 19 (May 21, 2010): https://www.cdc.gov/mmwr/preview/mmwrhtml/mm5919a4.htm.

50 Kim Kozlowski, "Virginia Tech Expert Helped Expose Flint Water Crisis," *Detroit News*, January 23, 2016, https://www.detroitnews.com/story/news/politics/2016/01/23/virginia-tech-expert-helped-expose-flint-water-crisis/79251004/.

51 Marc Edwards, "Our Sampling of 252 Homes Demonstrates a High Lead in Water Risk: Flint Should Be Failing to Meet the EPA Lead and Copper Rule," Flint Water Study Updates, September 8, 2015, http://flintwaterstudy.org/2015/09/our-sampling-of-252-homes-demonstrates-a-high-lead-in-water-risk-flint-should-be-failing-to-meet-the-epa-lead-and-copper-rule/.

52 Marc Edwards, "Commentary: MDEQ Mistakes and Deception Created the Flint Water Crisis," Flint Water Study Updates, September 30, 2015, http://flintwaterstudy.org/2015/09/commentary-mdeq-mistakes-deception-flint-water-crisis/.

53 CNN, "Flint Water Crisis Fast Facts."

54 Lindsey Smith, "After Blowing the Whistle on Flint's Water, EPA 'Rogue Employee' Has Been Silent. Until Now," *Michigan Radio*, January 21, 2016, https://www.michiganradio.org/post/after-blowing-whistle-flints-water -epa-rogue-employee-has-been-silent-until-now.

55 Hanna-Attisha, *What the Eyes Don't See*, 37.

56 Ibid., 40.

57 Ibid., 46.

58 Neal Augenstein, "Before Flint: D.C.'s Drinking Water Crisis Was Even Worse," WTOP News, April 4, 2016, https://wtop.com/dc/2016/04/flint-d-c-s -drinking-water-crisis-even-worse/.

59 Hanna-Attisha, *What the Eyes Don't See*, 47.

60 Hanna-Attisha, interview.

61 Hanna-Attisha, *What the Eyes Don't See*, 113–114.

62 Ibid., 110.

63 Ibid., 171.

64 Ibid., 201.

65 Ibid., 76.

66 Ibid., 186.

67 Ibid., 221–233.

68 Ibid., 256; Ron Fonger, "Elevated Lead Found in More Flint Kids after Water Switch, Study Finds," MLive, Updated January 20, 2019, https://www.mlive .com/news/flint/2015/09/study_shows_twice_as_many_flin.html.

69 Hanna-Attisha, interview.

70 Mona Hanna-Attisha et al., "Elevated Blood Lead Levels Associated with the Flint Drinking Water Crisis: A Spatial Analysis of Risk and Public Health Response," *American Journal of Public Health* 106, no. 2 (Winter 2016): 283–290

71 Hanna-Attisha, "Pediatrician Who Exposed Flint Water Crisis Shares Her 'Story of Resistance.'"

72 Hanna-Attisha, *What the Eyes Don't See*, 264.

73 Ibid.

74 Ron Fonger, "Crusading Doctor Shakes Head 'No' at Gov. Snyder's Flint News Conference," *mlive.com*, Updated January 20, 2019, https://www.mlive.com /news/flint/2016/01/hurley_doctor_says_she_couldnt.html.

75 CNN, "Flint Water Crisis Fast Facts."

76 Hanna-Attisha, interview.

77 Ibid.

78 Ibid.

79 Ibid

80 Ibid

81 Ibid.

82 American Public Health Association, "Lead."

83 Hanna-Attisha, interview.

84 Ibid.

85 Ibid.

Katharine Dexter McCormick. Photo courtesy of MIT Museum.

Katharine Dexter McCormick

Examining an Advocate's Path—Advancing Women's Reproductive Rights through Philanthropic Support for Oral Contraception Development

Mary Wachter and Erica Reed

Background

In the fall of 1922, Katharine Dexter McCormick smuggled over a thousand vaginal diaphragms into the United States, sewn into the voluminous linings of newly purchased items of European fashion. The diaphragms left France, passing through Le Havre's border guards and American customs with few questions asked, besides the obvious: "How could you possibly use all that clothing?"[1] Despite inheriting a large sum of money from both her family and her husband, McCormick did not conform to the traditional roles of late nineteenth-century women: daughter, wife, mother. Instead, she leveraged her social and economic status to pursue an education and a lifetime of work in philanthropy and advocacy that furthered women's causes, including the suffrage movement and the birth control movement. Cultivating independence and working for social change, she pioneered a course for herself that differed from the traditional role of white, affluent women of the time. While the bold, covert operation in 1922 was the first of many efforts on McCormick's part to pursue reproductive rights for women, it was far from her introduction to the twentieth-century feminist movement.

Some of McCormick's philanthropic work (along with the research and advocacy efforts of scientists, feminists, and reproductive rights leaders of that era) was flawed by the limited focus on white, middle-class women. Furthermore, the lack of protection provided to women participating in pharmaceutical trials to develop the pill reflects the ethnic and racial prejudices common in society during that time and the unfortunate history of human subject research in the United States. The problematic links between the reproductive rights movement and eugenics, and between the women's suffrage movement and racism, are also part of McCormick's story. This case study is presented with the acknowledgment that these injustices are part of our history. However, it remains important to know and understand McCormick's work and the social progress accomplished by the advent of oral contraception for women.

The dawn of the twentieth century saw transformative change in the roles of women and members of minority groups in America.[2] At the forefront of this revolution was the multifaceted feminist movement, populated with activists of diverse backgrounds and goals who grappled with issues of agency and autonomy. Of those issues, reproductive care and control were made primary in the face of high maternal mortality rates: "at the beginning of the 20th century, for every 1000 live births, six to nine women in the United States died of pregnancy-related complications, and approximately 100 infants died before age 1 year."[3] Making affordable, accessible birth control available was expected to be a transformative health-care achievement, broadening women's ability to make choices about their futures—from education to employment.

McCormick was born two years after the passage of the Comstock Act of 1873 (the Act), a national obscenity law that made it illegal to possess, distribute, or mail materials, devices, or medications regarding contraception and abortion.[4] The Act's passage was spearheaded by the New York Society for the Suppression of Vice, led by postmaster Anthony Comstock, for whom the legislation was named. The Act also banned the mailing or importation of materials from abroad. It was meant to regulate the rapidly changing role of women in America, as they entered the workforce and academia in increasing numbers and the average family size decreased. The restrictions targeted reproductive health and education, as well as women's ability to control reproduction. Today, pieces of the Act remain in existence—specifically, regulations criminalizing the transportation of information about abortion.

McCormick's lifelong dedication to the causes that she pursued with passion and commitment was rooted in her early exposure to her family's activism and successful entrepreneurship. Katharine Moore Dexter was born to Wirt and Josephine Dexter on August 27, 1875, in Dexter, Michigan. The town had been founded by her grandfather, Samuel William Dexter, a businessman and influential community leader whose home was said to be a stop on the Underground Railroad.[5] McCormick's great-grandfather, Samuel Dexter III, was secretary of war and then secretary of the treasury, in the administration of President John Adams.[6] Prior to McCormick's birth, Wirt and Josephine lived in Chicago, where Wirt was a successful lawyer and board member of the Chicago Relief and Aid Society, a charitable organization charged with helping the city's poor. After the devastating Great Chicago Fire in 1871, he led the public relief effort.[7] For several years during this time of crisis, including McCormick's early childhood, the Dexters's home served as the society's headquarters. It was also during this time when McCormick learned that her mother supported the suffrage movement. Josephine was active in charitable efforts to aid needy women and admitted to advocating the practice of "prudent sex," a term used by suffrage supporters of the time to describe the use of contraception for deliberate birth limitations.[8] These efforts to aid needy women occurred in the public or social sphere but were considered acceptable as an extension of the women's domestic sphere: "While both men and women . . . believed a woman's place was in the home, this sphere was often enlarged to incorporate those outside influences that would have an impact on the home and family."[9] McCormick's father also supported the rights of women when the topic gained public attention[10] and was outspoken in his denunciation of slavery.[11]

The Dexters were strong proponents of education and intellectual curiosity, which aided McCormick and her older brother, Samuel, in their educational quests. Samuel attended Harvard University and obtained a law degree. However, academic pursuits were not as easy for McCormick or women at large in the late 1800s. Although

McCormick passed the entrance exam of the Massachusetts Institute of Technology (MIT), she was required to complete three years of preparatory coursework before she could become a full-fledged degree student. Despite this and other obstacles, she graduated in 1904 as the only woman in her class, the second woman to graduate from MIT, and the first woman to receive a degree in science from the institution.[12] She planned to enter medical school to become a surgeon.[13] McCormick likely chose her educational path in science in part because of the tragic and premature deaths of her beloved father and brother, which deeply affected her. She was only fourteen years old when a heart attack suddenly claimed her father in her presence, and she was eighteen when her brother died from meningitis.[14]

However, McCormick did not continue to medical school after college. Instead, she married Stanley McCormick the same year that she graduated from MIT. Stanley was an old acquaintance from her youthful years in Chicago (McCormick and her mother had moved to Boston after the death of her father). While the Dexters were affluent as a result of her father's family's wealth and his successful career as an attorney, McCormick's husband's family had a much larger fortune from its agriculture business conglomerate, International Harvester, as well as other business ventures.[15] The family also founded and operated the investment firm William Blair and Co. and published and edited the famed *Chicago Tribune*.[16] This advantageous financial position, combined with McCormick's academic background in science, would prove beneficial for her later understanding and financing of both the care related to the unfortunate deterioration of Stanley's mental health and the birth control movement.

Shortly after McCormick's marriage to Stanley, he began to experience paranoid delusions and to engage in violent behavior, which required hospitalization. He continued to exhibit anxiety and anger around women, including his mother, sisters, and wife. In 1906, just two years into his marriage to McCormick, Stanley was diagnosed with dementia praecox, known today as schizophrenia. He would suffer from this severe affliction for the next forty-one years, until his death in 1947 at the age of seventy-three. McCormick remained

Stanley's loyal wife despite his confinement and round-the-clock care on the grounds of a McCormick family estate near Santa Barbara, California, called Riven Rock. Here Stanley lived out the remainder of his life largely isolated from human contact—including his mother, sisters, and wife—with the exception of his caregivers.

During Stanley's affliction, the knowledge and treatment of mental illness shifted significantly, with the introduction of Freudian psychoanalysis and the belief that the causes of such ills as schizophrenia included psychological factors. Simultaneously, scientists were exploring the impact of physiological deviations on mental health. McCormick dedicated much of her time and resources to identifying cutting-edge therapies and working with leading experts to discover a cure, or at least a more effective treatment, for Stanley's condition. Her sophisticated understanding of science enabled her to effectively advocate among medical thought leaders, and her wealth supported innovative research in the fields of mental health, endocrinology, and other therapeutic areas that might offer hope in the treatment of Stanley's debilitating illness. One such example was her decision to fund and influence the establishment of the Neuroendocrine Research Foundation at Harvard Medical School in 1927. She believed it would research her belief that Stanley's condition could be linked to a dysfunction of his adrenal glands, since traditional psychiatric treatment had failed to cure him.

McCormick's role as Stanley's medical advocate was not without conflict and controversy. His family strongly urged her to divorce him, but she vehemently refused for fear that their motives would not lead them to act in Stanley's best interest. Upon the court's determination of Stanley's incompetence in 1909, a judge appointed McCormick and two of Stanley's siblings to share in the direction and oversight of his care. This shared guardianship, which was wrought with tension, created lasting barriers to the implementation of treatment options that McCormick believed might yield better outcomes for Stanley, as well as her efforts to control the excessive costs of Stanley's care. His care plan, which was limited to psychological treatments, had incentives for the psychiatrists who continued to receive payment for intensive psychotherapy while ignoring McCormick's requests to bring in other consultants and try alternative physiological therapies in the hope of improving Stanley's condition. An egregious example emerged through a consulting agreement with two renowned psychiatrists, one of whom was paid $10,000 per month ($147,562 in 2019 dollars) for services. McCormick shared her expectation with the consulting psychiatrists that Stanley's care would be advanced through both psychological and physiological therapeutic approaches. However, when her repeated requests to try endocrine treatment for Stanley were rejected, she attempted to end the consulting arrangement. Her efforts to terminate the contract were thwarted when Stanley's two siblings, who themselves were receiving psychological counseling to understand their relationship with Stanley, secretly extended the arrangement. A very public court battle ensued that resulted in the termination of the psychiatrists' contract but also expanded Stanley's shared guardianship to include the deans of two prestigious medical schools, each of whom was to be paid $15,000 annually ($221,343 in 2019 dollars). Nonetheless, McCormick remained undeterred and outspoken in her advocacy on behalf of Stanley until his death.[17]

During the time when McCormick began her pursuit of treatment options and the advances in research that might help address her husband's unmet needs, she also began to redefine her work with the suffrage movement to help fight for women's rights. Both advocacy efforts were fueled by her passion and commitment, and both would have to overcome conflict and barriers. However, the experience she gained in challenging Stanley's care and physicians over those decades, combined with her science education, immersion into the research on mental illness, and understanding of hormonal therapy, would lead to her interest and subsequent investment in the scientific work that would result in her most significant contribution to public health, financially supporting the development of the birth control pill.

McCormick's relationship with the suffrage movement began at MIT. She became the first representative of the College Equal Suffrage League (CESL) at the university, though the institution refused McCormick's request to hold organized meetings of the CESL on campus.[18] After her graduation from MIT, McCormick joined the

National American Women's Suffrage Association (NAWSA), making a name for herself as one of the association's leading speakers. She also coordinated the funding for NAWSA's *Woman's Journal*, relying on much of her own money to support the publication. She was named both vice president and treasurer of NAWSA. In her acceptance speech, McCormick emphasized the power that suffrage had on the individual: "so much attention has been given to the growth and development of the movement for woman suffrage that the effect on women themselves has been lost sight of."[19] Under her leadership, NAWSA increased its membership and the funds it raised, and her speaking tours provided a clear and personalized brand for the organization and its goals. Her speeches made clear that the right to vote was important not just for the empowerment of women, but also for gender justice and equity.[20]

In an effort to make the goals of the movement more personal for its constituents, McCormick hired canvassers; created brochures, pamphlets, and news releases; trained delegates in effective use of publicity; and organized a writing campaign to newspapers around the country.[21] From her experience on CESL speaking tours, McCormick understood that the majority of women did not need to be "jollied or scolded to see that suffrage was a necessary part of their lives."[22] She traveled with other association members for months at a time, touring many of the towns and villages in eastern and central Massachusetts.[23] These tours were intended to cultivate connections with the community, which included seeking a central location for speeches and involving local newspapers to ensure media coverage.[24] McCormick thrived, blazing a trail informed by her sense of gender equity and the personal advantages she had because of her race, class, and education. She understood the value of equal opportunity and access to resources, and believed suffrage was a means of cultivating widespread social change for women across socioeconomic classes. This experience would serve her well when she became an advocate for women's right to contraception.

McCormick was introduced to Carrie Chapman Catt while representing the CESL at a convention in Massachusetts.[25] Catt, the founder of the International Woman Suffrage Alliance (IWSA) and a former president of NAWSA, urged McCormick to join the IWSA.

She "recognized the value of McCormick's European travel experiences and her fluency in both German and French."[26] McCormick was quickly elected to the IWSA's board as correspondence secretary. Through McCormick's time at the forefront of the suffrage movement, leaders such as Chapman relied on her ability to balance the responsibilities of various tasks and offices and meet them successfully.[27] McCormick's ability to divide her time and attention among many projects helped her to develop an expansive network of contacts.

At the 1912 NAWSA convention in Philadelphia, Alice Paul, an activist and leader of NAWSA's Congressional Committee, expressed dissatisfaction with the movement's "educational approach," calling for a strategy that would reposition suffrage as a political movement.[28] Paul's tactics were more militant in nature. Eight thousand suffragists attended a march led by Paul on the day before Woodrow Wilson's inauguration. The suffragists were vulnerable to attacks from both hecklers and police, which was widely reported in the press. At one point, the army cavalry was called out to separate the groups.[29] After the march, McCormick wrote to the *New York Times* in an effort to disassociate the larger NAWSA movement with Paul's street action.[30] McCormick was labeled antimilitant and her debate with Paul brought McCormick additional attention. Her relationship with her husband quickly attracted media coverage. Much to her frustration, public focus shifted from her leadership within the movement to Stanley's illness. The coverage revealed the "barriers facing women like herself who were attempting to gain respectable recognition."[31]

McCormick's leadership style prioritized education and research rather than political demonstration. She exhibited this in both her advocacy for her husband and in her personal involvement in supporting scientific research. A key component to McCormick's ability to create change was her privilege: this allowed her to leverage her personal assets, resources, and opportunities to better engage in social movement making. She did not allow her economic or social status to stand in the way of activism or deter her from understanding the positionality of women in dissimilar situations. Women within social movements "are almost always risking more—

challenging more—than male activists because their participation, even in movements that are not specifically about gender, challenge societal notions of what women should be doing."[32] The skills McCormick cultivated through her participation in the suffrage movement established her as a formative agent for equitable social change.

After nearly two decades of leading NAWSA through communications and financial planning, McCormick celebrated the historic passage of the Nineteenth Amendment to the U.S. Constitution on August 26, 1920, along with her fellow movement leaders. The amendment blocked voter discrimination on the basis of sex, a result of nearly a century of activism. In the wake of the amendment's passage, McCormick's activist and philanthropic interests divided. She turned much of her financial attention to finding a cure for Stanley, but she remained active in the women's movement and began her lifelong engagement with the birth control movement.

Margaret Sanger, the founder of what is now known as Planned Parenthood, formally joined the reproductive rights movement in 1911, the same year that McCormick was elected to NAWSA's board. In subsequent years, Sanger opened the first birth control clinics in New York City, launched a monthly newsletter (the *Woman Rebel*), and attended transnational conferences dedicated to birth control. She coined the term *birth control* in an early issue of the *Woman Rebel*.

McCormick first met Sanger in 1917, when both were attending the trial of a young man who had been arrested for distributing Sanger's pamphlets on contraception.[33] During that meeting, the women each "recognized [their] unique compatibility that centered on women's rights and freedom of choice."[34] Sanger saw that given McCormick's academic accomplishments and social activism, she could leverage her personal privilege for feminist social change— and most importantly, she would be an ally. Between their first meeting and 1925, McCormick assisted in organizing transnational birth control conferences, as well as financing the printing of Sanger's pamphlets on birth control and contraception.

In 1922, McCormick was selected as a delegate to the Fifth Annual International Birth Control Conference, to be held in London. As part of her preparation for the trip, she developed a plan to purchase hundreds of diaphragms to bring into the United States when she returned, an act that was illegal under the Comstock Act (as mentioned above). At the time, diaphragms were readily available to the majority of European women with manufacturers in Rome, Milan, Antibes, and Paris.[35] Amid the conference meetings and events, McCormick met with European manufacturers in the guise of a French or German scientist,[36] relying on her multilingualism and science degree. After she had placed her orders, boxes of diaphragms were sent to her family's Swiss château, where local seamstresses sewed the diaphragms inside the linings of her clothes. After passing through customs in New York City, McCormick delivered over a thousand diaphragms to Sanger, enough to supply the city's birth control clinics well into the following year.[37]

During this time, Sanger crusaded against conservative forces, both domestic and international, to advocate for comprehensive reproductive health care. To overcome the staunch opposition of the Catholic Church, Sanger had dedicated much of her time to uniting the birth control movement, including larger organizations such as the American Birth Control League as well as smaller birth control clinics.[38] As a result of Sanger's efforts, the Birth Control Federation of America was formed. It later changed its name to the Planned Parenthood Federation of America (PPF) and adopted a policy of avoiding religious controversy in favor of emphasizing the health and social value of family planning.[39]

Increased controversy followed Sanger and segments of the suffrage and birth control movements when the eugenics movement became entwined with the others. These movements had paralleled each other since their early days and at times grew increasingly close on issues such as population control and the avoidance of unwanted or unplanned children. As Sanger became a vocal enthusiast of eugenics and paid less attention to feminist arguments, her leadership position in the movement offered opponents a target to aim at.[40] While McCormick was well aware of Sanger's embrace of eugenic arguments and controversial public positions and statements, she remained undistracted in her quest to make an oral contraceptive a reality for women as a basic human right.[41]

At the time when the women's birth control movement was advancing, so too was the evolution of pharmaceutical drug development.[42] The decades following World War II were the so-called golden age of drug discovery. Following the large-scale development of penicillin in the 1940s, antibiotics rapidly moved from experiment to application. In just ten years, all the great families of antibacterial therapies were developed. Antihistamines were discovered and praised as "wonder drugs."[43] Valium (diazepam) was brought to the market by Roche in 1963, followed by the introduction of the monoamine oxidase inhibitor class of antidepressants and antipsychotic haloperidol.[44]

In the wake of Stanley's death in 1947, McCormick contacted Sanger to once again get involved in the birth control movement. Though McCormick had continued to support the movement through generous donations, she had become far removed from its day-to-day activism and operations. In 1950, as the settlement of her husband's estate was in its final stages, McCormick was financially prepared to reinvest in the movement. She set her sights on contraceptive research to address her greatest challenge, "the lack of easy and adequate contraceptive means in the U.S."[45] In the middle of the twentieth century, the timing of two monumental advances—one in social justice and the other in scientific innovation—coincided with a pivotal juncture for McCormick. She was now free to reengage in the women's movement and, with her introduction to a scientist named Gregory Goodwin Pincus, positioned to advance the first oral contraceptive therapy and change the course of reproductive equity.

Resolution

Sanger suggested that McCormick make a donation to the Committee of Contraceptive Research, a part of the National Research Council that was funding projects overseas, but McCormick was exclusively interested in American projects.[46] It did not take McCormick long to discover that very little research on contraception was occurring in the United States. Around the same time Sanger turned to the Ford Foundation for funds to kick-start research efforts, but her request was denied due to the controversy surrounding contraception.[47] Shortly after this rejection, Sanger wrote McCormick in 1952, describing the work of Pincus—whom she had met two years earlier. Pincus was a graduate of Cornell University, earning a bachelor's degree in agriculture. He then attended Harvard University, earning a master's and doctorate degree (ScD, 1927). He was a faculty member at Harvard, Clark, and Boston Universities, as well as Tufts Medical School, through the mid-twentieth century.[48] He eventually established the Worcester Foundation for Experimental Biology in Shrewsbury, Massachusetts, and started investigating the effects of administering progesterone on the reproductive systems of rabbits and rats.[49] In early 1952, Pincus informed Sanger that his studies had "demonstrated unequivocally that it is possible to inhibit ovulation . . . and that following the sterile period, normal reproduction may ensue."[50]

McCormick was scheduled to meet Pincus in June 1952, but he was not able to attend the meeting. McCormick quickly learned that PPF was not fully supporting Pincus's research. She leveraged her financial power (including a sizable donation) to secure a meeting with the board, in an attempt to convince the board to finance Pincus's work. She was successful, but PPF's funding was limited: its initial stipend was only $3,400 ($32,943 in 2019 dollars).[51] It was not until June 7, 1953, that McCormick finally met Pincus, toured his laboratory, and had a vigorous discussion about his research. Her intense curiosity was satisfied enough by the end of the visit that she wrote him a check for $20,000 ($192,329 in 2019 dollars) as start-up funding and made a commitment to provide an additional $20,000 later. While McCormick became the primary funding source of the project—her contributions totaled more than $2 million from 1953 to 1959 ($2 million in 1959 would be $17,646,667 in 2019 dollars)—she also proved to be an untraditional donor, given her demand for details and her scrutiny of the rationale behind the research.[52]

Another important research partner who joined Pincus in his work was John Rock, a devout Catholic and a physician with a thriving Boston practice. Despite Rock's religion, he believed that women had the right to govern their own bodies. His long history of public support for his beliefs and his stellar popular reputation in the community created a challenge for the Catholic leadership in the region. Motivated by his belief in the birth control movement and the potential for drug development, Rock began the first human testing of progesterone on his patients for the opposite purpose from Pincus's: to increase fertility. At that time in Massachusetts, it was illegal to discuss or prescribe contraceptives. Rock enrolled patients in his study who wanted to become pregnant and hypothesized that stopping ovulation for a period of time would increase fertility once the treatment was discontinued.[53] Rock's testing yielded positive results for his small number of patients. However, enrolling larger numbers of subjects would prove a major challenge, as doing so raised ethical and political questions.

The research protocols and clinical trial enrollment included a range of subjects including psychiatric hospital patients. For large-scale enrollment, researchers ultimately turned to Puerto Rico—which had an established network of clinics and was considered to be out of the eye of the press. Edris Rice-Wray, the medical director for the Family Planning Association of Puerto Rico and director of the training center for nurses at the Public Health Unit of Puerto Rico's Department of Health, supervised the study. Rice-Wray noted that the dosage of progesterone was 100 percent effective if taken correctly, but she was concerned both that healthy women would not take a daily pill and that the side effects might cause participants to drop out of the study. She recorded that 17 percent of the participants complained of side effects such as nausea, dizziness, headaches, stomach pain, and vomiting. A newspaper wrote about the study, and a significant number of women dropped out, afraid of what their priest would say. Others dropped out because of side effects. There was additional backlash by the media, which characterized the testing as racist and imperialist.[54] Rice-Wray's concerns about side effects were dismissed, and Pincus and Rock believed that the complaints were psychosomatic and the problems were minor compared to the benefits. No action was taken to investigate the complaints. Additional communities were included in the trials, and the study was completed in less than a year. Pincus was a share-holder and contract employee of G. D. Searle, the pharmaceutical company that would apply for drug approval from the U.S. Food and Drug Administration (FDA).[55]

The path to FDA approval of an effective oral contraception included setbacks and challenges that did not reduce McCormick's commitment. She understood that developing such an innovation was complicated and took a long time—especially in the case of a product that was as controversial as it was essential for reproductive equity. Clinical trials succeeded and G. D. Searle submitted the FDA application.[56]

Despite the backlash at the time of the Puerto Rico study, Pincus believed that he had conducted his drug trials according to the standards of the time. But in fact there were multiple problems with the study. Pincus chose Puerto Rico for a number of reasons: it was facing a population boom and had high rates of poverty; the local government supported contraception, including sterilization, as a means of controlling population growth;[57] and there were more than sixty-seven health clinics that dispensed allowed means of contraception to a stationary population, whose members were generally poor and uneducated. The selection of Puerto Rico as the scientists' study site and the manner in which the women were recruited for the study contradicted the principles of gender empowerment across all social classes that were espoused in McCormick's earlier activities with the women's suffrage movement. The women of Puerto Rico did not have the necessary information, education, and advocacy they needed to make an informed choice about their participation: the study participants believed that they were receiving a drug that prevented pregnancy. Furthermore, high doses were administered to prevent any pregnancies, and the reports of side effects were dismissed.[58] These actions were unethical and would not be permitted under today's standards. America's inappropriate tradition of using women of color as experimental subjects without proper knowledge, consent, and protections in projects of population control was demonstrated here.

There are now additional requirements for research carried out on human subjects. As noted in the Belmont Report, "scientific research has produced substantial social benefits. It has also posed some troubling ethical questions."[59] The author of the report, the National Commission for the Protection of Human Subjects of Biomedical and Behavior Research, was established and "directed to consider (i) the boundaries between biomedical and behavioral research and the accepted and routine practice of medicine, (ii) the role of assessment of risk-benefit criteria in the determination of the appropriateness of research involving human subjects, (iii) appropriate guidelines for the selection of human subjects for participation in such research and (iv) the nature and definition of informed consent in various research setting."[60] Researchers must take training programs that concern the protection of human research subjects, and institutional review boards must examine the methods and protocols proposed for research to ensure that they are ethical. Federal regulations require that the boards give special consideration to protecting the welfare of particularly vulnerable subjects such as children, economically or educationally disadvantaged people, and members of racial or ethnic minority groups.[61]

The fruit of McCormick's early and enduring partnership with and financial support of Pincus ultimately yielded FDA approval of Enovid, the first oral contraceptive, on June 10, 1957.[62] This was among the pharmaceutical industry's advances in health that had the greatest impact and farthest reach. According to the Centers for Disease Control and Prevention, access to family planning and contraceptive services is one of the top ten greatest public health achievements of the twentieth century because of its influence in altering the social and economic roles of women.[63] There are sixty-one million women in the United States of reproductive age (that is, ages 15–44). About forty-three million of them (70 percent) are at risk of unintended pregnancy: they are sexually active and do not want to become pregnant, but they could become pregnant if they or their partners fail to use a contraceptive method correctly and consistently.[64] In 2015–2017, 64.9 percent of women ages 15–49 in the United States were using contraception.[65] The pill is still the most popular method of female birth control, with 25 percent of women ages 15–44 who use contraception choosing it.[66] The pill is 99 percent effective when taken as directed.[67]

In 1959, six years since her initial contribution to Pincus's work, McCormick went to a pharmacy and filled a prescription for Enovid for a friend. In her many roles—from daughter to wife, student to scientist, and philanthropist to activist—McCormick never followed the traditional path for women at the time. She advocated for the changes she wanted to see in the world. She consistently leveraged her education and financial status to contribute to the creation of accessible, long-lasting social change. The acceptance speech she delivered when she was elected NAWSA's treasurer and vice president demonstrates her philanthropy and activism: "To come into contact with this movement means to some individuals to enter a larger world of thought than they had known before; to others it means approaching the same world in a more real and effective way. To all it gives a wider horizon in the recognition of one fact—that the broadest human aims and the highest human ideals are an integral part of the lives of women."[68]

While McCormick's name has disappeared from the forefront of the contemporary feminist movement, her contributions to and vision of equitable reproductive care for women and family planning continue to frame conversations and activism today. Reframing McCormick's contributions with today's knowledge requires a deeper look at her involvement with the suffrage movement and Sanger. McCormick was privileged to make a series of choices that were open to her because of her role in society. She prioritized education and research in her roles with NAWSA and the suffrage movement, her advocacy for her husband, and her support of Pincus and Rock. It is also important to acknowledge the bias embedded in the social and scientific communities that led to the devaluing of the lives of women of color within the clinical trials for the development of the pill.

McCormick's financial support was critical to the development of oral contraceptives. Even when the U.S. pharmaceutical industry was beginning to boom in the dynamic economic period that followed World War II—thanks to financial support for late-stage drug research from large pharmaceutical companies and increased federal funding through the National Institutes of Health—funding for basic discovery research posed a challenge, just as it does today.[69]

Taking a molecule from discovery to proof of concept and then on to development is laden with the risks embedded in the inherent uncertainty of the research and development process, the time needed to launch a successful product, and the costs that cannot be recovered if a product does not reach the market.[70] An emerging source of basic research funding during this period (and still used today) was individual investors who provided flexible support at a very early stage. McCormick was the equivalent of what today is referred to as an angel investor—an affluent individual who provides capital for a business start-up when the risks are high. However, while angel investors of today usually provide support in exchange for ownership equity or some financial gain, McCormick was motivated by the impact on reproductive rights and her deep understanding of scientific innovation.[71]

One of her last appearances took place a month before her death on December 28, 1967, at the age of ninety-two, when she attended the dedication of the new wing of the Stanley McCormick Hall at MIT. In 1959, when McCormick learned that MIT was unable to admit more women, pleading lack of housing, she agreed to fund the first female dormitory (named in honor of her husband), and she subsequently funded the addition of a second wing. When it opened in 1963, it provided rooms for 200 women—four times the number that the institution had previously been able to house. Women now make up nearly half of MIT's undergraduate student body.[72] In her final years, McCormick continued to provide funding to support the advancement and education of women, which served to strengthen her legacy.

Notes

1 Armond Fields, *Katharine Dexter McCormick: Pioneer for Women's Rights* (Westport, CT: Praeger, 2003), 182.

2 Jonathan Eig, *The Birth of the Pill: How Four Crusaders Reinvented Sex and Launched a Revolution* (New York: W. W. Norton, 2014).

3 Centers for Disease Control and Prevention, "Achievements in Public Health, 1900–1999: Healthier Mothers and Babies," *Morbidity and Mortality Weekly Report* 48, no. 38 (October 1, 1999): 849–58, https://www.cdc.gov/mmwr /preview/mmwrhtml/mm4838a2.htm.

4 Fields, *Katharine Dexter McCormick*, 175.

5   Sarah Richardson, "Patron of the Pill," *American History* 51, no. 6 (February 2017): 24.

6   Franklin Harvey Head, "Wirt Dexter," in *Great American Lawyers*, ed. William Draper Lewis (Philadelphia: John C. Winston Company, 1909), 322.

7   Ibid., 323.

8   Linda Gordon, *The Moral Property of Women: A History of Birth Control Politics in America* (Urbana University of Illinois Press, 2002), 59.

9   Linda J. Rynbrandt, "The 'Ladies of the Club' and Caroline Bartlett Crane: Affiliation and Alienation in Progressive Social Reform," *Gender and Society* 11, no. 2 (April 1997): 205.

10 Fields, *Katharine Dexter McCormick*, 11.

11 Head, "Wirt Dexter," 339.

12 Fields, *Katharine Dexter McCormick*, 52.

13 Genevieve Wanucha, "A Mind of Her Own," *Technology Review*, 114, no. 2 (March–April 2011): M16.

14 Fields, *Katharine Dexter McCormick*, 16.

15 Ibid., 33–58.

16 Miriam Kleiman, "Rich, Famous, and Questionably Sane: When a Wealthy Heir's Family Sought Help from a Hospital for the Insane," *National Archives* 39, no. 2 (Summer 2007): 2, http://www.archives.gov/publications/prologue /2007/summer/mccormick.html.

17 Ibid., 3–12.

18 Fields, *Katharine Dexter McCormick*, 31.

19 Quoted in ibid., 102.

20 Ibid., 92.

21 Ibid., 123.

22 Quoted in ibid., 92.

23 Ibid.

24 Ibid.

25 Ibid., 75.

26 Ibid., 77.

27 Ibid., 103.

28 Ibid., 109.

29 Ibid., 110.

30 Ibid.

31 Ibid., 111.

32 Georgina Hickey, "The Respectability Trap: Gender Conventions in 20th Century Movements for Social Change," *Journal of Interdisciplinary Feminist Thought* 7, no. 1 (2013): article 2, 3.

33 Fields, *Katharine Dexter McCormick*, 177.

34 Ibid., 178.

35 Ibid., 181.

36 Ibid., 182.

37 Ibid., 181.

38 Ibid., 246.

39 Ibid., 247.
40 Jennifer Latson, "What Margaret Sanger Really Said about Eugenics and Race," October 14, 2016, *Time*, https://time.com/4081760/margaret-sanger-history-eugenics/.
41 Gordon, *The Moral Property of Women*, 286.
42 Enrique Raviña, *The Evolution of Drug Discovery: From Traditional Medicines to Modern Drugs* (Weinheim, Germany: Wiley-VCH, 2011), 1–3.
43 Raviña, The Evolution of Drug Discovery, vii.
44 Alfred D. Chandler Jr., *Shaping the Industrial Century: The Remarkable Story of the Evolution of the Modern Chemical and Pharmaceutical Industries* (Cambridge, MA: Harvard University Press, 2009), 1–3.
45 Fields, *Katharine Dexter McCormick*, 255.
46 Ibid., 254.
47 Ibid., 255.
48 Editors of the Encyclopaedia Britannica, "Gregory Pincus: American Endocrinologist," accessed February 7, 2021, https://www.britannica.com/biography/Gregory-Pincus.
49 Fields, *Katharine Dexter McCormick*, 262–263.
50 Quoted in Eig, *The Birth of the Pill*, 99.
51 Fields, *Katharine Dexter McCormick*, 256.
52 Ibid., 261.
53 Eig, *The Birth of the Pill*, 181–184.
54 Gordon, *The Moral Property of Women*, 287–288.
55 Eig, *The Birth of the Pill*, 229–234.
56 Ibid., 191.
57 Bonnie Mass, "Puerto Rico: A Case Study of Population Control," *Latin American Perspectives* 4, no. 4 (Autumn 1977): 69.
58 Chana Gazat, dir., "The Pill," PBS, February 24, 2003, "https://www.pbs.org/wgbh/americanexperience/films/pill/.
59 National Commission for the Protection of Human Subjects of Biomedical and Behavioral Research, "The Belmont Report," April 18, 1979, https://www.hhs.gov/ohrp/regulations-and-policy/belmont-report/read-the-belmont-report/index.html.
60 Ibid.
61 The Office of Human Research Protections in the U.S. Department of Health and Human Services provides reference materials as well as regulations (including policy, compliance, and reporting requirements) and related materials.
62 Eig, *The Birth of the Pill*, 258.
63 Centers for Disease Control and Prevention, "Ten Great Public Health Achievements—United States, 1900–1999," *Morbidity and Mortality Weekly Report* 48, no. 12 (April 2, 1999): 241–243, https://www.cdc.gov/mmwr/preview/mmwrhtml/00056796.htm.
64 Guttmacher Institute, "Contraceptive Use in the United States," April 2020, https://www.guttmacher.org/fact-sheet/contraceptive-use-united-states.

65 Kimberly Daniels and Joyce C. Abma, "Current Contraceptive Status among Women Aged 15–49: United States, 2015–2017," National Center for Health Statistics Data Brief No. 327, December 2018, https://www.cdc.gov/nchs/data/databriefs/db327-h.pdf,

66 Guttmacher Institute, "Contraceptive Use in the United States" (April 2020), https://www.guttmacher.org/fact-sheet/contraceptive-use-united-states.

67 Planned Parenthood, "How Effective Is the Birth Control Pill?," accessed February 7, 2021, https://www.plannedparenthood.org/learn/birth-control/birth-control-pill/how-effective-is-the-birth-control-pill.

68 Quoted in Fields, *Katharine Dexter McCormick*, 102.

69 Institute of Medicine, *Breakthrough Business Models: Drug Development for Rare and Neglected Diseases and Individualized Therapies: Workshop Summary* (Washington: National Academies Press, 2009).

70 Gerben Bakker, "Money for Nothing: How Firms Have Financed R&D-Projects since the Industrial Revolution," *Research Policy* 42, no. 10 (December 2013): 1793–1814.

71 Tom McKaskill, "An Introduction to Angel Investing," (Australia: Breakthrough Publications, 2009), https://www.drexit.net/angelinvesting.html.

72 Wanucha, "A Mind of Her Own," M19.

Mary Engle Pennington. Photo courtesy of University Archives
and Records Center, University of Pennsylvania.

Mary Engle Pennington

Transforming Food Safety with the Power of Persuasion and a Steadfast Commitment to Good Science and the Public's Health

Akanksha Arya and Christina Tan

Background

In the first half of the twentieth century, women with advanced degrees were predominantly employed on the campuses of women's colleges and a few major universities and in the expanding normal school systems that supplied teachers to public school systems.[1] In 1907, a commencement speaker told the graduating class at Simmons Female College (today's Simmons University) the formula for success: "A woman who conceals her cleverness, one who is willing to do large and responsible work . . . who is willing to handle the reins without seeming to . . . is the one who gets the greatest success" and concluded that the "best job which may come to any woman is the conduct and nourishment of the home."[2] Born in 1872, Mary Engle Pennington did not conceal her cleverness as she pursued her interest in science. Pennington was one of the few female PhDs who worked in her field, initially as an instructor but then as an entrepreneur, government official, businesswoman, educator, patent holder, and consultant. Pennington's interests remained focused on the practical ways that businesses and housewives could improve the safety of their food. She described herself as "an expert in the handling, transportation and storage of perishables and the application of refrigeration."[3] Throughout her life, Pennington's actions can be characterized as methodical, conscientious, persuasive, and collaborative. Her influence in governmental public health and the private food industry changed the way food is processed, stored, packaged, and sold.

The oldest of two daughters, Mary Engle Pennington was born on October 8, 1872. She spent her first few years in Nashville, Tennessee, but her family then moved to Philadelphia to be closer to the Engles, her mother's family, who were Quakers (a group also known as the Society of Friends). Pennington, who considered herself a native Philadelphian, declared years later in an interview with the *New Yorker* that "I'd never have been born anywhere but Philadelphia if I'd had anything to do with it."[4] The impact that growing up in Philadelphia would have on Pennington can be seen in her childhood. Thanks to the success of her father's label-manufacturing business, the family lived comfortably in a three-story redbrick house close to the University of Pennsylvania (Penn). At that time, Philadelphia was one of the largest cities with a commercial port in the United States, and it had the first medical school, medical society, lending library, and philosophical society in the North American colonies.[5] Pennington enjoyed gardening with her father and going to the market with her mother, where she noticed that the variety of foods available for purchase diminished with each coming winter. She also accompanied her mother to Quaker Sunday meetings, where she witnessed and absorbed a spiritual drive for service and a sense of equality among all people.[6] Although Quaker men and women held separate monthly meetings related to the business of the Society of Friends, women participated actively and influentially in its governance and ministry.[7] Quaker women could serve as traveling ministers and had responsibility for charitable functions and financial record keeping. In a time of unequal education for men and women, Quakers promoted the education of both boys and girls.[8] The Penningtons encouraged their daughters to pursue their educational interests. Pennington's love for learning flourished as she read for hours at the public library. At the age of twelve, she became interested in a book on medical chemistry, and as she spent her summer studying a chapter on nitrogen and oxygen, her passion for chemistry grew. She later recounted in a *New Yorker* interview: "Suddenly, one day, I realized, lickity hoop, that although I couldn't touch, taste, or smell them [nitrogen, oxygen, and other elements] they really existed. It was a milestone."[9] Soon afterward, she marched up to the headmistress of her all-girls finishing school and demanded that the school teach her chemistry. Studying chemistry was considered unladylike at the time, and Pennington was rebuffed coldly: "I doubt that you can even spell it."[10] While this was ironically true at the time, Pennington's curiosity still burned.[11] She went to Penn and asked a professor to explain to her what she had read in her medical chemistry book. The professor promised to teach her when she was older and suggested that in the meantime she learn how to read and spell the words.[12] Pennington graduated from her school and returned home to find that the boys she had played with when she was younger had all moved on to study at Penn. Still driven by her passion to learn science, one afternoon Pennington walked into the office of Horace Jayne, dean of the Faculty of Arts and Sciences and asked for permission to study at the Towne Scientific School at Penn.[13] Jayne led her to the chemistry lab and introduced her to the professor there as his new pupil. Though initially shocked, Pennington's parents came to welcome the idea of their daughter preparing for a career.[14]

Completing her degree requirements in three years, Pennington at last satisfied her curiosity about sciences like chemistry, biology, and hygiene. However, when the time came for her to receive her bachelor of science degree, she was denied her diploma by Penn's Board of Trustees, who did not accept the idea of a woman being admitted to the university. Instead, the university gave her a certificate of proficiency, which alone was not sufficient for her to take the next step in her education: entering a PhD program. Impressed by Pennington, the science faculty declared her eligible to study for a PhD, citing an old college statute that allowed the university, in extraordinary cases, to enroll special students in graduate studies. However, this statute restricted applicants younger than twenty-two from applying for a PhD.[15] Pennington was then eighteen, so she continued to work and study at Penn in the electrochemical school under the tutelage of the renowned Edgar Fahs Smith. When she turned twenty-two, Pennington submitted her dissertation, titled "Derivatives of Columbium and Tantalum," in which she described her research on chemical compounds formed from these elements.[16] Without receiving a bachelor's degree, she earned her PhD in 1895 and became one of the first 228 women to receive a PhD in the United States and one of 13 women to receive a PhD in chemistry in the country before 1900.[17] Pennington also became the third woman to join the American Chemical Society.[18] She continued to study chemical botany (the chemical study of plants)[19] at Penn for two more years. She then accepted a one-year fellowship at Yale University to study physiological chemistry ("a branch of science dealing with the chemical aspects of physiological and biological systems").[20] Her work included a collaboration with Russell Chittenden, known as "the father of American biochemistry," to study the effect of colored light on plant growth.[21]

Despite years of developing her expertise and credentials, Pennington struggled to find meaningful work after graduation. In 1898, she returned to Philadelphia and took a position as a physiological chemistry instructor at the Women's Medical College. Simultaneously, she took steps to build her own business. In the mid-1890s, new bacteriological and chemical tests for disease were giving physicians additional diagnostic tools. Pennington saw an opportunity and decided to open her own business, a clinical laboratory. To ensure financial stability, she secured commitments from four hundred local physicians that each of them would request at least $50 of laboratory testing annually. In 1901, with physician commitments in place, Pennington partnered with Elizabeth Atkinson, a fellow Penn chemistry student, and Evelyn Quintard St. John, a physician at the Women's Medical College of Pennsylvania, to open the Philadelphia Clinical Laboratory, which provided chemical and bacteriological analyses for doctors and hospitals. The lab was a success, and she developed a local reputation for doing high-quality work.[22]

Due to this reputation, in 1904, Pennington was asked to head the bacteriological lab at the Philadelphia Department of Health and Charities. In this position, she chose to focus on unsafe milk, in recognition of its contribution to foodborne illness trends at that time. Contamination of milk started at the dairy farm. A physician who inspected one farm noted that "attendants upon the cattle were careless of their personal habits and frequently were suffering disease. . . . Cattle were frequently found covered with manure and other dirt . . . which readily dropped into the pails whilst milking was being done. They [the cattle] were many times found suffering from constitutional disease, as well as local affections of the udder . . . frequently the surface of the milk pails was covered with dead and dying flies . . . few, if any, facilities were found for boiling water to cleanse the utensils." Milk would then be transported and stored at fluctuating temperatures, which allowed bacteria previously introduced into the milk to multiply and reach infectious doses.[23]

Milk was used in daily meals and played an integral role in the diet of young children. Infants were given cow's milk in bottles, and as children were weaned off of bottles, experts recommended that milk account for 60 percent of the caloric intake for a one-year-old and 33 percent for a two-year-old. Milk represented purity, childhood, and maternal care, so the unsafe and adulterated milk widely sold at the time was tainted both metaphorically and chemically. Infants' and children's developing digestive systems were no match for unsafe milk, and diarrheal disease was a leading cause of infant mortality. Infant mortality from such disease displayed peaks during warm seasons, supporting the notion that poor dairy and food storage were culprits in these infant deaths.[24] Pennington's crusade against unclean milk was an effort to protect this vulnerable population.

Pennington studied every stage in the process of milk production to understand current practices and sources of mishandling of milk. Based on her research, she developed safety standards for the regulation of the milk industry, including hiring a team of investigators to conduct regular inspections of dairy farms that supplied milk to Philadelphia. Using her laboratory research and field tests, Pennington established practices that were novel at the time, adopted first locally and then nationally. Her methodical study also led to routine dairy farm inspections, which collectively with the adoption of safety standards contributed significantly to improving children's public health. With the adoptions of these and other measures to clean up the milk supply, seasonal peaks in infant diarrheal disease in large U.S. cities had vanished by the 1920s.[25]

Along with studying the production of milk, Pennington researched the cold storage of milk. Every year as the weather grew warmer, she watched as pushcarts selling ice cream to children appeared in Philadelphia's streets. Pennington grew concerned about poor preservation and storage of ice cream in these pushcarts and the harm that impure frozen treats would have on children's health. There were no laws at the time that gave her jurisdiction to enforce safety standards among ice cream vendors. Without any regulatory authority, Pennington realized that she would have to persuade the vendors to adopt safety standards voluntarily. Pennington believed that given accurate scientific information, people could choose to make the right decisions themselves. She showed vendors microscopic slides of the bacteria growing on their equipment. Horrified, the vendors agreed to adopt better sanitization practices by boiling their pots and utensils. Pennington was thus able to change the practices of local businesses and protect the public's health.[26]

Pennington's crusade against unsafe milk at home was a small part of a larger crusade nationwide to clean up the country's food system. In the late 1800s, technological innovations and changes in the population created seismic shifts in the demand for food, producers' abilities to meet those demands, and opportunities for contamination of the food supply. With the industrial revolution, urban population in the United States grew dramatically in the 1880s, as a second wave of immigration began and many people moved into cities. Local producers were unable to supply the demands of the new residents. As railroads crisscrossed the country, food manufacturers saw opportunities in mass production and marketing and transporting their products to more distant and larger markets. The development of mechanical refrigeration and competitive ice manufacturing plants provided food manufacturers with the tools and resources to increase the life span of their products at the same time as their reach expanded to consumers nationwide. Companies built their own railroad lines and refrigerated trains, giving them more control over food transport. Consumers were no longer limited to local food producers. The flourishing food marketing industry led consumers to develop a taste for new processed foods.[27]

While manufacturers could now better meet consumers' demand for a larger quantity and variety of products, the complexity of this new food system created multiple opportunities for impurities to be introduced and affect food quality. There were reports of unsanitary practices at production sites and poor packing and refrigeration during transport, as well as adulterants in food products—with an estimated 15–56 percent in value of all food products in the United States entering the market being adulterated and misbranded, valued at $3 billion in 1906. Harvey W. Wiley, head of the U.S. Bureau of Chemistry (predecessor to the Department of Agriculture), zealously answered the call for science to validate suspicions about the food industry. Between 1887 and 1893, the bureau published a series of reports on food adulteration, revealing "watered down milk; charcoal mixed with pepper; seeds in ground spices; beer without barley . . . bleaching agents, chemicals, and dyes in molasses; chicory, acorn, and seeds in coffee; and acids and metallic salts in canned vegetables."[28] When manufacturers of food additives claimed that there were no links between food adulterants and sickness, Wiley responded with a series of "Poison Squad"[29] experiments, in which twelve volunteers agreed to eat wholesome meals laced with common adulterants every day for at least six months, stopping only when they became too sick with nausea, vomiting, or in some instances, abdominal pains to function. Journalists amplified the details of these experiments, and the published reports captivated readers, feeding public demand for regulation of the food industry.[30]

Despite calls for action, legislators were slow to enact any such regulation. As Congress dragged its feet, journalists revealed economic ties between legislators and food lobbies, which angered the public. More likely to vote based on issues than party, voters organized and put political pressure on their representatives. Women's organizations in particular took on the crusade for food and drug reform, playing a large role in generating public pressure by organizing mass campaigns that organized demonstrations, educated voters, and lobbied politicians. Wiley later cited women's groups and the medical community as the two major reasons for the eventual passage of the Pure Food and Drug Act of 1906.[31]

Meanwhile, in the wake of tragedies caused by adulterated foods, European countries passed their own food safety regulations, boycotted adulterated U.S. products, and flooded U.S. markets with their own higher quality products, wooing consumers away from the goods sold by domestic food companies. Recognizing the effect that consumer mistrust and foreign competition would have on U.S. products, the domestic food industry saw the need for regulation to regain the public's trust. After attempts at self-regulation failed to satisfy consumers, the food industry began calling for government regulation. By the time Upton Sinclair's investigative *The Jungle* was published in 1906, horrifying the U.S. public with graphic descriptions of the unsanitary practices of the meat industry, the country was ready for food safety legislation.[32]

After many previous attempts to enact legislation, the Pure Food and Drug Act (often referred to as the Wiley Act) was passed in 1906. This legislation gave the federal government jurisdiction to regulate interstate food commerce, which was involved in a significant portion of the sales of mass-manufactured food made in the United States. However, little research had been done to develop food science, and terms in the act like *safe* and *unsafe* were not scientifically defined. The dearth of food science research limited the act's enforceability and the ability for regulatory actions to be upheld in court. Recognizing the need for food safety science to give the act teeth, the Bureau of Chemistry established the Food Research Laboratory, and Wiley had the perfect person in mind to lead the new lab.[33]

A family friend of the Penningtons, Wiley had been following Pennington's work with milk production and storage in Philadelphia. Impressed by her skills and ability to work collaboratively with industry, he had previously enlisted Pennington's help in answering another research question. In 1905, a publicity story from the poultry industry had quickly gained attention from the press and the public. The story was about a banquet at which turkeys were served that the seller had preserved in cold storage for ten years. Not only did the guests survive to tell the tale, but they reported enjoying their meal. Intrigued by the story and aware of the shortage of scientific research on refrigeration, Wiley tasked Pennington with researching the effects of cold storage on poultry. Using her characteristic methodological approach of conducting a thorough scientific investigation to understand a problem, Pennington examined the entire poultry production process. She studied the chickens' feeding stations, the slaughtering process, the cold storage warehouse, the retail market, and the dressed chicken. While she could not find any poultry to study that had been stored for ten years, she concluded that poultry retained its quality and safety if kept stored at temperatures below 32 degrees Fahrenheit for up to a year. Through her work with milk and poultry, Pennington began to build the foundations of the scientific understanding of cold storage of perishables.[34]

When Wiley asked Pennington to lead the new Food Research Laboratory, she took the civil service exam. But she was reluctant to do so, as she was skeptical that a woman would be given the position of director. Unbeknown to her, Wiley submitted her exam under the name "M. E. Pennington," and she scored the highest on the exam. The civil service offered Pennington the position but then revoked the offer when it discovered that she was a woman. Pennington was furious that Wiley had submitted her exam using only her initials. However, convinced that Pennington was the right person for the job, Wiley advocated on her behalf and convinced the civil service to hire her. Despite Wiley's entreaties that she work in Washington, D.C., Pennington sought to avoid political and administrative burdens, and she set up her new office in the same building as her old office in Philadelphia.[35] She began her tenure with four employees, including her sister, Helen M. P. Betts, and St. John, the physician at the Philadelphia Clinical Laboratory.

For her first project at the Food Research Laboratory, Pennington expanded her study of poultry by focusing on the slaughtering, packaging, and transportation processes. She slaughtered thousands of chickens herself as she sought to find the most hygienic method. While most producers at the time used a block-and-axe method to slaughter poultry, Pennington discovered that using a small knife to pierce the chicken's brain and then cut the jugular veins provided superior results. This method made it easier to pluck the chicken and leave it intact, allowing for better transportation and reducing the opportunities for bacterial growth. The standard practice was to draw poultry by removing a chicken's feathers, blood, visceral organs, feet, and head before transport. While many states had laws against transporting undrawn chickens, Pennington persuaded all of them to change those laws by convincing them that undrawn chickens functioned as "sealed packages" that had less chance of bacterial invasion.[36] At the time, chickens were transported in barrels of chipped ice and would reach their destinations waterlogged and floating in tepid water. Pennington devised a method to remove the animal heat from chickens immediately after slaughter, allowing for a more hygienic system of packing the chickens dry in boxes and transporting them by refrigerated cars. Pennington also studied the quality of poultry, conducting chemical and microscopic exams to assess changes in color, texture, and chemistry. She concluded that if each step of processing was hygienic and refrigerated, poultry could be safely stored at 0 degrees Fahrenheit and retain a high quality of flavor. Pennington's research was essential in providing standards for federal legislation. After public outcry against the cold storage industry culminated in Congressional hearings in 1910, Pennington's research and testimony played a key role in setting a standard limit of one year for the cold storage of food entering interstate commerce—a step toward the establishment of the concept of the "cold chain" that persists to the present, regarding guidelines for refrigerated processing, storage, and transportation.[37] Initially the new standards were opposed by industry, but Pennington avoided taking an adversarial role. She presented the scientific evidence to support the superiority of cold-stored foods and connected it with the impact on consumers and markets. She was able to negotiate with industry and government to find common ground.

As consumers stopped keeping chickens at home, the mass-produced egg industry grew. Mass production often resulted in a percentage of cracked, oversize, or scarred eggs. These eggs were known in the industry as "dirties" and could not be sold in the market. Companies were founded that bought these "dirties" and then froze, canned, or dried them and sold the resulting products to bakers and confectioners. The limited regulation of this industry led to poor handling, storage, and transportation of the products, which in turn resulted in high counts of bacteria in them. Fueled by investigative journalism of poor practices and recent wins with food safety legislation, public outcry against these unsanitary practices grew.[38] The egg-breaking industry would test Pennington's scientific expertise, rigorous research capabilities, and powers of persuasion.

The debate over what to do about unsanitary practices in the egg-breaking industry moved to the U.S. District Court in Trenton, New Jersey. During an inspection, the U.S. Department of Agriculture (USDA) condemned 443 cans of egg product from the New Jersey–based H. J. Keith Egg Company on the basis that the eggs were "deteriorated and decomposed" and "injurious to health."[39] Concerned about the impact that this would have on its reputation, the Keith Company sued the USDA, claiming that it had falsely stated the problems with the eggs. Wiley believed the Keith Company would "put up a stiff fight,"[40] and he requested that the Food Research Laboratory examine the condemned egg product and send a representative to testify in court. Pennington offered to conduct the investigation herself. However, she warned Wiley that thus far the Food Research Laboratory had conducted only preliminary research on eggs and might not be able to provide evidence to support the government's position.

True to Wiley's concerns, the Keith Company fought hard, employing William T. Sedgewick, a renowned epidemiologist at the Massachusetts Institute of Technology (MIT) and a well-known defender of the cold storage industry, to test the eggs and testify on the company's behalf. H. J. Keith, the company's owner, wrote to Pennington, suggesting that she share her practices and collaborate with Sedgewick on the analysis of the product. Pennington declined. Keith had also recently been appointed as an assistant professor at MIT, an association that provoked Wiley's skepticism. When the time came to testify, Sedgewick argued that the high amount of bacteria in the eggs did not mean that they were harmful. He claimed that the eggs had no odd odor and tasted fine when cooked, and therefore the eggs had not decomposed. He concluded that the basis for the seizure of the eggs was unfounded because there were no standards set for egg purity. The Keith Company won the case in Trenton.

The USDA appealed the ruling, and the case moved to the U.S. Court of Appeals for the Third Circuit. There, Pennington testified that liquid egg products should be held to the same standards as milk, referring to a limit of 500,000 bacterial organisms per cubic centimeter—over which the likelihood of food poisoning increased. She reported that in Food Research Laboratory tests guinea pigs injected with the condemned egg products had all died of infections. Wiley added that the Pure Food and Drug Act prohibited the sale of food that had decomposed parts and that the USDA did not have to prove that the food was injurious to a person's health. The court ruled in the USDA's favor, but the Keith Company appealed the decision to the U.S. Supreme Court in 1912. Among its many arguments, the Keith Company highlighted flaws in the Pure Food and Drug Act, including that the USDA's jurisdiction did not apply to the ingredients of food, such as liquid eggs intended for baking, and that standards still had not been created for determining the safety of eggs. In 1912 the Supreme Court ruled in favor of the Keith Company.[41] As Pennington predicted, the dearth of scientific evidence to back the food safety legislation led to the USDA's losing the case.

Through the course of this case, Pennington insisted on rigorous research of eggs to develop the foundation for new standards. She pushed back against Wiley's entreaties for her to immediately start developing standards for liquid eggs, insisting instead on building a foundation of research about the processing of eggs to give scientific validity to any standards developed in the future. She studied each step of an egg's journey from the farm to the table to look for opportunities for improvement. She also studied the bacterial content of different forms of processed eggs, including those that were frozen, dried, or liquid. Based on her research, she began setting evidence-based standards for egg processing and developing ways to support the egg industry in meeting those standards. She encouraged farmers to improve the health and quality of eggs produced during warm weather by collecting them more frequently. She also invented the modern egg crate to help prevent the cracking of eggs in transit. Pennington said, "There is a thrill when a scientific idea suddenly strikes home in the form of a practical solution."[42] Her work helped address the root causes of egg decomposition and improve the quality of eggs entering the market.[43]

In 1911, spurred by media reports of the unsanitary conditions of egg-breaking factories, the secretary of agriculture threatened to ban the factories altogether. Concerned about the impact that this would have on egg farmers across the country, Pennington offered to support the industry in improving its practices. Her ability to balance industry and public health concerns convinced three midwestern factories to adopt her hygienic recommendations, including installing refrigeration, adopting special egg-breaking machines, and incorporating aseptic working conditions. Consumers responded positively, and these factories experienced an immediate increase in business—which resulted in the adoption of these standards by the rest of the industry to remain competitive.[44] Pennington was able to convince egg breakers that improving their practices and earning consumers' trust was good for business. Even without the support of strong regulations, she was able to use her scientific expertise, powers of persuasion, and ability to create solutions that benefited multiple parties to improve and save the egg-breaking industry.

After the Keith Company case, Pennington avoided involving herself or other Food Research Laboratory employees in future court hearings, seeking to separate her office from politics and focus on research. She moved on to research fish. She improved the sanitation of fish processing and harvesting by developing a standardized system for scaling, skinning, quick freezing, and dry packing fish. Her work at the Food Research Laboratory resulted in over forty articles' appearing in scientific journals and earned Pennington a star in the 1910 edition of *American Men of Science*.[45] Her food safety work on a range of products—milk, poultry, eggs, and fish—helped build evidence-based safety standards, supported industry in meeting those standards, and provided the scientific evidence that would make the Pure Food and Drug Act enforceable.[46]

In 1917, as trains carried food thousands of miles across the country to feed troops during World War I, Pennington crisscrossed the country to support the war effort. She was the only woman in a group with twenty-seven men working in the perishable products division of President Herbert Hoover's War Food Administration. The division members called themselves the "imperishables," and they had been tasked with finding ways to better feed the military by increasing the life span of perishable foods.[47] Although Pennington's efforts to improve the availability of fresh foods were not known to consumers, "shipping and packing officials saw her so frequently they called her 'Auntie Sam.'"[48] To gather data on food perishability and transport infrastructure, Pennington made around five hundred train trips across the country, testing food perishability in varied (including extreme) climates. She established a link between humidity and perishability and concluded that of the forty thousand refrigerated train cars in the country, only three thousand had adequate insulation and air circulation. Based on her data, Pennington, a team of railroad representatives, and a USDA official developed recommendations for insulation and ventilation for refrigerated railroad cars. In 1919, Pennington received the Notable Service Award from the Hoover administration for her support with the war effort.[49]

In the same year, Pennington left the Food Research Laboratory, taking her expertise in food safety, refrigeration, and regulation to the private sector. She had groomed two scientists to follow rigorous scientific processes and lead the laboratory in her place. While Pennington's successors were strong researchers, she could not pass on her skills of persuasion or her political skill. The following year, Congress took away the laboratory's appropriation, thus closing it for good. After three years of leading the research department of the American Balsa Company, Pennington opened her own business, an independent consulting company to food storage and shipping companies. Her only employee was a secretary. The business was so successful that in 1936 Pennington was able to move her office to the prestigious Woolworth Building in Philadelphia.[50]

In the early 1900s, while Pennnington's career flourished at the Food Research Laboratory and as an independent consultant, the ice refrigerator was a must for every modern kitchen. By the time she moved into the Woolworth Building, the innovation in the electric refrigerator industry was disrupting the status quo. Originally a box that held both ice and food, the ice refrigerator evolved into an appliance that separated ice and food into two compartments, protecting the food from melted water. Before the late 1800s, ice companies had mined natural ice. After the adoption of steam- and electric-powered refrigeration, which resulted in mass-manufactured clear ice that appeared pure to the consumer, the ice refrigeration industry exploded in the early 1900s, leading to a surplus in ice and the industry's seeking to expand its market. The industry created the National Association of Ice Industries (NAII) to develop new markets and educate consumers about the benefits of ice.

The ice refrigeration industry initially did not fear electric refrigeration and chose not to invest in innovation. Domestic science textbooks, used in high schools and colleges to prepare future homemakers (usually women), gave generations of future consumers lessons about ice refrigeration. In 1923, the purchase cost of an ice refrigerator was $30, while the cheapest electric refrigerator was $450—which made the ice refrigerator the more economical option for consumers. Not only were electric refrigerators expensive, but they also had flammable refrigerants and frequently broke down. Kitchens usually only had one outlet, forcing homemakers to choose whether to plug in a refrigerator or a light source for their kitchen.

However, the electric refrigeration industry made a series of innovations that avoided the problems of ice refrigeration. Thanks to technological advancements, between 1923 and 1929, the cost of an electric refrigerator was cut in half, and by 1935, the costs of buying and maintaining ice and electric refrigerators were equivalent. Electric refrigerators eliminated the hassle of having to regularly buy a supply of ice—an often unpleasant task, as homemakers perceived ice deliverymen to be unclean, rude, and likely to cheat by undersupplying them. The installation of cheap ice refrigerators by landlords left tenants unsatisfied, diminished the reputation of ice refrigerators, and led consumers to lobby apartment buildings to provide centralized electric refrigerators. In a marketing and semantic war with the ice refrigeration industry, the electric refrigeration industry sought to claim the term *refrigerator* for just electric refrigerators and refer to the competing product with the antiquated term *ice box*.

As the ice refrigeration industry watched the electric refrigeration industry capture its market, its members banded together in an attempt to save it. The NAII raised funds through many means, including a voluntary levy on ice sales by members and revenues raised from a film it produced, called *How Would You Like to Be the Ice Man*? Using these funds, the NAII launched a campaign to educate consumers about ice and increase home sales of ice refrigerators. It established the Household Refrigeration Bureau to manage the engine for this campaign.

In 1923, the NAII approached Pennington to head the Household Refrigeration Bureau. She had first attracted the NAII's notice in 1908, when she met J. F. Nickerson, editor of the NAII's newsletter, *Ice and Refrigeration*. Nickerson was so impressed by Pennington's expertise that he recommended that the secretary of agriculture send her as a representative to the First International Congress of Refrigeration, in Paris. Nickerson and his colleagues at the NAII believed that she would be the best person to research and promote household ice refrigeration.[51]

Despite her extensive work to improve the cold chain from production to manufacturing and transportation, Pennington believed that her work was incomplete without addressing the cold chain at the point of the consumer. Would the NAII opportunity allow her to implement the NAII's objectives to increase sales and fulfill her personal mission to reform the last part of the cold chain through the education of households about cold storage?

Resolution

Pennington chose to take the NAII's job offer even though the salary was half what she had made at the Food Research Laboratory—a testament to her belief in the importance of this position in taking the last step in her efforts to completely reform the cold chain. In the new job, she "saw opportunities to do research and education in domestic refrigeration as a way of improving the last link in the 'cold chain' that stretched all the way from the farm to the consumer."[52]

Pennington recognized the central role of housewives in maintaining the nutrition and health of the family, and she focused her efforts on educating women about the importance of home refrigeration. Over the next seven years, Pennington used her background as a bacteriological chemist to educate readers on the scientific principles involved in home refrigeration and food safety. She published thirteen pamphlets on food safety and refrigeration and distributed 1,250,398 copies of the pamphlets to a mailing list of 35,000, which included home economics teachers, home demonstration agents, women's clubs, and welfare agencies. Pennington aimed to supply educators with teaching material to help inform the next generation of homemakers.

Scientists disagreed on what was healthy food: chemists claimed that the chemical nutrition in food was most important, while bacteriologists claimed that food's freshness was an indicator of the absence of harmful bacteria. Pennington's pamphlets attempted to bridge this divide by showing that the appearance and freshness of foods kept adequately refrigerated were indicators of the foods' nutritional value. She recommended that consumers seek refrigerators with adequate humidity to prevent food deterioration and food waste. As the purpose of her role was to increase sales of ice refrigerators, she made sure to include information about how an ice refrigerator was the best device for hygienically storing food. Drawing on her previous research on humidity and perishability, she described the high humidity of an ice refrigerator as ideal for maintaining food quality and freshness in her pamphlets.

Pennington invoked women's roles as homemakers and caregivers in educating women on refrigeration and persuading them to make healthy decisions. She appealed to their desire to keep their families healthy. Pennington was able to build on the developing field of home economics, which incorporated science into tasks associated with the home and offered greater opportunities for women interested in science.[53] Pennington's pamphlets include *Safeguarded by Your Refrigerator* and *The Care of the Child's Food in the Home*. In *Safeguarded by Your Refrigerator*, she applied her previous research on dairy products to direct mothers on how to protect their children from spoiled milk, encouraging them to "take such exemplary care of the milk after she gets it that no shadow of blame can attach to her should trouble arise."[54] In *The Care of the Child's Food in the Home*, she showed how high-quality insulation in ice refrigerators would maintain low temperatures that prevent bacterial growth and provide shelter for food from unhygienic flies and dust. She insisted that "when a baby's health hangs in the balance the intelligent mother will see to it that the ice supply never runs too low."[55] While fulfilling her commitment to the NAII, Pennington recognized the importance of women in home food safety and sought to empower them with information.

Pennington recognized the importance of the influence of other women on homemakers and lobbied the reluctant NAII for funds to hire a female workforce of "home service workers" educated in the science of home economics who would educate other women about refrigeration.[56] In addition, Pennington hired Margaret H. Kingsley as her assistant director. Every year, Kingsley conducted a week-long training session to prepare the home service workers to demonstrate the benefits of ice refrigeration, lead discussions with groups of women at schools and clubs, and develop a network linking the ice refrigeration industry and consumers and home service industries. Graduates of this training went forth to promote ice refrigerators in a variety of ways, including giving public lectures on ice refrigeration and cooking demonstrations of recipes that used ice. Pennington believed that these women would combat consumers' perceptions of the ice industry as a rough and male-dominated industry; however, the NAII was loath to change its established system of marketing and sales. The NAII provided only lukewarm support for this initiative, always requiring that Pennington undergo annual funding renewals for this program and preventing home service workers from completing sales, to avoid competition with the industry's salesmen.

Concerned about the dearth in research and innovation in the ice industry, Pennington lobbied the NAII to increase funding for research on ice refrigeration. For her education-based approach to be a success, she needed scientific evidence to back her claims of the virtues of ice refrigeration. She was also concerned that the techno-logical gains of the electric refrigeration industry would leave the ice industry behind. However, the NAII was less concerned about these gains by its competitors and remained convinced that ice refrigera-tors would always win out over electrical refrigerators as the most economical choice. Pennington had difficulty convincing the NAII to provide meaningful research funding. She received some funding to develop a standardized grading scale for ice refrigerators and to part-ner with the USDA's Bureau of Home Economics to design a study of home refrigeration. Aware that she would not receive sufficient funds to conduct research herself, she reached out to the home economics departments at Cornell and Columbia Universities and encouraged them to conduct various research projects on ice refrigerators. She convinced the NAII to provide each of these universities with $250 and free ice refrigerators for tests. Interested in improving ice refrig-erators, Pennington wanted to know more about what materials pro-vided the best insulation, how cabinet size affected outcomes, and the impact of different foods and environments on ice refrigerator temperatures. She knew the ice refrigerator would survive only if it could work at least as well as, if not better than, electric refrigerators. Unfortunately, the NAII did not prioritize research and innovation and failed to give Pennington sufficient funding.

In 1931, Pennington left the NAII's Household Refrigeration Bureau, frustrated by the lack of funding for research and her edu-cation campaigns. The NAII did not develop any new pamphlets after her departure, and the distribution of educational materials declined. Despite innovations leading to the economic equivalence between electric and ice refrigerators for consumers, the NAII had difficulty raising additional funds from its members to sustain the Household Refrigeration Bureau and its campaign. Under new leadership, the bureau shifted its focus from education to sales. While home service workers were still integral to the bureau's campaign, the NAII remained reluctant to hire women workers. And while the electric and gas industries adopted approaches sim-ilar to Pennington's in marketing to an audience often referred to as "Mrs. Consumer," the bureau lost the NAII's support and funding in 1941. The ever-innovative electric refrigeration industry eventually made the ice industry obsolete.[57]

After working with the NAII, Pennington took a position with the Institute of American Poultry, which was more generous in funding her studies. She never retired from her consulting business and continued to conduct research, publish scientific papers, and innovate in the field of insulation and other food storage technologies.[58] She received patents for a poultry-cooling rack, a bacteria-resistant method of treating eggs, and a sterile food container. In 1941 Pennington became the first woman to be elected to the Poultry Historical Society Hall of Fame. She was inducted into the National Women's Hall of Fame in 2002 and the Inventors Hall of Fame in 2018.

At home, Pennington prepared refrigerated, canned, and frozen foods in her kitchen, confident that foods from all over the United States were now safe to eat. Never married, she shared a Riverside Drive penthouse in New York City with her Persian cat, Bonny. Throughout her life, she attended Quaker services. Her domestic activities included knitting, gardening, and sewing, and she continued to be engaged in promoting cold storage and delivering lectures to businesses.[59] On vacations, she described her travels and surroundings in great detail in letters that would be passed around by her sister, nephew and niece, and four grandnieces. During those vacations, she also met with banks and businessmen to lecture them on the social and financial benefits of modern refrigeration.[60] On December 27, 1952, Pennington died of a heart attack in St. Luke's Hospital in New York. She was buried in Philadelphia.[61]

Throughout her career, Pennington's commitment both to rigorous research and to public health protection shaped how she made decisions that ultimately furthered the field of food science and enabled homemakers to protect their households. In addition, in each of her professional endeavors she promoted women's leadership and employment by hiring other women. The following convictions "were present throughout Pennington's career: (1) care for the well-being of innocent and powerless persons (often women and children) who were liable to be injured by inadequate and unscientific food processing, transportation, and preservation, and (2) a faith in the effectiveness of science-based education to change behavior and thus reduce risks to those who were endangered by such problems."[62] Her legacy lives today through the everyday use of modern refrigeration and the evolution of food safety science.

Notes

1 Sally Gregory Kohlstedt, "Sustaining Gains: Reflections on Women in Science and Technology in 20th-Century United States," *NWSA Journal* 16, no. 1 (Spring 2004): 1–26, www.jstor.org/stable/4317032.

2 Quoted in Elaine R. Ognibene, "Moving beyond 'True Woman' Myths: Women and Work," *Humboldt Journal of Social Relations* 10, no. 2 (Spring–Summer 1983): 11, www.jstor.org/stable/23262316.

3 Quoted in Barbara Heggie, "Ice Woman," *New Yorker*, September 6, 1941, 23.

4 Quoted in ibid.

5 Susan Brandt, "'Getting into a Little Business': Margaret Hill Morris and Women's Medical Entrepreneurship during the American Revolution," *Early American Studies*, 13, no. 4 (Fall 2015): 774–807, doi: 10.1353/eam.2015.0034.

6 "Mary Engle Pennington," in *Encyclopedia of World Biography*, 2nd ed., Andrea Henderson, ed., vol. 22 (Detroit, MI: Gale, 2005): 352–355.

7 Jean R. Soderland, "Women's Authority in Pennsylvania and New Jersey Quaker Meetings, 1680–1760," *William and Mary Quarterly* 44, no. 4 (October 1987): 722–749, https://www.jstor.org/stable/pdf/1939742.pdf ?refreqid=excelsior%3A569e445fd3f4c314f91b23de288f7a17.

8 Bryn Mawr was founded in Pennsylvania in 1833 as a liberal arts college for Quaker women. Quakers were also among the first to encourage women to go into medicine, founding the Female Medical College of Pennsylvania in 1850. In the institution's first year, eight women, five of them Quakers, enrolled as candidates for the degree of doctor of medicine. See "Rights of Women," Quakers in the World, accessed February 8, 2021, http://www .quakersintheworld.org/quakers-in-action/166.

9 Quoted in Heggie, "Ice Woman, 23."

10 Quoted in ibid.

11 Ibid.

12 "Mary Engle Pennington: The 'Cold Chain' of Food Safety," U.S. Food and Drug Administration, Virtual Exhibits of FDA History, March 28, 2018, https://www.fda.gov/AboutFDA/History/VirtualHistory/HistoryExhibits /ucm341862.htm.

13 Elizabeth D. Schafer, "Pennington, Mary Engle (1872–1952)," Encyclopedia .com (March 15, 2021) https://www.encyclopedia.com/women/encyclopedias -almanacs-transcripts-and-maps/pennington-mary-engle-1872-1952.

14 Heggie, "Ice Woman."

15 Ibid, 24.

16 Mary Engle Pennington, "Derivatives of Columbium and Tantalum," *Journal of the American Chemical Society* 18, no. 1 (1896): 38–67, doi: 10.1021 /ja02087a007.

17 Margaret W. Rossiter, "Doctorates for American Women, 1868–1907," *History of Education Quarterly* 22, no. 2 (Summer 1982): 159–183, www.jstor.org/stable /367747.

18 Schafer, "Pennington, Mary Engle."

19 Lillie J. Martin, "Plan for Laboratory Work in Chemical Botany," *Botanical Gazette* 11, no. 11 (November 1886): 311–313, https://www.jstor.org/stable /2993914?seq=1#metadata_info_tab_contents.

20 "Physiological Chemistry," Merriam-Webster, accessed February 8, 2021, https://www.merriam-webster.com/medical/physiological%20chemistry.

21 Prabook, "Russell Henry Chittenden," accessed March 18, 2021, prebook.com /web/Russell.chittenden/1899466.

22 Schafer, "Pennington, Mary Engle."

23 G. Lloyd Magruder, "Milk as a Carrier of Contagious Disease, and the Desirability of Pasteurization," *New England Medical Monthly* 29, no. 5 (1910): 160–161.

24 Sarah Komisarow, "Public Health Regulation and Mortality: Evidence from Early 20th-Century Milk Laws," *Journal of Health Economics* 56 (December 2017 https://www.sciencedirect.com/science/article/abs/pii/S0167629616304842 ?via%3Dihub.

25 Ibid.

26 Heggie, "Ice Woman."

27 I. D. Barkan, "Industry Invites Regulation: The Passage of the Pure Food and Drug Act of 1906," *American Journal of Public Health* 75, no. 1 (January 1985): 18–26, PMC1646146.

28 Ibid., 20.

29 Ibid., 21.

30 Carol Lewis, "The 'Poison Squad' and the Advent of Food and Drug Regulation," *FDA Consumer* 36, no. 6 (November–December 2002): 12–15, http://esq .h-cdn.co/assets/cm/15/06/54d3fdf754244_-_21_PoisonSquadFDA.pdf.

31 Jillian London, "Tragedy, Transformation, and Triumph: Comparing the Factors and Forces That Led to the Adoption of the 1860 Adulteration Act in England and the 1906 Pure Food and Drug Act in the United States," *Food & Drug Law Journal* 69, no. 315 (2014): 315–34

32 Barkan, "Industry Invites Regulation"; see Upton Sinclair, *The Jungle* (New York: Doubleday, Page, 1906; repr., New York: Penguin Books, 1985).

33 "Mary Engle Pennington," *Encyclopedia of World Biography*.

34 Heggie, "Ice Woman."

35 "Mary Engle Pennington," *Encyclopedia of World Biography*.

36 Heggie, "Ice Woman, 26."

37 Lisa M. Robinson, "Establishing the Cold Chain: The Work of the United States Food Research Laboratory, 1907–1919," *Journal of Agricultural and Food Information* 7, no. 1 (published online October 24, 2008): 19–37, doi: 10.1300 /J108v07n01_04.

38 "Mary Engle Pennington," *Encyclopedia of World Biography*.

39 Lisa Mae Robinson, "Regulating What We Eat: Mary Engle Pennington and the Food Research Laboratory," *Agricultural History* 64, no. 2 (Spring 1990): 149, http://www.jstor.org/stable/3743804.

40 Ibid.

41 Four Hundred and Forty-Three Cans of Frozen Egg Product v. United States, 226 U.S. 172 (1912), https://cite.case.law/us/226/172/.

42 Quoted in Malcolm Forbes and Jeff Bloch, *Women Who Made a Difference*, (New York: Simon and Schuster, 1990), 238.

43 Robinson, "Regulating What We Eat.

44 Heggie, "Ice Woman."

45 Mary R. S. Creese, *Ladies in the Laboratory? American and British Women in Science, 1800–1900: A Survey of Their Contributions to Research* (Lanham, MD: Scarecrow, 1998), 257.

46 "Mary Engle Pennington," *Encyclopedia of World Biography*.

47 Heggie, "Ice Woman."

48 Forbes and Bloch, *Women Who Made a Difference*.

49 "Mary Engle Pennington," *Encyclopedia of World Biography*.

50 Heggie, "Ice Woman."

51 Karl D. Stephan, "Technologizing the Home: Mary Pennington and the Rise of Domestic Food Refrigeration," in *1999 International Symposium on Technology and Society—Women and Technology: Historical, Societal, and Professional Perspectives. Proceedings. Networking the World*, (New York: Institute of Electrical and Electronics Engineers, 1999), https://drive.google .com/file/d/0B08kTWc1vxHcbWZzNm9PNnc4WDA/view; Lisa Mae Robinson, "Safeguarded by Your Refrigerator: Mary Engle Pennington's Struggle with the National Association of Ice Industries," in *Rethinking Home Economics: Women and the History of a Profession*, ed. Sarah Stage and Virginia B. Vincenti (Ithaca, NY: Cornell University Press, 1997), 253–270, http://www.jstor.org/stable/10.7591/j.ctv2n7jkd.25.

52 Quoted in Stephan, "Technologizing the Home," 291.

53 Sasha Chapman, "The Woman Who Gave Us the Science of Normal Life," *Nautilus*, March 30, 2017, http://nautil.us/issue/46/balance/the-woman-who -gave-us-the-science-of-normal-life.

54 Quoted in Robinson, "Safeguarded by Your Refrigerator," 261.

55 Quoted in ibid, 259.

56 Ibid.

57 Stephan, "Technologizing the Home;" Robinson, "Safeguarded by Your Refrigerator."

58 Robinson, "Safeguarded by Your Refrigerator."

59 Heggie, "Ice Woman."

60 Ibid.

61 Schafer, "Pennington, Mary Engle."

62 Stephan, "Technologizing the Home," 290.

Florence Schorske Wald. Photo in the public domain.

Florence Schorske Wald

Standing by Her Principles—Not by a Title—to Bring Hospice to the United States

Patricia A. Findley, Suzanne Willard, and Jacqueline Hunterton-Anderson

Background

At the beginning of the twentieth century, the United States—particularly New York City—faced turbulent times, with significant growth in terms of population, industry, and wealth. An influx of immigrants increased New York's ethnic, racial, class, and religious diversity.[1] There was a rise of activism in unions, as illustrated by radical groups like the Industrial Workers of the World (also known as the Wobblies), as well as a push for the Nineteenth Amendment to the Constitution, giving women the right to vote. Overshadowing this rising activism was the 1918 flu pandemic, in which over fifty million people worldwide—including 675,000 Americans—died.[2] In 1917, during these tumultuous times, Florence Wald (then Schorske) was born in the Bronx, New York City. Raised by social activist parents, Wald chose a path rich in education, and her strongly held beliefs about social justice helped her become a leader who challenged the way health-care professionals delivered medical care for people at the end of life. Wald left a lasting legacy for compassionate end-of-life care and an interdisciplinary care model known today as hospice care.

Wald's early experiences laid the foundation for the roles she would play throughout her life. She lived with her parents and brother in a Bronx apartment overlooking the Harlem River. Her father was a banker, and her mother worked in the shipping industry. Wald's paternal grandfather owned a cigar-making business and was a labor organizer.[3] Her maternal great-grandfather, Meyer Thalsmessinger, was a radical German revolutionary and a commissioner in New York City who served on one of the first slum clearance committees and as a trustee for New York's public schools.[4] The family was immersed in politics, art, literature, and music.[5] Her parents often involved their children in their activist work, as they helped immigrants acculturate to the United States.[6] Her mother was also a volunteer at a health clinic that served the poor.[7] As a child, Wald learned the value of social justice, or "the objective of creating a fair and equal society in which each individual matters, their rights are recognized and protected, and decisions are made in ways that are fair and honest."[8] She was quick to speak her mind and advocate for her ideas, behavior her parents had modeled for her.

Wald's father's strong opinions and personality had a lasting impact on her life. However, he was chauvinistic and often mocked the idea of women's liberation. In a world in which women fought for the right to vote, her father's beliefs in this area posed a conflict for Wald. Her education did not lessen her general inner conflict and insecurity about the role of women in society.[9] This insecurity lasted well into her adulthood, as she struggled to find her place in a world that did not always welcome a woman's strength of character or abilities outside the home.[10]

As has been the case with many leaders, several incidents shaped Wald's character. A sickly child, she developed a respiratory condition that required her to be hospitalized for several months.[11] She was later diagnosed with scarlet fever and needed to be isolated. During this illness she met Eunice Biller, who was her private nurse. The care that Biller provided was holistic, not focused just on physical care. Biller ensured that Wald was able to play and listen to music in her convalescence. In addition to helping Wald get better, Biller instilled in her the importance of helping others and considering the patient's body, mind, spirit, and emotions when providing care. Biller also instilled in Wald a desire to provide such care.

Another important incident was her beloved grandmother's death when Wald was ten years old. It was customary during this time for the family to hold a viewing in their home to allow people to come and pay their respects to the deceased. When she saw her grandmother, Wald thought that she was sleeping, and she bent to kiss her on the lips and was surprised and frightened by how cold they were. She found that no one offered to comfort her or wanted to discuss her sadness and grief over this significant loss. Even as a child, she was troubled by the experience and the taboo about discussions of grief and death.

During the 1930s, in the depth of the Great Depression, young women like Wald found that they had few choices in life. Sparse resources led families like Wald's to support sons in their educational pursuits and to encourage daughters to marry. Wald's brother Carl, whom she idolized, was given an education at Columbia and Harvard Universities.[12] Wald and Carl were very close and shared many childhood experiences. She wanted to have an education like her brother, to be a nurse, and to incorporate the tenets of social justice learned from her parents into the role of caregiver. Carl understood that when Wald sought to go to college, she was overcoming the insecurity she had felt as a child. Her father was not supportive, but it was an issue of inequality in the family. With the help of her brother and unbeknown to her parents, she applied to several colleges. When she told her father of the acceptances she had received, he reluctantly agreed that she could matriculate, but he wanted her close and to attend Barnard College, in New York City. However, Wald saw that the prestigious Mount Holyoke College, in Massachusetts, had an innovative program whose credits would be accepted by Yale University toward a graduate degree in nursing. It was Carl's persistent advocacy in support of Wald with their father that allowed her to pursue her desire not only to be a nurse but also to have an advanced education.

Wald graduated from Mount Holyoke in 1938 and received a master's degree in nursing from Yale in 1941. It was at Yale that Wald first encountered a model of care in which the patient was the center, where it was important to "have the patient feel like a person and not as a contagious disease."[13] While Yale's nursing school had a strong focus on responding to the patient as a human being, hospitals and the health-care professions had a different but equally strong emphasis on a medical model that was physician-centered and paternalistic. The late 1930s and early 1940s were a turning point in the treatment of illness. New anesthesia agents, penicillin (which was discovered in 1928 and became commercially available in the 1930s), vaccines (for polio, diphtheria, tetanus, and pertussis), innovative medical treatments that could prevent and cure disease, and the increased availability of technology created the belief that medical treatments were more relevant than nursing care. These conflicting views of roles are "embedded in the 'care' and 'cure' ideologies respectively embraced by most nurses and physicians."[14] The medical model of practice often placed dying patients out of sight at the end of a hospital hall.[15] A patient who was dying was seen as a failure of curing. Strict policies on visiting hours limited family members' involvement in a patient's care and often left relatives with little access to doctors. In addition, there was little interest in a holistic approach to the sick and dying.

After graduating from Yale, Wald accepted a position at the Henry Street Settlement's visiting nursing program, returning to the place where her parents had taken her in their advocacy work with immigrants. Consistent with the dynamic evolving at the time, the Henry Street Settlement had separated its visiting nurse service from the social service organization. The visiting nurse service changed from a patient-focused and nurse-driven organization to one focused on the disease, not on the whole person. Dissatisfied with this medical model, Wald left the Visiting Nurse Service of New York after two years. During the final stages of World War II, she served in the Women's Army Corps. Always an activist, she wanted to contribute to the effort to fight the atrocities that were happening in Germany. Instead, she was assigned to a maternity hospital.[16] After the war, she became part of a research team at the New York City Eye Bank and in the Surgical Metabolism Unit of the College of Physicians and Surgeons at Columbia University.[17]

Later, a job at Babies and Children's Hospital in New York City gave Wald an opportunity to see how she could make a difference as she successfully advocated to include parents in caring for their sick children. This advocacy recognized the child's emotional and physical needs by allowing parents to stay with their children (even when they slept) and assist in their care. Wald was able to attend to the mental health needs of the patients and their families, not just to the disease. She saw that she needed more training and soon returned to Yale for additional education.

In 1950, the National League for Nursing required all schools of nursing to include content on mental health, following an increased interest in mental health training within the nursing profession.[18] Innovative educational programs related to mental health were developed and mental health research and new treatment approaches were often funded by the federal government: Yale had one of these innovative programs to provide formal education and clinical training in mental health. In 1956 Wald received a second master's degree from Yale, this time in mental health nursing.

One of the leaders in nursing with an emphasis on mental health at that time was Hildegard Peplau, a nursing theorist with a PhD. As a primary contributor to mental health law reform, Peplau led the way toward the humane treatment of patients and the therapeutic relationship between the nurse and the patient.[19] She was also a prolific writer, whose words captivated Wald. Peplau developed the first graduate-level program for the preparation of advanced practice clinical specialists in psychiatric nursing.[20] After graduating from Yale, Wald, now thirty-eight years old, joined Peplau as a faculty member at the College of Nursing (now known as the School of Nursing) at Rutgers University.

In 1957, Yale recruited Wald as an assistant professor of psychiatric nursing and leader of the new mental health nursing program. She found that things were not what they had appeared to be. The school was in chaos and threatened with a shutdown: Yale intended to shift the university away from disciplines of practice such as nursing. The school of nursing needed leaders and its curriculum reform, but the external push for the closing drove the nursing school faculty members behind closed doors. Some were looking for new jobs. However, Wald found that some were willing to take a stand to enhance the curriculum. She helped develop a new curriculum and presented it to the university's president, who accepted it and offered Wald the deanship of the school. Wald became dean in 1959, knowing that she had the support of a group of faculty members invested in teaching advanced nursing practice and research methods.[21]

As dean of the Yale School of Nursing, Wald was well positioned to make some critical reforms in nursing education and advocate for nursing as a scholarly clinical discipline. These reforms would have a significant impact on health care, health-care education, and interdisciplinary relationships among health-care team members. She drew upon the other schools at Yale to broaden the scope of nursing education and added a strong research focus. During this time, she reconnected with Henry Wald, an engineer, whom she had known during her time at Columbia University and who was now a widower with two young children.[22] Henry and Wald married in 1959.

In the late 1950s and into the 1960s, there was a major transformation in U.S. mental health policies, services, and treatment. The most significant change was the transition of mental health care from institutions to community-based programs. The public saw institutions as warehouses and state-run institutions as expensive to maintain. Prevailing thought leaders felt that these institutions could be closed by transferring care to community-based programs. However, those programs were often inaccessible, and patients were left without much support and landed in the street.[23] Wald saw this lack of support, and as dean, she was able to form an interdisciplinary team with members from the fields of nursing, public health, and psychiatry, along with community members, to create the Connecticut Mental Health Center in 1966.[24] The work was groundbreaking: it allowed nursing faculty members to have joint appointments, promoting nurses to the same status as other professionals such as social workers, physicians, and psychologists, who could practice and teach—as well as collaborate on care and conduct research—regardless of professional title.[25] This collaboration implemented the interprofessional care model that Wald advocated.

During her tenure as dean, Wald emphasized advanced nursing practice and a focus on the care for people with mental illness. Wald, a well-trained researcher and clinician, understood the complexity of care. Her own experience of poor physical health seemed to have made her more empathetic and fueled her desire to make changes to help the needy, the sick, and the dying.[26] These traits were first noted in nursing school by her instructor and other students, and Wald went on to demonstrate a leadership style described as characterized by "quiet, unswerving commitment, sense of inclusion, consensus building, and collegiality."[27]

Wald used her research as a way to challenge the system. Her focus was on illuminating the needs of the dying, with the hope that they would express their feelings. This was in contradiction to the standard practice of care for the dying, and Wald found that physicians did not involve patients in any discussion of their illness or treatment. There was a closed awareness, meaning that the patient was unaware of his or her impending death. Wald witnessed how doctors and nurses were afraid to speak with patients and their families about dying. The emotional needs of the dying patient were not a focus. Wald understood that patients desperately wanted to have their voices heard. Peplau described "the patient as an active participant in understanding and solving his problem rather than as a passive recipient of advice and instruction."[28] Despite resistance, Wald felt something needed to be done to change the delivery of health care and, most importantly, the delivery of end-of-life care.

Wald was the principal investigator in her research. This was unusual at the time, given that female scientists were denied proper credit for their work and instead saw their research attributed to male colleagues.[29] Wald promoted the belief that the principal investigator has the right to independent thought regardless of gender or position. She was responsible for the preparation, conduct, and administration of her projects, ran her research team meetings, and analyzed the data. She was promoting systemic change with this new approach of having not only a woman but a nurse leading a research team.

Interestingly, Wald's need to change health care coincided with a time of unrest in the United States, when authority was questioned, an unpopular war was waged halfway around the world, and the civil rights movement awakened many people to injustices across the nation. Wald used her role at Yale to fight for the civil rights and antiwar movements, as well as other causes. During that time, Wald recalled, "the women's movement gave promise that the gender barrier between doctors (predominantly men) and nurses (predominantly women) would be lowered—that doctors would hear what nurses said and nurses would challenge doctors. The healthcare hierarchy was shaken. Nurses became more capable of expressing themselves and began to expect recognition."[30]

A pivotal moment for Wald came in 1963 when she met Cecily Saunders, a nurse, social worker, and physician from Great Britain. Saunders came to Yale to speak to the medical students. One School of Nursing faculty member, Virginia Henderson, attended the lecture. She told Wald that Saunders's topic was the "essence of nursing" and asked Saunders to speak the next day at the school. Saunders gave Wald the context in which to advocate for better patient care at the end of life. Wald recounted how Saunders "just opened the door for [her]."[31]

Saunders had a unique approach to working with terminally ill patients. This approach diverged from the medical view that promoted prolonging life as long as possible. Instead, Saunders's approach empowered patients to die in the way they wanted. She felt that pain management was critical to mitigate suffering at the end of life so patients could speak with family members as they all prepared for death.[32] Saunders felt that the approaches to the patient of all members of the care team should be aligned. In her conversations with Saunders, Wald found support for her own concerns that nurses felt at odds with physicians in the care of the terminally ill.[33] Wald realized the impact that Saunders was having on end-of-life care. Her team approach, which focused on opening up end-of-life conversations between the patient and his or her family, was definitely a concept that Wald favored and that was included in the Yale curriculum.

The radical movements of the 1960s; the publication in 1969 of Elisabeth Kübler-Ross's *On Death and Dying*, which placed the taboo topic of death in the national discourse;[34] and Wald's introduction to Saunders helped set the stage for Wald to ignite the hospice movement in the United States. As a researcher, Wald felt that the work

Saunders was doing could provide the evidence to change practice of end-of-life care in the United States. She also felt that a good foundation for this approach could be in the hospice movement.[35]

Wald accomplished much at Yale, but when she found a new passion in hospice care, she believed that her time as dean had come to an end. In 1969, she traveled to England with her husband and spent a month learning every aspect of the hospice program at St. Christopher's Hospice in London. Wald knew that traditional models of caring for the ill and dying were dependent on the patient's family. When no family member was available, religious institutions took over, incorporating a spiritual component into care. St. Christopher's Hospice exposed Wald to the modern concept of hospice care, and she was impressed that it had been the first place to accept patients with all diagnoses and of all religions and social classes. This unique practice was impressive in this time of civil unrest, when an individual's diagnosis, religion, race and ethnicity, or social class could separate individuals for differential treatment. Wald faced a decision as hospice fit well with her roots in social justice and her ideals as a nurse, but it was unclear if the United States and the health-care community were ready to embrace the use of hospice care.

Resolution

When Wald and her husband returned to Connecticut from their visit to St. Christopher's to learn about hospice care, Wald knew this would be her new focus. She set up a lunch meeting with people she felt would join her in the quest to explore the possibilities of hospice. Her guests were from the religious community, given how hospice care was provided at St. Christopher's Hospice, as well as physicians interested in medical sociology. As most of the patients requiring hospice care were dying of cancer, Wald added Ira Goldenberg, a well-respected oncologist, to the team exploring hospice. Wald had accompanied Goldenberg on his rounds to increase her knowledge about the needs of terminal oncology patients. Her observations of Goldenberg's approach to care highlighted some of the deficiencies in care given to the dying. In particular, she felt that ineffective care was being delivered and going unchallenged because of the lack of collaboration among the providers involved.

Wald set in motion a movement in the United States to make significant changes in the delivery of health care for people who were dying. She envisioned equality when she brought various professionals together for any of her research projects, just as she insisted that teamwork and collaboration were critical practices in the proposed hospice facility.[36]

In the 1960s, when Wald was introducing hospice care and the interdisciplinary model of care as a core component of hospice, the medical community was not ready to embrace change. In hospice care, the physician is seen as "one among a number of equal members of an interdisciplinary team and had no automatic entitlement to the position of leader."[37] Wald pushed for health-care professionals to collaborate as equal partners. At the time, nurses were still seen as being subordinate to physicians, a view compounded by social dynamics: nurses were primarily female, in their twenties, and had a diploma rather than a college degree, and they were paid much less than physicians.[38] In contrast to the typical nurse, Wald was older, and she had a bachelor's degree and two master's degrees from major universities. She came from a family whose members were highly educated and respected in their fields. Wald had the experience, education, and passion to make observations about the role of nurses in relation to that of doctors. She found that the role of nurses limited their creativity in ways to treat patients: the doctor writes the orders, and the nurse is left to carry them out.[39] Wald was not happy with these roles, since compared to the doctor, the nurse spent more time with the patient and had a greater understanding of the patient's needs, family, and perceptions about his or her own care. Wald planted the roots for hospice care in the United States through her informal presentations of her research findings as well as her call to change nursing education.[40] By 1969, nurses were taking on an expanded role. With the increased demand for health care given the availability of new technology and with the expansion of treatment paradigms, nurses began to perform some of the tasks previously reserved for physicians, particularly at times when the latter were not available.[41]

The concept of evidenced-based practice, now widely used and respected, was in its infancy in the 1960s. Wald recognized that to create a monumental shift in practice, she would need to produce evidence to support the change. She conducted the *Interdisciplinary Study of the Patient and His Family (1968–1971)* and another research study titled: *A Nurse's Study of the Terminally Ill Patient and His Family* to build an evidence base for the development of hospice care. Wald based this work on what she learned during visits to St. Christopher's Hospice, where she observed and experienced an equal and collaborative model in operation. She wanted hospice to center on the care and comfort of the patient who was dying. In the *Interdisciplinary Study of the Patient and His Family*, Wald interviewed twenty-two patients and collected extensive diaries and transcripts of observations of how patients interacted with interdisciplinary team members and with their family members when confronting death. She turned to two famous qualitative researchers, Barney Glaser and Anselm Strauss, who pioneered *grounded theory* and its methodology.[42] This form of analysis helps the researcher develop theories by collecting and examining qualitative data for patterns, concepts, and themes. Wald worked closely with a faculty colleague from Yale, Donna Diers, on her research. Despite Diers's help with navigating the qualitative method, Wald rejected her own attempts to develop categories from the diaries and transcripts and determined the categories were "trash."[43] She later stated that common social science concepts used to evaluate the emotional responses in the diaries and transcripts did not reflect the material properly. When she used clinical terms to describe patients' and families' responses and experiences she could organize and present the data to accurately reflect those experiences. Wald understood the standards for publication in medical journals and the criticisms she could face from the medical investigators—particularly Goldenberg, who felt Wald's *Interdisciplinary Study of the Patient and His Family* study participant sample size was too small to provide any generalizable information.[44] Therefore, she admitted defeat,[45] and the studies were not published. Wald turned her attention back to the development of hospice care. However, she did want information from her research to get out, so she presented her work informally by speaking about her findings with colleagues and at professional meetings.[46]

Wald embodied transformational leadership in the founding of the hospice movement in the United States. She used her observations, research, clinical knowledge, and leadership experience to help people understand and embrace the hospice movement. Wald demonstrated an "ability to challenge intellectual and moral norms and elevate the consciousness of those who became the first American hospice founders."[47] Interdisciplinary collaborative care was the model that hospice needed to use to achieve the best outcomes.[48] She had a respect for human life, and she valued human dignity, spiritual needs, and the rights of patients and their families to make decisions at the end of a patient's life.[49] Over time, her physician colleagues recognized the importance of this work.

Wald built the first hospice in the United States, Hospice, Inc. (later renamed Connecticut Hospice), which opened in 1975 in New Haven.[50] She engaged supporters—and valued the inclusion of patients, families, and the community—in its development and construction. Wald saw that raising consciousness about hospice care for both the health-care team as well as the community at large was critical. She kept the focus on consciousness-raising by requiring an unwavering focus on improving the care for the dying and developing an interdisciplinary team. Wald wanted the program to be replicated and embraced. She documented core principles and included them in the model of research, educational pursuits, and conferences to share this work. She focused on community outreach to raise awareness and financial support for physical construction, as well as to build capacity to support social change.[51]

Wald was an energetic and engaged change agent. As founding member of Hospice, Inc., she, along with her husband, oversaw the construction of its building and the establishment of its interdisciplinary team. Her husband had quit his job and acquired a degree in health facility planning to help Wald construct the hospice facility as she wanted it to be.[52] To advance the hospice model further,

Dennis Rezendes, a consultant, was engaged to secure the necessary state approvals and permits, in addition to financial support. However, like many visionaries, Wald did not tolerate people with ideas that were not aligned with hers.[53] This created difficulties, and soon the board of directors of Hospice Inc. was receiving complaints about Wald's demanding to be part of all aspects of programming.[54] Wald was committed to the concept of hospice, but she accepted that this concept and the crucial work of caring for the dying was more important than command and controlling the aspects specific to administrative approvals and reimbursement, so she resigned her position, and Rezendes was named director of the hospice. A Wharton Business School graduate, he had a corporate and administrative mind-set that was similar to the concept of the physician as captain of the ship. Unlike Wald's focus on clinical care and consensus building, Rezendes' charge was to lead Hospice, Inc. through the state's application process for a certificate of need and secure a facility license.

Wald remained an active leader in promoting hospice across the United States and developed a hospice model for correctional systems. While her time at Hospice Inc. was not long, her contribution to the hospice movement in the United States was extraordinary and recognized by several organizations.[55] Yale awarded her an honorary degree, introducing her as "the mother of the American hospice movement."[56] She was not comfortable with this title, which she viewed as "a completely incorrect description," and she stated, "There were many, many people in those days who were just as inspired and motivated as I was."[57] She was the first recipient of Leading the Way Award of the Hospice and Palliative Nurses Association. In 1998, she was inducted into the National Women's Hall of Fame. And in 2001, she was named a living legend by the American Academy of Nursing.

Wald's influence continues to impact current practice. Hospice care affects primarily quality and only secondarily quantity of life, but it needs to be started soon after a patient and/or the family elects to use only comfort measures to relieve suffering and provide practical, emotional, and spiritual support. Since the creation of hospice care, individuals and their families have had end-of-life journeys that involve a team effort. Wald envisioned hospice care to be family centered and involve multiple disciplines to provide the best patient care at the end of life. This approach allows for the management of patient care by physicians, nurses, social workers, chaplains, and volunteers, as well as home health aides, bereavement counselors, dieticians, and pharmacists, among others.[58] Involving multiple people in planning improves the care given and provides for the comfort of the patient and family members. Wald worked to change the narrative of hospice care from giving up to one of care based on comfort, support, and involvement of patients and their families.

Hospice care is now considered part of the health-care continuum in the United States.[59] Although still underutilized, its use has grown significantly in the past few years due to increasing awareness of resources and options. Decisions about end-of-life care are some of the most difficult for patients and families. More than 65 percent of Americans spend the final stages of life in hospice care. Medicare recognized and authorized hospice coverage in 1982, under the Tax Equity and Fiscal Responsibility Act. According to the Hospice Association of America and the National Hospice and Palliative Care Organization, there are 4,639 hospice programs certified by Medicare representing an increase of 13.4 percent since 2014.[60] Of these hospices, 26.9 percent are not-for-profit organizations. In 2018, 1.55 million Medicare beneficiaries received hospice care.[61]

Being born into a turbulent political time and raised in a family whose members believed in advocacy and social justice set Wald on a trajectory to effect profound change in health care. She developed a passion for being a nurse, and she quickly focused on the care of patients at the end of life. She is recognized as a pioneer for her work in bringing the hospice model and its interdisciplinary model of care to the United States.[62]

Diers points out that Wald's leadership had a significant impact on the care patients receive at the end of life.[63] Her work affected ethical decision making, public policy on how care is delivered, how care was financed, and even—with her husband's help—the architecture of hospice centers. Wald was a "vanguard woman of her time, leading the way and encouraging others of us to take the risks to go forth and make concrete the visions we had been given to address some of society's inequities and maladies. . . ."[64] Wald had a rich and fruitful life that was influenced by many factors. She used all of her strengths and talents to lead a movement to create hospice care in the United States. She challenged the way health-care professionals in different disciplines interacted, promoted equality in communication among people in different disciplines to enhance patient outcomes, and believed that no single profession had all the answers. She modeled what we now know as interprofessional care. She did this by focusing on promoting the best outcomes for patients. Wald was a bold woman for her time, and she spoke her mind in advocating for others. She fought hard for health-care teams to work collaboratively with the patient and for the interprofessional practice of care rather than its leadership by the person with the highest-ranking title.

Wald died in 2008 at the age of ninety-one. She is remembered for her unswerving commitment to and respect for the rights of patients, particularly the rights of those at the end of life. She built consensus and found trusted partners as she made innovations in nursing education related to mental health. Wald advanced "nursing as a scholarly clinical discipline based in specialist nursing practice"[65] and was a leader in the development of hospice care in the United States. She had a role in changing the ways health-care professionals treat patients and professional colleagues interact. She was a woman of her time, but she promoted a model in which patients are the center of care long before the medical establishment was ready to embrace it.

Notes

1 Lawrence A. Cremin, *American Education: The Metropolitan Experience, 1876–1980*, vol. 3 (New York: Harper Collins, 1998).

2 Jeffrey K. Taubenberger, Ann H. Reid, and Thomas G. Fanning, "The 1918 Influenza Virus: A Killer Comes into View," *Virology* 274, no. 2 (2000): 241–245.

3 Dorian Block, "The Roots of a Rebellious Nurse," *Illness, Crisis and Loss* 17, no. 4 (2009): 285–298.

4 Ibid.

5 Ibid.

6 Mary L. S. Vachon, "Alchemy, Compassion, and the Healer's Art: A Tribute to the Life and Work of Florence Wald," *Illness, Crisis and Loss* 17, no. 4 (2009): 319–330.

7 Emily K. Abel, *Prelude to Hospice: Florence Wald, Dying People, and Their Families* (New Brunswick, NJ: Rutgers University Press, 2018).

8 "Social Justice," Oxford Reference, accessed February 9, 2021, https://www .oxfordreference.com/view/10.1093/oi/authority.20110803100515279.

9 Block, "The Roots of a Rebellious Nurse."

10 Paula Baker, "The Domestication of Politics: Women and American Political Society, 1780–1920," *American Historical Review* 89, no. 3 (June 1984): 620–647, https://www.jstor.org/stable/1856119.

11 Vachon, "Alchemy, Compassion, and the Healer's Art."

12 Carl E. Schorske studied at Columbia University as an undergraduate and received a master's degree and PhD from Harvard University. During World War II, he worked for the Office of Strategic Services, the precursor to the CIA. After the war, he taught at Wesleyan University for fourteen years, moving in 1960 to the University of California, Berkeley, where he was a faculty leader who challenged the university's restrictions on political expression during the turmoil of the mid-1960s Free Speech Movement. Schorske later taught at Princeton University, where he was Dayton-Stockton Professor of History until his retirement. He was a Pulitzer Prize–winning historian, recipient of the so-called genius grant from the MacArthur Foundation, and popular classroom lecturer, whose *Fin-De-Siècle Vienna: Politics and Culture* (New York: Vintage, 1981) is widely regarded as a classic work of intellectual scholarship. See Associated Press, "Carl E. Schorske Dies at 100: Pulitzer-Winning Historian Taught at Berkeley and Princeton," September 18, 2015, https://www.latimes.com/local/obituaries /la-me-carl-schorske-20150919-story.html.

13 Quoted in Beth P. Houser and Kathy N. Player, *Pivotal Moments in Nursing: Leaders Who Changed the Path of a Profession* (Indianapolis, IN: Sigma Theta Tau International Honor Society of Nursing, 2007), 371.

14 William D. Corser, "The Contemporary Nurse-Physician Relationship: Insights from Scholars outside the Two Professions," *Nursing Outlook* 48, no. 6 (November–December 2000): 263–268, https://doi.org/10.1067/mno .2000.109154.

15 Mary Ann Krisman-Scott, "Origins of Hospice in the United States: The Care of the Dying, 1945–1975," *Journal of Hospice and Palliative Nursing* 5, no. 4 (2003): 205–210.

16 Donna Diers, "Before Hospice: Florence Wald at the Yale School of Nursing," *Illness, Crisis and Loss* 17, no. 4 (2009): 299–312.

17 Ibid.

18 Peter Nolan, *A History of Mental Health Nursing* (Cheltenham, UK: Nelson Thornes, 2000).

19 Hildegard E. Peplau, *Interpersonal Theory in Nursing Practice: Selected Works of Hildegard E. Peplau*, ed. Anita Werner O'Toole and Sheila Rouslin Welt (New York: Springer, 1989).

20 Ibid.

21 Houser and Player, *Pivotal Moments in Nursing*.

22 Block, "The Roots of a Rebellious Nurse."

23 Ellen L. Bassuk and Samuel Gerson, "Deinstitutionalization and Mental Health Services," *Scientific American* 238, no. 2 (1978): 46–53.

24 Diers, "Before Hospice."

25 Ibid.

26 Block, "The Roots of a Rebellious Nurse."

27 Zelda Foster and Florence Wald, "A Crossroads," *Illness, Crisis and Loss* 9, no. 1 (2001): 45.

28 Quoted in Patricia D'Antonio et al., "The Future in the Past: Hildegard Peplau and Interpersonal Relations in Nursing," *Nursing Inquiry* 21, no. 4 (December 2014): 315, https://doi.org/10.1111/nin.12056.

29 Jessica Fink, "Gender Sidelining and the Problem of Unactionable Discrimination," *Stanford Law and Policy Review* 29, no. 1 (2018): 311–324.

30 Quoted in "Wald, Florence Sophie," Encylcopedia.com, https://www.encyclopedia.com/history/encyclopedias-almanacs-transcripts-and-maps/wald-florence-sophie, updated March 16, 2021.

31 Quoted in Abel, *Prelude to Hospice*, 10.

32 "Florence Sophie Wald," in *Encyclopedia of World Biography*, 2nd ed., Andrea Henderson, ed., vol. 24 (Detroit, MI: Gale, 2005).

33 Foster and Wald, "A Crossroads."

34 Elisabeth Kübler-Ross, *On Death and Dying* (London: Routledge, 1969).

35 Florence S. Wald, "Emerging Nursing Practice," *American Journal of Public Health and the Nation's Health* 56, no. 8 (1996): 1252–1260.

36 Abel, *Prelude to Hospice*.

37 Ibid., 114.

38 Arlene W. Keeling, *Nursing and the Privilege of Prescription, 1893–2000* (Columbus: Ohio State University Press, 2007).

39 Abel, *Prelude to Hospice*, 20.

40 Wald, "Emerging Nursing Practice."

41 Abel, *Prelude to Hospice*.

42 Barney G. Glaser, Anselm L. Strauss, and Elizabeth Strutzel, "The Discovery of Grounded Theory: Strategies for Qualitative Research," *Nursing Research* 17, no. 4 (1968): 364.

43 Quoted in Abel, *Prelude to Hospice*, 89.

44 Ibid.

45 Ibid., 90.

46 Ibid.

47 Cynthia C. Adams, "The Leadership of Florence Wald: Listening to the Voices of the Early Hospice Founders and Colleagues," *Illness, Crisis and Loss*, 17, no. 4 (2009): 379–398.

48 William Rock, "Interdisciplinary Teamwork in Palliative Care and Hospice Settings," *American Journal of Hospice and Palliative Medicine* 20, no. 5 (2003): 331–333, https://journals.sagepub.com/doi/10.1177/104990910302000502.

49 Adams, "The Leadership of Florence Wald."

50 Abel, *Prelude to Hospice*.

51 Adams, "The Leadership of Florence Wald."

52 Abel, *Prelude to Hospice.*

53 Ibid.

54 Ibid.

55 Ibid.

56 Ibid.

57 Quoted in ibid.

58 Elaine M. Wittenberg-Lyles et al., "Assessing the Nature and Process of Hospice Interdisciplinary Team Meetings," *Journal of Hospice and Palliative Nursing* 9, no. 1 (2007): 17–21.

59 Karen Ogle, Brian Mavis, and Tammy Wang, "Hospice and Primary Care Physicians: Attitudes, Knowledge, and Barriers," *American Journal of Hospice and Palliative Medicine* 20, no. 1 (January 1, 2003): 41–51, doi:10.1177/104990910302000111.

60 Hospice Association of America and the National Hospice and Palliative Care Organization, "NHPCO Facts and Figures: 2020 edition," (August 20, 2020): 1–24, https://www.nhpco.org/factsfigures/.

61 Ibid.

62 Diers, "Before Hospice."

63 Ibid.

64 Sally S. Bailey, "Reflections on the Spirituality of Florence Wald," *Illness, Crisis and Loss* 17, no. 4 (2009): 313–316.

65 "Florence Schorske Wald '41," Yale School of Nursing, accessed February 9, 2021, https://nursing.yale.edu/alumni-giving/distinguished-alumnaei-award/90-yale-nurses/florence-schorske-wald-41.

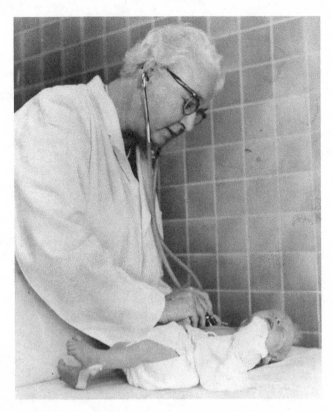

Virginia Apgar. World-Telegram photo by Ed Palumbo.

Virginia Apgar

Focusing on Prevention, She Structurally Transformed Maternal and Child Health for Generations

Mary E. O'Dowd and Colleen Blake

Background

Virginia Apgar developed innovations in maternal and child health practice and strategically advocated for the implementation of a public health infrastructure that has allowed her foundational efforts to be expanded and remain relevant for decades. Throughout her career, she produced groundbreaking research, advocated for improvements in clinical practice based on scientific evidence, and convened policy makers and experts who collectively have made repeated improvements in the care for pregnant women and infants for generations. Children in the United States take their first test, the Apgar test, within moments of birth. The newborn's score can have a dramatic impact on the entire family's life. The test, created in the early 1950s, is so common that most people who find themselves in a delivery room do not think about it long enough to consider the enormous impact that it has had on the care of infants and their mothers. Many people may not know who created this test that has survived so long, although without realizing it, they usually know her name.

The Apgar test, a newborn scoring system, was revolutionary. It was "the first clinical method to recognize the newborn's needs as a patient. It helped spur the development of neonatology as a medical focus, establishing the need for protocols and facilities such as the newborn intensive care unit to provide specialized care."[1] The scoring system became so ubiquitous that "every baby born in a modern hospital anywhere in the world is looked at first through the eyes of Virginia Apgar."[2] Apgar made her way through a career in academic medicine as a physician, researcher, advocate, and teacher. As a teacher, she taught her students, "Do what is right and . . . do it now."[3] She was always ready to respond to an emergency, carrying medical equipment (including a laryngoscope) in her purse "whether in the hospital, on the sidewalk, the highway or in church"[4] and saying "nobody, but nobody, is going to stop breathing on me!"[5] Living in an era before the passage of Good Samaritan laws, many physicians and students were counseled to "protect their own welfare before treating a patient, [while Apgar] was outspokenly teaching the opposite."[6]

Apgar's approach to life and her career was "forthright, direct, realistic, and practical."[7] Her personality, persistence, curiosity, and commitment to continued learning led to the elevation of anesthesia as a specialty and improved care for infants at the time of birth. She laid the foundation for improved data collection and research on birth defects that continues to increase knowledge and lead to the development of prevention tools in the United States today. Apgar used her communication skills and humor to translate scientific research into standard practice for providers, and she empowered parents with the knowledge to help prevent birth defects in their children.

Apgar was born in Westfield, New Jersey, on June 7, 1909, to Helen May Clarke and Charles Apgar. Her father, an insurance executive, was also an amateur inventor and astronomer. Influenced by her father's interest in science and by the childhood illnesses that affected her two older brothers, Apgar displayed an early interest in pursuing a career in medicine.[8] In 1904 her oldest brother, Charles, died before the age of five from tuberculosis. Her second brother, Lawrence, was born in 1907 and suffered from chronic childhood illnesses.[9] During her early life, infant and childhood mortality was relatively common. In 1900, children younger than five years accounted for 30 percent of all deaths in the United States, and in 1915, the infant mortality rate was approximately a hundred deaths per thousand live births. Since that time significant improvements in living standards; public health interventions; and advances in technology, medical science, and clinical practice have led to dramatic progress in the survival of infants.[10] In 2018, the Centers for Disease Control and Prevention (CDC) reported that the overall U.S. infant mortality rate was 5.7 deaths per thousand live births.[11] However, the improvements have not been equitably experienced among all racial and ethnic groups, with the highest rate among non-Hispanic Blacks reporting a rate of 10.8 and the lowest rate for Asians at 3.6 deaths per thousand live births in 2018.[12] In addition, significant geographic variations exist between individual states which individually report rates that range from 3.5 in New Hampshire to 8.41 in Mississippi.[13]

During the time that Apgar was pursuing her early education, positive changes were occurring in the care of mothers and infants. In the early 1900s, a significant amount of attention was focused on the high rates of infant and maternal deaths. Many public health initiatives, along with advances in clinical care, were implemented to address this problem. The discovery and use of antimicrobial agents, improved access to prenatal care, and a focus on milk hygiene improved infant survival. In addition, the CDC notes that 40 percent of the high maternal mortality rates during 1900–1930 was due to sepsis.[14]

From 1925 to 1929, Apgar attended Mount Holyoke College, in Massachusetts. During those years, friends described her as a highly energetic woman who performed exceptionally well in her many varied interests and activities. A zoology major, she supported herself financially by working at part-time jobs and seemed to have "endless energy, already noted by her high school yearbook editor ('. . . frankly, how does she do it?')[, which] became her trademark in college. She played on seven sports teams, reported for the college newspaper, acted in dramatic productions, and played violin in the orchestra."[15] This extraordinary energy continued after she graduated and pursued her career in medicine.

In 1933, Apgar, then twenty-four years old, graduated fourth in her class from the College of Physicians and Surgeons at Columbia University, in New York City. Columbia had begun accepting women only in 1917, and Apgar was one of just nine women in her class of ninety students. After graduating in the midst of the Great Depression, she found herself with significant financial debt.[16] At this point in their medical training, people choose to specialize in a particular field and complete residency programs to gain hands-on knowledge. Apgar began a surgical residency and displayed a level of honesty that would become one of her well-known and cherished characteristics. After one of her patients died of complications, Apgar worried that she had made a mistake by clamping an artery. When confronted with the fact that no autopsy was going to be performed, "she secretly went to the morgue and opened the operative incision to find the cause. That small artery had been clamped. She immediately told the surgeon. She never tried to cover a mistake. She had to know the truth no matter what the cost."[17]

After beginning a two-year surgical internship at Columbia, she transitioned to anesthesia.[18] Several factors may have influenced her decision to pursue a specialty in anesthesia. Allen Whipple, chair of Columbia's Surgery Department, has been repeatedly cited as having steered Apgar toward anesthesia. Various biographers who describe Whipple's advice have proposed different rationales for it. One biographer suggests that Whipple may have felt that the practice of anesthesia would benefit by having the intellect of Apgar engaged in improving the standards of care.[19] Alternatively, it has been implied that Whipple was concerned about the economic realities that she faced as a woman in the field of surgery, where he thought she would have limited employment opportunities.[20] Anesthesiology was an emerging area of medical care traditionally provided through the practice of nursing, and therefore it was more accepting of women practitioners. Given the significant underrepresentation of women in the medical profession at that time, anesthesia has been described as a specialty that presented women with greater opportunities for employment and leadership. Between 1920 and 1940, women physicians were more common in anesthesia than other medical fields, and the International Anesthesia Research Society had three women presidents.[21] It is possible that the confluence of these factors led Apgar to pursue training as an anesthesiologist rather than continue her training as a surgeon.

In January 1937, Apgar left Columbia and started the first portion of her anesthesiology residency training at the University of Wisconsin, in a program led by Ralph Waters. He had created the first academic residency program for anesthesiology in the United States after joining the Wisconsin faculty in 1927. Apgar "faced the usual woman physician problem, lack of housing for trainees, and had to sleep in Waters' office for 2 weeks until a room was found for her, in the maids' quarters. Her diary from this time recorded the usual disasters of learning anesthesia. She also recorded her anger at having to miss department events held in male-only dinner clubs."[22] After six months of training in Wisconsin, Apgar returned to New York City to complete her residency training at Bellevue Hospital in a program led by Emery Rovenstine. Rovenstine had trained under Waters and had left Wisconsin to become the director of anesthesia at Bellevue in 1935.[23]

In 1933, the White House Conference on Child Health and Protection had issued a report titled "Fetal, Newborn, and Maternal Morbidity and Mortality." The report provided "a brief presentation . . . of particularly important views and conclusions in regard to causes for the present maternal, fetal and neonatal mortality and morbidity, and to their possible elimination."[24] It discussed a broad range of topics, including the specialty of providers who cared for newborns, anesthesia techniques, the impact of resuscitation on infants, and the influence of social and economic factors.[25] During the 1930s and 1940s, the number of infants born in hospitals rather than at home increased. This shift away from home births and the improvements made in the hospital setting allowed maternal mortality to decrease by 71 percent between 1939 and 1948.[26] Hospitals and the medical community began to make changes in how they reviewed deaths, while increasing the level of professional education for people who delivered babies. The report brought a new focus on care for newborns just as Apgar began her professional career. At the same time, a renewed emphasis on professional education was occurring.

In 1938, after completing her residency training, Apgar left Bellevue to became the first woman to head a specialty division at the Columbia-Presbyterian Medical Center: she was the director of the new Anesthesiology Division within the Department of

Surgery.[27] Apgar designed the division's structure with Whipple and remained its director and only staff member until the mid-1940s, due to the difficulty in recruiting physicians to the specialty because of its lower pay and lower respect.[28] To develop the educational component of the division, Apgar collaborated with a nurse-anesthetist, Anne Penland, to create a teaching handbook, "Notes on Anesthesia," for students in her program. However, much of the teaching was informally conducted through hands-on clinical experience.[29]

As a physician, Apgar was well respected and trusted. She met with patients, "radiating confidence, gentleness, and concern as well as good humor; and she always had a little joke."[30] Examples of the sympathetic approach she used when caring for patients include carrying a child down the stairs to avoid a feared elevator ride and joking about her own hysterectomy to put a woman about to undergo the procedure at ease.[31] Apgar was doing serious work as a physician and teacher, her communication style used humility and humor to engage her patients and students effectively.

Under her leadership, the anesthesia division grew in terms of the number of its physicians and the size of its budget, as well as its reputation within the surgical field. In 1941, she threatened to quit if her request for adequate funding was rejected.[32] Apgar built the division with a focus on education and clinical care. The educational component demanded a significant amount of her time and therefore limited her ability to supervise or conduct research—which had been part of the original design for the division. At that time, her lack of formal research experience became a liability for her professional advancement.[33] In 1949, when the division was upgraded to the level of a department, Apgar was not named to head it. Instead, the university administration gave the post to a male colleague, and Apgar became the director of obstetric anesthesia[34] and was made a full professor within the department. This was the first time a woman had achieved that rank at Columbia.[35] As a department, anesthesia now had a better platform with which to provide education and conduct research.

Apgar's status as a physician and a full professor was significant by itself. However, Apgar's accomplishments were quite remarkable for the time. Around the time of Apgar's birth, women made up just 5 percent of the physician workforce. Fifty years later, when Apgar was named a full professor, this share had increased to only 6 percent.[36] Apgar had an optimistic perspective and felt that "being female had not imposed significant limitations on her medical career. Though she sometimes privately expressed her frustration with gender inequalities (especially in the matter of salaries)."[37] While this perspective may have been influenced by the context of her time, it is clear that she confronted challenges with a positive attitude toward reinvention and professional growth.

In her role at Columbia, Apgar developed into an "honest and encouraging teacher who inspired numerous doctors in their practice of medicine and research,"[38] and she was well positioned to complete what would become her renowned research. One day in 1952, over breakfast in the cafeteria, medical students were discussing how to evaluate newborns at the time of delivery. In response, "Apgar said, 'That's easy you'd do it like this.' She grabbed the nearest piece of paper . . . and scribbled down the 5 points of the Apgar Score. She then dashed off to the labor and delivery suite to try it out."[39] Drawing upon her skills as a scientific researcher and using the perspective of an anesthesiologist, she developed and tested a systematic way to evaluate the health status of a newborn.

Later that year, Apgar presented her research at the Twenty-Seventh Annual Congress of Anesthetists, and in 1953 she published. Her article, "A Proposal for a New Method of Evaluation of the Newborn Infant," described "a practical method of evaluation of the condition of the newborn infant one minute after birth."[40] Apgar outlined five signs to be evaluated: heart rate, respiratory effort, reflex irritability, muscle tone, and color. She explained their relative importance and the most effective way to conduct the evaluation and provide a score. Throughout the article, she emphasized the various ways that each step of the evaluation had been reviewed and made a concerted effort to present the most objective, practical, and accurate way to complete the test. The presentation of her proposed method of newborn evaluation to her peers laid the groundwork for the acceptance and implementation of a new standard of care for newborns.

While conducting her research, Apgar saw a problem in the lack of care given to women and newborns within the field of anesthesia. In addition to identifying the problem, she saw an opportunity to use her skills as a physician, educator, and researcher to better understand the causes of death and morbidity and the means of preventing them. Perhaps as a woman physician leader who, with persistence, had managed to advance within her profession despite the gender inequities she faced in medicine, she was uniquely qualified to identify and address this challenge. In 1955, Apgar wrote:

> It is my impression that the field of obstetric anesthesia has been neglected by anesthesiologists. At present anesthesia stands third or fourth on the list of causes of maternal mortality, and it is widely known that the death rate of infants under one day has decreased very little in the past thirty years. In the majority of these deaths, respiratory inadequacy appears to be the main cause. With the anesthesiologists' wide experience with respiratory obstruction, apnea, and shallow ventilation, it is logical to think that we may be able to contribute to a decreasing incidence of death, as well as to learn much of practical use in pediatric anesthesia, by closer observation of the newborn infant.[41]

With these words, Apgar recognized the structural sexism within the field of anesthesiology and called upon her colleagues to prioritize women and children as patients. She further argued that the anesthesiologist, within the context of newborn delivery, should care for both the mother and the infant. This proposal was consistent with her professional efforts to improve the status of anesthesiology as a medical specialty.

Of particular note, Apgar highlighted the fact that, given the variety of complications that can occur during birth with both mother and infant, "teamwork is especially important at this time."[42] Apgar had collaborated with nurses to develop medical training tools for anesthesia, and she may have been more accustomed than most health-care providers at the time to interdisciplinary clinical care and its benefits. Noting the rare availability of a pediatrician at the time of birth, she made a clear and detailed case for the use of a multispecialty team in caring for patients. Apgar suggested that "all three, obstetrician, anesthesiologist, and obstetric nurse, need to be thoroughly familiar with the immediate problems of the newly born infant."[43] She advocated teaching medical and nursing students in these specialties, in addition to pediatricians, how to care for infants immediately after birth to improve outcomes. Her scoring system itself was "a useful, rapid method of shorthand communication between services and specialties."[44] Apgar argued that a focus on the perinatal period, the education of providers as an intervention, and taking a team approach to care would help reduce maternal and infant mortality.

Apgar used multiple strategies to create change in her field and to broaden the influence of her work. Noting that during the time of birth it was not always possible for all of the specialized doctors to be present, she advocated that all members of the team, including anesthesiologists, physicians in training, and nurses receive training on how to evaluate the health of the newborn. This accomplished two objectives simultaneously. First, it recognized the value of the team members other than the obstetrician and put them at the same level in terms of newborn evaluation training. Second, it created a platform for providing education to all of the health-care providers in the room in a consistent way. This training elevated the status of the anesthesiologist and increased the use of the test by providing all team members with the skill to use it properly. Whether or not Apgar intended to do so, she created an environment that incentivized the obstetrician to know the Apgar test and use it consistently. In any case, the other trained physicians and nurses in the room would know it and have the ability to evaluate its use or complete it independently. This created both an element of teamwork and shared accountability. Apgar was thoughtful, scientific, and thorough in her advocacy for change. She recognized that the obstetrician and was the lead physician and described that person's primary role as addressing the health of the mother. She suggested that other providers must therefore be ready to assist in the evaluation of the secondary patient, the newborn.

Apgar continued to build upon her research. The implementation of a consistent and comparable infant scoring system provided a new ability to measure the health of an infant immediately after birth. The system made additional research possible on the effect of different types of anesthesia on the infant. Apgar's continued work created an evidence base of measured outcomes according to the type of anesthesia agent used. This helped physicians recommend and choose the type of anesthesia, balancing the mother's pain management and the best health outcomes for infants.

Working with two physician colleagues, Duncan Holaday and Stanley James, Apgar conducted additional research that tied low Apgar scores to low levels of blood oxygen.[45] She was known as a practitioner who looked at new and old ideas objectively and was committed to learning. James remembered that at one time cyclopropane was one of her favorite anesthetic agents for delivery, "which she firmly believed to be completely safe and harmless for the infant. When her research fellows found that infants born under cyclopropane were significantly more depressed, she was horrified. After looking at the data, she accepted the verdict and announced, 'There goes my favorite gas.'"[46] Apgar stopped using this type of anesthesia and coauthored a research paper in the *Journal of Pediatrics*, disseminating the knowledge for other doctors to follow suit.

Despite the successful practice of the scoring system and her subsequent work to refine its use, and consistent with her personality and humility, Apgar did not seek to name the tool after herself. L. Joseph Butterfield, a physician colleague, created the name as a mechanism to help students remember the evaluation process. He moved this name into the public sphere without sharing it with Apgar in advance or asking for her permission: instead, he submitted a letter to the *Journal of the American Medical Association* (*JAMA*) explaining the name. In an interview, Butterfield tells the story of Apgar's reaction to his letter, which took place: "In 1962 I wrote a letter to *JAMA* [*Journal of the American Medical Association*], which described . . . an epigram that I devised to remember the five dimensions of observation in the Apgar score. These were: 'a' for appearance, 'p' for pulse, 'g' for grimace, 'a' for activity, 'r' for respiratory effort. And she [Apgar] was in Denver just shortly thereafter at a medical society meeting. . . . One of the medical students helping her with the exhibit leaned down from the stage and he said, 'Dr. Apgar, what does the "g" in your name stand for?' And for one of the only times in her life, she was speechless. She had not read the *JAMA* in March of that year, I believe. And she later wrote me a very nice letter thanking me."[47] In a letter to Butterfield in response to learning of his teaching tool, Apgar responded with humor: "I chortled aloud when I saw the epigram. It is very clever and certainly original. You might like to hear a greeting I received at Boston Lying-In one day by a secretary, who said 'I didn't know Apgar was a person, I thought it was just a thing.'"[48]

Apgar was a female physician in an era when there were very few such people. She chose a career in anesthesia, which at the time was a new specialty for medicine. Anesthesiology presented her with an opportunity to build and advance professionally with less competition from her male counterparts. Apgar took advantage of this and built a research career in an area that had ample opportunity for growth by further focusing on a specific issue: the health and well-being of mothers and infants from the perspective of anesthesiology. Her curiosity and honest approach to her work led her to realize that certain medical practices were causing problems and even death for patients. Apgar developed tools to help address these problems, and her achievements showed that sound and well-researched interventions could prevent maternal and infant deaths. Her research remains relevant: in May 2019, the CDC estimated that seven hundred women in the United States die each year from pregnancy-related complications and noted that the majority of these deaths are preventable.[49]

During her two decades at Columbia, Apgar attended over seventeen thousand births, developed and refined her scoring system, and taught many students. Due to her professional focus on newborn evaluations, she became increasingly aware of birth defects and interested in the ways that they could be prevented or ameliorated. By this point, she had already demonstrated that "learning was the focal point of her life. Her curiosity was insatiable, and new knowledge held a continuing fascination for her."[50] Acting on this devotion to learning, in 1958 Apgar took a sabbatical leave from

Columbia to pursue a master's degree in public health at the Johns Hopkins School of Public Health. She intended to develop her statistics skills in this program and return to Columbia.[51]

At this time, the March of Dimes (MOD), then known as the National Foundation, was a major organization involved in changing the landscape of health and health research in the United States. In 1958, Basil O'Connor, leader of the MOD and a friend of President Franklin D. Roosevelt, announced that the organization would adopt the new mission of preventing birth defects.[52] This transition presented a dramatic change for the organization, which had been solely dedicated to the eradication of polio through funding research, advocacy, and education. The MOD had spearheaded the development of a safe and effective polio vaccine, which was the key to eliminating polio in the United States.[53] Widespread acceptance and use of the vaccine required the MOD—a victim of its own success—to transform itself or cease to be relevant. The coincidence that this occurred at the same time as Apgar's return to school because of her growing interest in birth defects led to a new opportunity to change her career path.

Resolution

In 1959, Apgar joined the MOD as the head of its division on congenital birth defects. The MOD refers to her as a pivotal figure for the organization and as "the 'founder' of our interest in prematurity, for it was she who first brought attention to the problems of premature birth, as early as 1960. Virginia Apgar was a charismatic and tireless advocate for those affected by birth defects, and she never missed an opportunity to focus on the well-being of the newborn in the delivery room in her educational outreach."[54] The MOD had gained a widely respected physician and researcher, and Apgar stepped onto a national platform with greater visibility and broader impact.

Apgar's new role took advantage of her personality and the skills in communication and humor that had served her well in the past. She had an uninhibited communication style and often used a shock factor to emphasize a point,[55] and she now applied this approach in public. As a national spokesperson, "She taught everywhere—in the air, in hotel dining rooms, even in church. In later years she carried a small bottle containing an 8-week old fetus, as a teaching device, in her purse. The fetus had a failure of closure of the neural tube and therefore had a visible defect which could clearly be seen at that early age. . . . The fetus was even named Billy, and at a recent dinner meeting of the Spina Bifida Association of America, she produced Billy. He was handed round and examined by all the parents. No one was shocked. All were fascinated and intrigued. It was a perfect educational vehicle."[56] Apgar leveraged her position and unique style to convincingly advocate for change by educating the public, the health-care community, and even Congress.

In 1964 and 1965, the United States experienced an epidemic of rubella, a contagious disease caused by a virus. The CDC estimated that during that epidemic "an estimated 12.5 million people got rubella, 11,000 pregnant women lost their babies, 2,100 newborns died, and 20,000 babies were born with congenital rubella syndrome (CRS),"[57] which can have severe and lifelong impacts that include heart defects, intellectual disabilities, liver and spleen damage, deafness, and other consequences.[58] In the aftermath of this epidemic, Apgar used her role at the MOD to initiate a campaign to advocate for universal rubella vaccination, which prevents CRS by protecting the mother from the disease. Testifying before Congress in 1969, Apgar argued that widespread immunization of children with the rubella vaccine would prevent future epidemics and subsequent birth defects. She explained that the MOD had pledged to collaborate with health departments and medical societies to foster public understanding through education efforts. Part of that work included producing direct mailings for 145,000 health professionals and millions of educational flyers for the general public. She urged Congress to support these efforts by providing funding for immunizations.[59] Apgar engaged the public, the medical community, and Congress in a multifaceted approach to achieve vaccine coverage rapidly and avoid future epidemics. As a result of increased vaccination rates, the number of rubella cases in the United States decreased to the point where the disease was eliminated from the country in 2004.[60]

Despite leaving Columbia, Apgar did not stop teaching medical students or conducting research. She became the first medical professional in the United States to specialize in birth defects, and she taught teratology (the scientific study of congenital abnormalities and abnormal formations) at Cornell University from 1965 to 1974. Apgar continued to conduct research and publish in academic journals within the new specialty of birth defects. In 1966, she published "The Drug Problem in Pregnancy," in which she outlined the progress made and remaining questions related to current academic understanding of the impact of medications and drugs on the developing fetus. Apgar highlighted the fact that an "important change in thinking has taken place in the past decade. The idea that the placenta is a barrier to the transfer of drugs from the mother to the fetus has been disproved. Rather, the placenta is a sieve. Almost everything ingested by or injected into the mother can be expected to reach the fetus in a few minutes."[61] She articulated the necessity for future research to increase understanding of the causes of and preventions for birth defects related to medications and other drugs. Consistent with her approach while implementing the Apgar score, she recognized the need for the tools and platforms so that researchers could do this work. Apgar argued that a birth defects registry must be established to account for and quantify cases, stating that "until such a registry is established, there is no way to know whether birth defects are increasing or decreasing, or whether a cluster of defects is significant or not."[62]

Building upon this position, Apgar teamed up with a statistician, Gabriel Stickle, to publish "Birth Defects: Their Significance as a Public Health Problem" in 1968. According to the article, "an estimated 7% of the live-born [in the United States] have significant defects which are evident at birth or during infancy."[63] They further approximated that 10 percent of these babies die in infancy but that another cohort of the population are born with defects such as diabetes that are undetectable at birth. Collectively, the article estimated that, at that time, fifteen million Americans were living with a defect that affected their daily life. Apgar and Stickle further noted that birth defects were the second leading cause of death in the country. The authors then outlined a comprehensive plan to mitigate and prevent birth defects through the development of a national registry to improve data quality, the expansion of medical education to focus on the collection of family histories and pregnancy data, and mandating uniform recording and reporting of major birth defects at any age. They made the case for building a public health system that would make it possible to use a methodical approach to better understand, detect, and prevent birth defects while simultaneously helping connect people who were affected by them with services and supports.[64] In 2020, this tracking system is in effect and continues to grow. The CDC indicates that 3 percent of babies born in the United States have a birth defect, and forty-three states have tracking programs for such defects. In addition, the CDC funds fourteen population-based state programs that collect data and use them for prevention and to provide service referrals.[65] New Jersey, where Apgar was born, hosts one of these programs and highlights its work in tracking more than 100,000 babies born each year. Not only does New Jersey track births, but it was the first state in the country to mandate screenings for critical congenital heart defects, which it did as of August 2011.[66] The plan that Apgar outlined and advocated for was implemented and continues to save lives today.

In 1968, Apgar became the vice president of medical affairs at the MOD and continued to reshape its mission. Through her continued pioneering research, commitment to education, and advocacy, Apgar effectively led the evolution of the MOD from an organization with a singular focus on polio to one with a broad perspective on perinatal health, encompassing the health of all pregnant women and babies. In an effort to effect change, the MOD provided grants to promote the development of neonatal intensive care, genetic counseling, and perinatal networks, in addition to training medical professionals.[67] In the midst of this work, Apgar remained focused on communicating directly with the public, patients, and mothers in particular. In 1972, she coauthored *Is My Baby All Right?*, a book that provided direct consumer education on the causes of birth defects and opportunities for prevention. Describing the science behind genetic mutation and abnormalities with diagrams and pictures, Apgar and her coauthor explained the current understanding of medical research. They coupled this with stories of patients with experience in dealing with sickle cell anemia, cleft lip, cerebral palsy, congenital heart defects, and many more.[68] Jane Brody, a well-known health columnist for the *New York Times*, (and the subject of a case study in this volume) wrote in the blurb that appeared on the book's back cover that the "unquestionably readable and well-researched [book provides] detailed descriptions of the countless things that can go wrong in the process of creating a new human life. [It also] may give the hope, understanding, and love needed to care for an afflicted child."[69] The book ends with a list of resources that could provide a variety of types of assistance for parents and offers guidance on how to contact these organizations.

The capstone of Apgar's career, according to the MOD, was her effort in 1972 to "convene the first Committee on Perinatal Health, [a] joint effort of the American Medical Association, the American College of Obstetricians and Gynecologists, the American Academy of Family Physicians, the American Academy of Pediatrics, and the March of Dimes."[70] One product of this four-year deliberative process was the publication in 1976 of *Toward Improving the Outcome of Pregnancy*. This report, endorsed by so many influential organizations, led to the introduction and implementation of a new system of regionalized perinatal health care that contributed to the improvement in survival rates for newborns in the following twenty years.[71] This process was replicated and provided updated recommendations in 1993 and 2011, modeled on the thoughtful, collaborative, and interdisciplinary professional approach that was started by Apgar, and continues to drive improvement in health-care delivery and prevent birth defects.

While working for the MOD, Apgar lived in Tenafly, New Jersey, and cared for her mother, who died in 1969 at the age of ninety-five.[72] "Apgar never married, insisting: 'It's just that I haven't found a man who can cook.'"[73] She never stopped working, dying of liver disease on August 7, 1974, at Columbia-Presbyterian Medical Center—where she had trained, worked, and taught for many years. She received many awards for her work, including the issuance of a United States postage stamp with her photo on it in 1994. In 1995, she was inducted into the National Women's Hall of Fame.[74] She was an influential leader who had an impact on people and organizations beyond her immediate authority by devoting her seemingly boundless energy to the creation of practical and evidenced-based public health strategies. One of her colleagues said of her leadership style that she had the "ability to get the best out of people without antagonizing them."[75] Apgar was able to continuously excel in competitive male-dominated environments, saying that "women are liberated from the time they leave the womb."[76] Embodying the meaning of those words, Apgar appears to have persistently transformed any obstacle in her professional life into an opportunity to reinvent herself and expand her work. She was committed to continuous learning and affecting the world around her. Apgar's impact has been so significant that a U.S. surgeon general was quoted saying that she had "done more to improve the health of mothers, babies and unborn infants than anyone [else] in the 20th century."[77]

Apgar was directly involved in promoting change in clinical practice, medical education, and the structure of the health-care system to improve the lives of many people by preventing the causes of disease and death that affect children and adults. She conducted scientific research, published her work within the scientific community and to educate the public, and advocated for strategic policies that created public health registries and systems to ensure that their implementation had lasting effects. She authored more than seventy publications, and countless studies have been based on her life's work. The foundation that she laid continues to support work on maternal and child health. Apgar's strong sense of optimism is pervasive in her work to prevent negative outcomes for patients as well as in her personal journey. When she commented on her own success, she remained humble: "I've been lucky all my life, I can hardly believe it. So often, I have been asked by interviewers, 'what obstacles did you meet, as a woman, as you became a physician?' Their faces uniformly fall when I tell them that there were no obstacles at all in my career, such as it is. True, I did not achieve everything for which I aimed, but these failures constitute probably less than ten percent of the opportunities presented."[78]

Notes

1 David Rose, "Virginia Apgar," March of Dimes Archives, May 28, 2009, https://www.marchofdimes.org/mission/virginia-apgar.aspx.

2 Quoted in Virginia Apgar and Joan Beck, *Is My Baby All Right? A Guide to Birth Defects* (New York: Trident, 1972), 9.

3 Quoted in L. Stanley James, "Fond Memories of Virginia Apgar," *American Academy of Pediatrics* 55, no. 1 (1975): 2.

4 Ibid.

5 "Virginia Apgar: Biographical Overview," U.S. National Library of Medicine, U.S. National Library of Medicine, accessed February 10, 2021, https://profiles.nlm.nih.gov/spotlight/cp/feature/biographical.

6 James, "Fond Memories of Virginia Apgar," 2.

7 Ibid, 1.

8 "Virginia Apgar: Biographical Overview."

9 "Changing the Face of Medicine: Dr. Virginia Apgar," U.S. National Library of Medicine, last updated June 3, 2015, cfmedicine.nlm.nih.gov/physicians/biography_12.html.

10 Institute of Medicine, *When Children Die: Improving Palliative and End-of-Life Care for Children and Their Families,*" ed. Marilyn J. Field and Richard E. Behrman (Washington: National Academies Press, 2003), "Chapter 2: Patterns of Childhood Death in America," https://www.ncbi.nlm.nih.gov/books/NBK220806/.

11 Centers for Disease Control and Prevention, "Infant Mortality," accessed March 21, 2021, https://www.cdc.gov/reproductivehealth/maternalinfanthealth/infantmortality.htm.

12 Ely, Danielle and Driscoll, Anne. "Infant Mortality in the United States, 2018: Data From the Period Linked Birth/Infant Death File," National Vital Statistics Reports. Volume 69, Number 7: 4, accessed March 21, 2021, https://www.cdc.gov/nchs/data/nvsr/nvsr69/NVSR-69-7-508.pdf.

13 Centers for Disease Control and Prevention, "Infant Mortality Rates by State," accessed March 21, 2021, https://www.cdc.gov/nchs/pressroom/sosmap/infant_mortality_rates/infant_mortality.htm.

14 Centers for Disease Control and Prevention. "Morbidity and Mortality Weekly Report." Achievements in Public Health, 1900–1999; Healthier Mothers and Babies, (1999): 849–858, accessed March 21, 2021, https://www.cdc.gov/mmwr/preview/mmwrhtml/mm4838a2.htm.

15 "Virginia Apgar: Biographical Overview."

16 Ibid.

17 James, "Fond Memories of Virginia Apgar." 2.

18 Selma H. Calmes, "Dr. Virginia Apgar and the Apgar Score: How the Apgar Score Came to Be," *Anesthesia and Analgesia* 120, no. 5 (May 2015): 1060–1064.

19 Ibid.

20 "Virginia Apgar: Biographical Overview."

21 Calmes, "Dr. Virginia Apgar and the Apgar Score.": 1061.
22 Ibid, 1061.
23 Douglas Bacon and Hussain Darwish, "Emery A. Rovenstine and Regional Anesthesia," *Regional Anesthesia* 22, no. 3 (1997): 273–279.
24 Fred Lyman Adair and Hugo Ehrenfest, "Fetal, Newborn, and Maternal Morbidity and Mortality: Report of the Subcommittee on Factors and Causes of Fetal, Newborn, and Maternal Morbidity and Mortality," White House Conference on Child Health and Protection (New York: Appleton-Century Co., 1933), 3.
25 Ibid.
26 Centers for Disease Control and Prevention, "Achievements in Public Health, 1900–1999: Healthier Mothers and Babies," *Morbidity and Mortality Weekly Report* 48, no.38 (October 1, 1999): 849–858, accessed on March 22, 2021, https://www.cdc.gov/mmwr/preview/mmwrhtml/mm4838a2.htm.
27 "Virginia Apgar: Biographical Overview."
28 "Changing the Face of Medicine."
29 "Establishing a New Specialty, 1938–1949," U.S. National Library of Medicine, U.S. National Library of Medicine, The Virginia Apgar Papers, accessed March 22, 2021, https://profiles.nlm.nih.gov/spotlight/cp/feature/specialty.
30 James, "Fond Memories of Virginia Apgar," 2.
31 Ibid., 2.
32 "Virginia Apgar Biography," *Encyclopedia of World Biography*, accessed February 10, 2021, https://www.notablebiographies.com/An-Ba/Apgar -Virginia.html.
33 "Establishing a New Specialty, 1938–1949."
34 "It Happened Here: The Apgar Score," New York-Presbyterian, accessed March 27, 2019, https://healthmatters.nyp.org/apgar-score/.
35 "Virginia Apgar Biography."
36 Staff Care, "Women in Medicine: A Review of Changing Physician Demograph-ics, Female Physicians by Specialty, State and Related Data," (Irving, CA: Staff Care, 2015).
37 "Virginia Apgar: Biographical Overview."
38 "Virginia Apgar Biography."
39 Calmes, "Dr. Virginia Apgar and the Apgar Score." 1062.
40 Virginia Apgar, "A Proposal for a New Method of Evaluation of the Newborn Infant," *Anesthesia & Analgesia* 120, no. 5 (May 2015): 1059, https://doi.org/10 .1213/ANE.0b013e31829bdc5c.
41 Virginia Apgar, "The Role of the Anesthesiologist in Reducing Neonatal Mortality," *New York State Journal of Medicine* 55, no. 16 (1955): 2365.
42 Ibid., 2366.
43 Ibid.
44 James, "Fond Memories of Virginia Apgar," 3.
45 Siang Yong Tan and Catherine A. Davis, "Virginia Apgar (1909–1974): Apgar Score Innovator," *Singapore Medical Journal* 59, no. 7 (July 2018): 395–396.
46 James, "Fond Memories of Virginia Apgar," 3.

47 L. Joseph Butterfield, MD, interview by Russell Nelson, MD, Oral History
    Project, American Academy of Pediatrics, June 24, 1997, accessed on
    March 22, 2021, https://downloads.aap.org/AAP/Gartner%20Pediatric%20
    History/Butterfield.pdf.

48 Virginia Apgar, letter to L. Joseph Butterfield, August 1, 1961. Virginia Apgar
    papers, Five College Compass Digital Collections, accessed on March 22,
    2021, https://compass.fivecolleges.edu/object/mtholyoke:21642.

49 Emily E. Petersen et al., "Vital Signs: Pregnancy-Related Deaths, United
    States, 2011–2015, and Strategies for Prevention, 13 States, 2013–2017,"
    Morbidity and Mortality Weekly Report 68, no. 18 (May 10, 2019): 423–429.

50 James, "Fond Memories of Virginia Apgar," 1.

51 "Virginia Apgar: Biographical Overview."

52 David Rose, "History of the March of Dimes," March of Dimes Archives,
    August 26, 2010,t https://www.marchofdimes.org/mission/a-history-of-the
    -march-of-dimes.aspx.

53 David Oshinsky, Polio: An American Story (Oxford: Oxford University Press,
    2005).

54 Rose, "History of the March of Dimes."

55 James, "Fond Memories of Virginia Apgar," 2.

56 Ibid.

57 Centers for Disease Control and Prevention, "Rubella in the U.S.," accessed
    February 10, 2021, https://www.cdc.gov/rubella/about/in-the-us.html.

58 Centers for Disease Control and Prevention, "Pregnancy and Rubella,"
    accessed February 10, 2021, https://www.cdc.gov/rubella/pregnancy.html.

59 Virginia Apgar, "Statement by Virginia Apgar, M.D. Vice President for
    Medical Affairs, The National Foundation-March of Dimes, Subcommittee
    on Health, Senate Committee on Labor and Public Welfare," June 30, 1969,
    accessed on March 22, 2021, https://profiles.nlm.nih.gov/101584647X92.

60 Centers for Disease Control and Prevention, "Rubella in the U.S."

61 Virginia Apgar, "The Drug Problem in Pregnancy," Clinical Obstetrics and
    Gynecology 9, no. 3 (1966): 623.

62 Ibid., 627.

63 Virginia Apgar and Gabriel Stickle, "Birth Defects: Their Significance as a
    Public Health Problem," Journal of the American Medical Association 204, no. 5
    (1968): 372–373.

64 Virginia Apgar and Gabriel Stickle, "Birth Defects: Their Significance as a
    Public Health Problem," Journal of the American Medical Association 204, no. 5
    (1968): 371–374.

65 Centers for Disease Control and Prevention, State-Based Birth Defects
    Tracking Systems," accessed February 10, 2021, https://www.cdc.gov/ncbddd
    /birthdefects/states/index.html.

66 State of New Jersey Department of Health, "Newborn Screening & Genetic
    Services," accessed February 10, 2021, https://www.nj.gov/health/fhs/nbs
    /critical-congenital-heart-defects/.

67 Rose, "History of the March of Dimes."

68 Apgar and Beck, *Is My Baby All Right?*

69 Jane Brody, cover endorsement for *Is My Baby All Right?* by Virginia Apgar and Joan Beck.

70 Rose, "Virginia Apgar."

71 S. D. Berns, ed., *Toward Improving the Outcome of Pregnancy III: Enhancing Perinatal Health through Quality, Safety and Performance Initiatives*, reissued ed. (White Plains, NY: March of Dimes Foundation, 2011), https://www.marchofdimes.org/materials/TIOP%20III%20.pdf.

72 "Helen May Clarke Apgar," Find a Grave, accessed February 10, 2021, https://www.findagrave.com/memorial/32636815/helen-may-apgar.

73 Quoted in Robert J. Waldinger, *Notable American Women: The Modern Period, A Biographical Dictionary*, ed. Barbara Sicherman and Carol Hurd Green (Cambridge, MA: Belknap Press of Harvard University Press, 1980), 28, accessed on March 22, 2021, https://hdl.handle.net/2027/mdp.49015002851013.

74 "Virginia Apgar: Biographical Overview."

75 James, "Fond Memories of Virginia Apgar." 3.

76 Quoted in "Virginia Apgar: Biographical Overview."

77 Quoted in Tan and Davis, "Virginia Apgar," 395–396.

78 Quoted in James, "Fond Memories of Virginia Apgar," 4.

Marilyn Gaston. Photo courtesy of National Library
of Medicine.

Marilyn Gaston

Changing the Face of Health Care through Research, Public Service, and Community Health

Denise V. Rodgers and Grace Ibitamuno

Background

Marilyn Hughes Gaston believes that one individual can make a difference but that the power of a community of people committed to a goal can change the whole world.[1] Her life is evidence that she is right on both counts. As an individual, she has contributed to medical research that has made a difference by changing the lives of children and adults with sickle cell anemia. As a member of a group committed to the goal of improving health care for minority populations, she has left an impact on the U.S. infrastructure for healthcare delivery through federally qualified health centers (FQHCs). Gaston remains committed to changing the world and addressing health disparities by working with Black women to improve their own health.

In 1986, Gaston was the lead author of a study published in the *New England Journal of Medicine* titled "Prophylaxis with Oral Penicillin in Children with Sickle Cell Anemia" (hereafter, "Prophylaxis with Penicillin Study").[2] The results of a randomized trial reported in this article clearly demonstrated that children with sickle cell anemia ages three months to three years who were given penicillin prophylactically were significantly less likely to experience morbidity and mortality from *Streptococcus pneumoniae* septicemia. This finding significantly changed the management of children with sickle cell disease (SCD) and provided compelling evidence of the need to screen newborns for the disease.

This seminal article was the result of the work of the national Prophylactic Penicillin Study group, which was led by Gaston as the deputy branch chief and deputy director of the Sickle Cell Disease Branch in the Division of Blood Diseases and Resources at the National Heart, Lung, and Blood Institute (NHLBI) at the National Institutes of Health (NIH). Gaston served in these roles from 1976 to 1989. Within a year of the article's publication in 1986, the NIH Consensus Development Panel recommended universal SCD screening for all newborns in the United States and the initiation of penicillin prophylaxis for newborns living with the disease beginning at three months of age. In that same year, forty-four states, the District of Columbia, Puerto Rico, and the Virgin Islands enacted laws requiring newborn SCD screening—which is now required in all fifty states. Today, clinical guidelines from the NIH recommend prophylaxis with penicillin beginning at two months of age for infants suspected of having sickle cell anemia, whether or not a definitive diagnosis has been made.[3]

Gaston came to her work on SCD as a result of her commitment to helping poor, underserved, and disadvantaged patients. This commitment, which grew in part from her own experience, shaped her work throughout her career. Marilyn Gaston (then Hughes) was born on January 31, 1939, in a public housing project in Cincinnati, Ohio. Her father, Myron Hughes, worked as a waiter, and her mother, Dorothy, was a medical secretary. Gaston grew up with her brother and half-brother in a family that, while poor, knew much joy.[4] From a very young age, she wanted to be a doctor. Yet many of her school counselors and teachers said it could never happen because she was a "Negro," a girl, a Catholic, and poor. However, her parents had raised her to believe in herself. Gaston remembers her mother saying, "Girl, do not pay those people any attention—besides every *no* you hear in life is just a *yes* waiting to happen!"[5] Her mother frequently read her the story of *The Little Engine That Could*, so "I think I can, I think I can" has been an enduring theme throughout her life.[6]

Gaston says that she faced outright racism when she was growing up in the projects. However, her life was filled with family support and examples of exceptionally strong black women that helped her deal with racism. "My godmother single-handedly integrated the public pool," recalls Gaston. "Every Saturday morning, she got us up and forced us to go swimming. We didn't want to go, we'd say, 'They don't like us! They'll call the police!'" But every summer Saturday, Gaston and her peers were unwilling civil rights activists. The black children went into the pool, the white children got out of the pool, and the police came. The episodes went on not for weeks or months, but for years. "People saying things to you, calling the police on you. That does toughen the skin," says Gaston.[7]

When Gaston was a young girl, her mother fainted at home due to vaginal bleeding caused by what would later be found to be metastatic cervical cancer—a disease that ultimately took her life. Because the family was too poor to afford health insurance or to pay for care for the condition, her mother succumbed to what is now a preventable (or at least treatable) disease. After her mother's death, Gaston realized that throughout her own life, her mother had always put the health of her husband and children before her own and therefore did not seek care in the early stages of her disease. This theme of Black women caring for others before themselves would reemerge later in Gaston's career.

In 1953, Gaston entered Miami University in Oxford, Ohio, graduating four years later with a bachelor's degree in zoology. In 1964, she graduated from the University of Cincinnati's College of Medicine. When Gaston enrolled at the college, she was "one of only six female students, and the only black female. 'I probably faced more discrimination as a woman than as an African American,' says Gaston. She credits those Saturday morning swims for carrying her through a daily gauntlet of rude comments that caused some of her white classmates to drop out."[8] She went on to complete a one-year rotating internship at Philadelphia General Hospital in 1965. It was then that she first encountered a patient with sickle cell anemia. When the child first presented to the emergency department in Philadelphia, Gaston and her supervising resident initially suspected the child was a victim of child abuse because of the swelling and symptomology of pain typical in sickle cell crises. They determined later that the child had SCD and was given appropriate treatment.

This episode led Gaston to learn more about this disease, which most frequently affects individuals of African descent.[9]

From 1965 to 1967, Gaston was a pediatric resident at Cincinnati Children's Hospital, and in 1968, she completed an ambulatory pediatric fellowship there. While still a pediatric resident, she joined a group of local community leaders to found the Lincoln Heights Health Center, the first FQHC in Ohio. The center, which officially opened on October 8, 1967, was founded by Dolores Lindsay, a local community member, several volunteer physicians, and local leaders. Soon after it opened, funds became available from the University of Cincinnati's Department of Pediatrics to pay Gaston as a physician on staff at the center once she had completed her residency.[10]

The first FQHCs were established based on provisions of the Economic Opportunity Act of 1964, which was part of President Lyndon B. Johnson's War on Poverty. What is now known as the FQHC program was implemented through provisions of the Omnibus Budget Reconciliation Act (OBRA) of 1989 and expanded under the OBRA of 1990. This legislation increased Medicare and Medicaid reimbursement for specified services.[11] According to the Health Resources and Services Administration, FQHCs "may be Community Health Centers, Migrant Health Centers, Health Care for the Homeless, and Health Centers for Residents of Public Housing."[12]

From 1968 to 1974, Gaston served as the part-time medical director of Lincoln Heights Health Center. In 1974, the center received a grant from the Ohio Department of Health to expand pediatric and obstetrical services, and Gaston became the center's first full-time medical director. "She was the consummate leader of the medical team and a visionary. She brought Pediatric Nurse Practitioners and Physician Assistants on staff before they were widely accepted by the general medical community. She saw the value they would bring to the team."[13] From 1972 to 1976, Gaston was also an associate professor of pediatrics at the University of Cincinnati's College of Medicine and the director of the Comprehensive Sickle Cell Center at Cincinnati Children's Hospital. She was also raising her two young children.

While she was in Cincinnati, Gaston met Clarice Reid, who in 1959 had become the third Black person to graduate from the College of Medicine. From 1962 to 1968, Reid was the only Black pediatrician in private practice in Cincinnati. In 1973, she joined the National Sickle Cell Disease Program at the NHLBI.[14] Her appointment followed President Richard Nixon's signing of the National Sickle Cell Anemia Control Act on May 16, 1972. Congress passed this legislation with the goals of finding a cure for sickle cell anemia and helping people living with the disease. The legislation also led to the establishment of the Cooperative Study of Sickle Cell Disease and the establishment of the National Sickle Cell Disease Program. It should be noted that a factor leading to this act's passage was the activism of the Black Panther Party, which had begun widespread community-based sickle cell screening in the early 1970s. In 1972, leaders of the party brought national attention to the disease in an interview about sickle cell anemia with John Lennon and Yoko Ono, during their stint as hosts of the *Mike Douglas Show*.[15]

Gaston moved to Washington, D.C., in 1976, when her husband accepted a job offer at Howard University. Reid quickly recruited her to work at the National Sickle Cell Disease Program, where Gaston became the deputy director. It was during this time that Gaston and her coauthors published "Prophylaxis with Penicillin Study," the "ground-breaking study . . . which . . . drastically influenced the world of SCD. . . . One of the most important immediate results of Gaston's study was that early treatment greatly improved chances of survival as well as quality of life for SCD patients, making such treatment 'a central policy of the U.S. Public Health Service'" (USPHS).[16] It is also noteworthy that several other prominent Black physician leaders in public health brought attention to sickle cell disease in the early days of sickle cell disease research. One of those leaders was David Satcher, who would become the sixteenth surgeon general of the United States, an assistant secretary for health, and director of the Centers for Disease Control and Prevention.[17] Another was Louis Sullivan, a hematologist, who worked on SCD and published an editorial in the *New England Journal of Medicine* titled "The Risks of Sickle-Cell Trait" in September 1987.[18]

In 1985, a report titled *Report of the Secretary's Task Force on Black and Minority Health* was released. It was a comprehensive effort to better understand and make recommendations to address the causes and effects of health disparities in minority populations. Thomas E. Malone, a deputy director at the NIH and chair of the task force, wrote in the report's cover letter, "The levels of awareness and sensitivity to the issues surrounding minority health have been greatly heightened among the individuals serving on the Task Force and through them, within the agencies, divisions, and programs of the Department. As a result, [of their participation], we are better prepared to serve as emissaries for positive action within the Department, our communities and professional organizations."[19] Gaston was an alternate member of the task force and a member of its subcommittee "charged with investigating the physiological, cultural, and societal factors that, in combination, perpetuate health inequities for minorities"[20] in the priority area of infant mortality. As a pediatrician working with children with SCD, she too frequently witnessed infants dying before their first birthday. This was particularly true before publication of the "Prophylaxis with Penicillin Study." The research that went into the creation of the task force's report documented comprehensively how pervasive the disparity in infant mortality between blacks and whites was in the United States. The task force found that 80 percent of disparities in health outcomes in minorities were caused by six problems: cancer, cardiovascular disease or stroke, chemical dependency (cirrhosis), diabetes, homicide or accidents, and infant mortality. In a section of the report called "Developing Strategies within the Federal Sector," one critical recommendation was that "the Department should conduct both intra- and interdepartmental reviews to identify and provide for collaboration between the various activities currently being supported within the Department and other elements of the Executive Branch, respectively. The reviews should focus on programs that have impact on the actual or potential availability of health professionals to minority communities."[21] Malone wrote, "I believe this report is a landmark effort in analyzing and synthesizing the present state of knowledge of the major factors that contribute to the health status of Blacks, Hispanics, Asian/Pacific Islanders, and Native Americans. It represents the first time the Department of Health and Human Services (DHHS) has consolidated minority health issues into one report. This report should serve not only as a standard resource for departmentwide strategy, but as the generating force for an accelerated national assault on the persistent health disparities which led you [Margaret Heckler, the secretary of health and human services] to establish the Task Force a little more than a year ago."[22]

Gaston was inspired to take action by her participation in the preparation of the report. The recognition that came from the "Prophylaxis with Penicillin Study"—as well as the success of the implementation of SCD screening and penicillin prophylaxis in the United States and abroad—opened the doors to greater opportunities for Gaston. The question she faced was what opportunity would be worth leaving her current position and Reid, her colleague and friend?

Resolution

In March 1989, Sullivan, was named secretary of the DHHS in the administration of President George H. W. Bush.[23] Gaston was tapped to head the Division of Medicine in the Bureau of Health Professions at the Health Resources and Services Administration (HRSA). Gaston and Sullivan knew each other and had similar research interests, and her confidence in his leadership helped convince her to leave the NIH and move to HRSA. The following year she left the Bureau of Health Professions to become the director of the Bureau of Primary Health Care (BPHC, another part of HRSA) and assistant surgeon general. At that time, she also rose to the rank of rear admiral in the USPHS.

Another contributing factor in her decision to leave her work in SCD was her desire to expand her efforts to broader areas of health, with a specific focus on the elimination of health disparities. She realized that at the BPHC she could play a key role in implementing the recommendations of the report that focused on the federal government's taking strategic actions to improve access to care for poor, underserved, and minority communities. Gaston became the first Black woman to direct a bureau of the USPHS and the second Black woman to achieve the rank of assistant surgeon general and rear admiral in the USPHS. While it was a difficult decision to leave Reid and the SCD studies she had worked on at the NIH, the moves to the Bureau of Health Professions and then to the BPHC presented "a larger opportunity for impact nationally—in terms of [expanding] access to primary care for poor, disadvantaged and minority populations both nationally and internationally—as well as the opportunity to have a major impact on changing health outcomes."[24]

Gaston's early experiences—including her mother's illness, her early encounter with a child with sickle cell disease, and her role in helping establish and staff a community health center—would resonate for most of her life. The multidimensionality of her life and career also created tension for her, as she struggled to determine which career path would allow her to make the greatest difference in the lives of those she was committed to serve. When asked why she chose to leave the NIH, she said:

> I left NIH as it was a major promotion—to assistant surgeon general—and better pay (the kids were going to college soon). I wanted to be in charge of the single program in the Public Health Service focused mainly on getting health care to poor and uninsured, and underserved people and communities, and improve the quality of care and decrease disparities. That goal was why I even went into medicine in the first place! Remember my mother and how she precipitated that goal for me when she fainted from metastatic cancer! And also, I started my career on the front lines of an FQHC in a very poor Black neighborhood. I started with Bureau of Health Professions and the opportunity to increase [the number of] Black health professionals working in those communities to improve access. And then of course [I] moved to the Bureau of Primary Health Care with a five-billion-dollar budget and many more programs taking direct care of target populations— improving quality of care and decreasing disparities.[25]

In the context of this effort, Gaston was able to leverage her leadership of the BPHC to play a major role in implementing the third recommendation of the task force's report, which encouraged the

DHHS to "continue to investigate, develop, and implement innovative models for delivery and financing of health services."[26] The directed goal of this effort was to improve the delivery of health care to "facilitate access to services by minority populations, improve efficiency of service and payment systems, and modify services to be more culturally acceptable."[27] The move to the BPHC took Gaston back to her roots, caring for the underserved as she had done at the Lincoln Heights Health Center. It allowed her to oversee the provision of health care to people like her mother, people with potentially preventable illnesses who did not have access to care because of poverty.

In her previous work at the Lincoln Heights Health Center and in traveling the country in her new roles, Gaston heard the same thing much too often: "Health care for poor people is just poor care."[28] She knew better and set out to prove it at the helm of the BPHC. Taking her mission a step further, her goal became the improvement of health-care quality and health-care access in all FQHCs. This goal is rooted in Gaston's overall leadership philosophy. When asked about her philosophy, she stated:

> We must be servant leaders. We must serve the people who utilize our services, and we must serve the people who do the work, those who work with us. As a leader I believe it is important to recognize that I don't know everything, and I must be willing to learn from the people I work with. I often learned something new every day from those who worked for me. As a servant leader, I was evaluated by those who reported to me and considered being evaluated by the patients we served. I also believe that if you are faced with making a difficult decision and you consider the people you are trying to serve, then make the decision that is in their best interest, and most of the time you will make the right decision.[29]

Gaston's first action as director of the BPHC was to make sure that FQHCs could receive federal funding only if they were accredited by the Joint Commission or the National Committee for Quality Assurance, to ensure that all centers met similar operating and quality adherence standards. An innovative approach at the time, this stipulation paved the way for the improvement and mainte-nance of health-care quality provided at FQHCs today.

Gaston worked on increasing health-care access for the under-served. Based on her efforts and those of her team, the national annual FQHC budget increased from about $500 million in 1990 to over $1 billion in 2001, at the end of her tenure at the BPHC. The number of FQHCs around the country available to serve patients went up by 50 percent—from about 500 in 1990 to 748 in 2001.[30] The number of patients served almost doubled: in 1990, 5.8 million patients were cared for at FQHCs,[31] and by 2001, that number had increased to nearly 10.0 million.[32]

The vast majority of FQHC clients were (and still are) members of racial or ethnic minority groups and low-income and uninsured people; 40 percent were children. Based on Gaston's work, while 75 percent of the nation's uninsured reported not having a usual source of care, 99 percent of FQHC clients reported having a usual source of care.[33] Continuity of care in the long term was also established at higher rates at FQHCs than in other primary care settings. Uninsured FQHC clients were more likely to receive life-style counseling (related to diet, physical activity, smoking cessa-tion, drinking, drug use, and sexual health) and cancer screenings than uninsured people cared for elsewhere.[34]

Gaston's background as an NIH researcher directed her leader-ship approach at the BPHC. She applied rigorous scientific methods to improving health-care quality at FQHCs. In 1998, the BPHC col-laborated with the Institute for Healthcare Improvement, five clin-ical networks, and five FQHCs to create a model for improving quality in the management of chronic illnesses. The model, which came to be known as the Health Disparities Collaborative (HDC), had three main components: the MacColl Chronic Care Model, a model for quality improvement, and learning sessions.[35] HDCs focused on creating informed and empowered patients, as well as prepared and proactive clinical teams.[36] Learning sessions encour-aged collaboration among team members from several FQHCs.[37]

Gaston's work improved the quality of care that patients received. Compared to other medical centers, FQHCs had more encounters with patients with chronic conditions like hypertension and diabetes. However, FQHC patients reported higher rates of well-controlled blood pressure—90 percent versus 50 percent in a comparable group—and more than twice the rate of on-time HbA1c readings for people living with diabetes. Clinical processes of care and outcomes improved, and an analysis of the diabetes-focused HDC implementation showed a cost-effectiveness ratio of over $33,000 per quality-adjusted life-year.[38] All of this shows that Gaston not only achieved her goal of improving health care at FQHCs, but she also reduced the cost of caring for patients with chronic illness at FQHCs throughout the country. The HDC model of care has since been adopted in public health to address everything from chronic illness to behavioral and mental health concerns in all demographic groups and in various settings.

In her roles as director of the BPHC and assistant surgeon general, and managing a budget of $5 billion, Gaston started an initiative of the bureau called One Hundred Percent Access and Zero Health Disparities. In 1999, Gaston said that the goals of the initiative were "that every person, in every underserved community will have access to primary and preventive care . . . and that there will be no disparities in health status due to race, ethnicity or income."[39] She continued: "We cannot achieve the vision alone. . . . We need the help of every state, every national organization, every business, every academic institution and committed people from communities across the country."[40] This goal was accepted across HRSA.[41]

The backdrop of the development of the initiative was the appointment of David Satcher as the eleventh assistant secretary for health and surgeon general on February 13, 1998. This was the first time one individual held both positions simultaneously. Satcher was extremely committed to the elimination of health disparities by race and ethnicity, and in January 2000, he launched the DHHS Healthy People 2010 national health promotion and disease prevention agenda. The two overarching goals of Healthy People 2010 were to increase the quality and quantity of healthy life and to eliminate health disparities. This was the first time in the history of the United States that a goal to eliminate, not just reduce, health disparities was explicitly adopted by the entire DHHS.

It should be noted that on November 8, 1999, Massachusetts Senator Edward Kennedy introduced the Minority Health and Health Disparities Research and Education Act, which became law on November 22, 2000. This law resulted in the creation of the National Center on Minority Health and Health Disparities at the NIH. The launch of the BPHC initiative, combined with the Healthy People 2010 agenda, allowed Gaston to move aggressively to achieve disparity elimination goals that she had recognized as a priority from the beginning of her career.

The publication of the task force report resulted in Gaston's spending a growing amount of time speaking publicly about health disparities and the need to eliminate them. A seminal event that solidified Gaston's focus on the health of midlife Black women was an appearance on a program on Black Entertainment Television in the mid-1990s with Sharon Pratt Kelly, then mayor of Washington, D.C.; the actress Pam Grier; and Gayle Porter, a friend and collaborator of Gaston's who was both a physician and a clinical psychologist. The program focused on Black women's health, and Gaston recalls that the panelists were inundated with questions from the program's live audience as well as from viewers who called in. After the show ended, several viewers tracked down contact information for the physicians, Gaston and Porter, to ask them more questions and gather more information.[42]

When Gaston and Porter searched for health resources for midlife Black women, they found very few. Thus, they began working on a book which would become *Prime Time: The African American Woman's Complete Guide to Midlife Health and Wellness*.[43] They did not anticipate how difficult it would be to find a publisher after the book was finished. Gaston recalls being told by a number of publishing houses that "Black women don't read books like this."[44] Finally, they met with a Black woman editor at Random House, who stated that "this book is revolutionary and I want it" and agreed to publish the book.[45]

George W. Bush was elected president in 2000, and the priorities of the new administration differed somewhat from those of the administration of President Bill Clinton, particularly as they related to eliminating health disparities. With a new administration came new leadership for HRSA. In March 2002, Elizabeth Duke was officially named the administrator for HRSA, although she had been involved in leading it before her official confirmation. In the Bush administration, HRSA embarked on a major initiative to create new access points for care and to expand the number of patients served by FQHCs. However, once Duke arrived, it quickly became clear to Gaston that she and her new boss had different ideas about how to accomplish health center expansion, and it was time for her tenure at the BPHC to end.[46]

Thus in 2002, Gaston had to make another difficult career decision. She had spent enough time working for the federal government that she could comfortably retire. However, the national data on the health status of midlife Black women was a clear call for her to use her voice and expertise in a different way to address the obvious and preventable disparities. Gaston and Porter had intended their book to be a practical guide about prevention, with clear recommendations for health improvement. They did not originally intend to create Sister Circles, groups that give midlife Black women opportunities to come together in short-term support groups that strive to promote wellness, change behavior, and improve the outcomes of chronic diseases. However, as the authors traveled around the country promoting their book, Sister Circles became a natural outgrowth of the publication. This realization led Porter and Gaston to form a not-for-profit organization called the Gaston and Porter Health Improvement Center, Inc., in 2002.

The organization facilitates the development of Prime Time Sister Circles. In 2016, Gaston and Porter were awarded a five-year research grant to conduct a randomized trial to document the impact of the circles on hypertension control among the participants.

Gaston approached her work with Sister Circles as a researcher but also based on her personal experience and with humility: "I was 45 when I finally quit smoking. It was almost as challenging as finishing medical school."[47] Both she and Porter also understood Black women's mistrust of the medical system and that "it doesn't matter whether we are well-educated or have money. African American women suffer disproportionately from life-threatening diseases. They are twice as likely as American Caucasian women to suffer from cardiovascular disease, three times more likely to have diabetes, and at twice the risk for cancer. They are also more likely to experience stress and depressive symptoms."[48] Gaston and Porter's work brought psychology to medicine and is intended to change "how women approach their own health, and thus the health of their families and communities."[49]

Gaston has come full circle and intends to devote the rest of her life's work to the promotion of Black women's health. She now does the kind of work that might have saved her mother from premature death. Throughout her career, Gaston has led with passion, intellect, good humor, and an unwavering commitment to improving health outcomes for those most in need in this country. When she speaks at a conference, after being introduced, she generally dances her way into the room, encouraging members of the audience to join her by clapping their hands and swaying to the music.[50] The joy she radiates provides an important antidote as she then discusses the enormous challenges faced by the poor, the uninsured, and minority populations in the United States. She encourages everyone in attendance to join the quest to improve health outcomes.

Gaston says that she is "proud of the fact that her passion for health and health outcomes and access to care got [her] to one of the highest levels of the public health service" and that she "has been blessed and privileged to do this important work,"[51] as she was able to "go to the neediest communities, to make sure they had access to care leading to improved health outcomes."[52] Early in her life she decided that she would make a difference in people's lives. Clearly, she has done just that.

Notes

1   County Cable Montgomery, "Marilyn Gaston," June 6, 2019, video, 5:06, https://archive.org/details/Marilyn_Gaston.
2   Marilyn H. Gaston et al., "Prophylaxis with Oral Penicillin in Children with Sickle Cell Anemia," *New England Journal of Medicine* 314, no. 25 (June 19, 1986): 1593–1599, DOI: 10.1056/NEJM198606193142501.
3   National Heart, Lung, and Blood Institute, "Evidence-Based Management of Sickle Cell Disease: Expert Panel Report 2014: Guide to Recommendations," 2014, https://www.nhlbi.nih.gov/sites/default/files/media/docs/Evd-Bsd _SickleCellDis_Rep2014.pdf.
4   Marilyn Gaston, "Excellence Forever," keynote address at the University of Cincinnati chapter of the Student National Medical Association, Midwest

regional conference. Cincinnati, OH, October 20, 2018.; See also County Cable Montgomery, "Marilyn Gaston."

5   County Cable Montgomery, "Marilyn Gaston."

6   Ibid.

7   "Marilyn Gaston and Gayle Porter," Encore.Org, accessed February 11, 2021, https://encore.org/purpose-prize/marilyn-gaston/.

8   Ibid.

9   "Changing the Face of Medicine: Dr. Marilyn Hughes Gaston," U.S. National Library of Medicine, last updated June 3, 2015, https://cfmedicine.nlm.nih .gov/physicians/biography_124.html.

10 Marilyn Gaston, telephone conversation with Denise V. Rodgers, August 21, 2020; see also "50 Years of Providing Accessible & Quality Health Care Services to the Underserved, 1967–2017," The HealthCare Connection, 2017, 2, accessed on March 26, 2021, https://healthcare-connection.org/wp-content /uploads/2020/05/50th-History-Book.pdf.

11 Center for Health and Research Transformation, "Federally Qualified Health Centers: An Overview," July 22, 2013: 3, https://chrt.sites.uofmhosting.net /wp-content/uploads/2013/07/CHRT_Federally-Qualified-Health-Centers -An-Overview-.pdf?_ga=2.219507225.1242103987.1616000058-1816842856 .1616000058.

12 Health Resources and Services Administration, "Federally Qualified Health Centers," accessed February 11, 2021, https://www.hrsa.gov/opa/eligibility -and-registration/health-centers/fqhc/index.html.

13 "50 Years of Providing Health Care Services," 4.

14 "Changing the Face of Medicine: Dr. Clarice D. Reid," U.S. National Library of Medicine, last updated June 3, 2015, https://cfmedicine.nlm.nih.gov /physicians/biography_262.html.

15 "The Black Panther Party Stands for Health," Columbia University Mailman School Of Public Health, February 23, 2016, https://www.mailman.columbia .edu/public-health-now/news/black-panther-party-stands-health.

16 Amy Huggins, "Marilyn Hughes Gaston, M.D.," Archives of Maryland, 2006, https://msa.maryland.gov/megafile/msa/speccol/sc3500/sc3520/014500 /014533/html/14533bio.html.

17 Fitzhugh Mullan, "David Satcher Takes Stock," Health Affairs 21, no. 6 (November–December 2002), 154–161: DOI: 10.1377/hlthaff.21.6.154.

18 Louis W. Sullivan, "The Risks of Sickle-Cell Trait: Caution and Common Sense," The New England Journal of Medicine 317, no.13 (1987): 830–831, https://www.nejm.org/doi/full/10.1056/NEJM198709243171309.

19 Margaret M. Heckler, Report of the Secretary's Task Force on Black and Minority Health, vol. 1 (Washington: Department of Health and Human Services, August 1985), viii, https://archive.org/details/reportofsecretaroousde/page /n7.

20 Ibid., 4.

21 Ibid., 23.

22 Ibid., vii.

23 Gwen Ifill and Morris S. Thompson, "Louis W. Sullivan," *Washington Post*, December 23, 1998, https://www.washingtonpost.com/archive/politics/1988/12/23/louis-w-sullivan/23ae2f72-898a-4188-a0f9-4d3454671a3d/.

24 Marilyn Gaston, email to Denise V. Rodgers, October 8, 2019.

25 Marilyn Gaston, telephone conversation with Denise V. Rodgers, May 10, 2019.

26 Heckler, *Report of the Secretary's Task Force on Black and Minority Health*. 15.

27 Ibid., 15.

28 Marilyn Gaston, "The Revolution Continues: Past, Present and Future," Northwest Regional Primary Care Association Fall Conference, December 9, 2015, https://www.youtube.com/watch?v=VoBjPnmHDYI.

29 Gaston, telephone conversation with Denise V. Rodgers, May 10, 2019.

30 Center for Health and Research Transformation, "Federally Qualified Health Centers," 3–4.

31 Institute of Medicine, *America's Health Care Safety Net: Intact but Endangered* (Washington: National Academies Press, 2000:120, https://doi.org/10.17226/9612.

32 Robert M. Politzer et al., "Inequality in America: The Contribution of Health Centers in Reducing and Eliminating Disparities in Access to Care," *Medical Care Research and Review* 58, no. 2 (June 2001): 236, doi:10.1177/107755870105800205.

33 Ibid., 241.

34 Ibid.

35 Marshall H. Chin, "Quality Improvement Implementation and Disparities: The Case of the Health Disparities Collaboratives." *Medical care* vol. 48, no.8 (August 2010): 668–675. DOI:10.1097/MLR.0b013e3181e3585c. Also see *Improving Chronic Illness Care*, Improvingchroniccare.Org (2019), http://www.improvingchroniccare.org/index.php?p=The_Chronic_Care_Model&s=.

36 Chin, "Quality Improvement Implementation," 2–3; also see *Improving Chronic Illness Care*.

37 Chin, "Quality Improvement Implementation," 2.

38 Politzer et al., "Inequality in America."

39 Quoted in Tawara D. Goode, "Engaging Communities to Realize the Vision of 'One Hundred Percent Access and Zero Health Disparities': A Culturally Competent Approach," Policy Brief 4, National Center for Cultural Competence, Georgetown University Child Development Center, University Center for Excellence and Developmental Disabilities, (Spring 2001): 2.

40 Ibid.

41 Ibid, 1–2.

42 Gaston, telephone conversation with Denise V. Rodgers, May 10, 2019.

43 Marilyn Hughes Gaston and Gayle K. Porter, *Prime Time: The African American Woman's Complete Guide to Midlife Health and Wellness*, rev. ed. (New York: One World/Ballantine, 2003).

44 Gaston, telephone conversation with Denise V. Rodgers, August 22, 2020.

45 Quoted in ibid.

46 Ibid.
47 "Marilyn Gaston and Gayle Porter."
48 Ibid.
49 Ibid.
50 "The Revolution Continues: Marilyn Gaston, M.D.," YouTube, December 9, 2015, video, 52:00, https://www.youtube.com/watch?v=VoBjPnmHDYI.
51 Gaston, telephone conversation with Denise V. Rodgers, August 22, 2020.
52 Gaston, telephone conversation with Denise V. Rodgers, May 10, 2019; see also County Cable Montgomery, "Marilyn Gaston."

Jane E. Brody. Photo courtesy of Don Kim.

Jane E. Brody

Using Journalism to Impact Personal Health, One Column at a Time

Dawn Thomas and Christina Chesnakov

Background

"I'm sort of like a horse with blinders on, because once I found what I loved, I never looked back and I never changed,"[1] Jane Brody said in an interview. Her passion and personality led her in 1976 to become the first personal health columnist for the *New York Times*, providing her with a platform to educate and influence the population on health. *Time* best summarized Brody's personality and style: "Nervy attacks, not attacks of nerves, are the usual hallmark of the brassy dynamo who has been successfully lecturing and hectoring the American public for the past decade."[2] For more than four decades as a personal health columnist, Brody has been working to educate the public on health and prevention.

Brody's "Personal Health" column quickly became the most popular feature on the *New York Time news services*[3] and earned her the title of "High Priestess of Health"[4] from *Time*. Brody has written more than a dozen books, including the best-selling *Jane Brody's Nutrition Book*[5] and *Jane Brody's Good Food Book*.[6] She has also written magazine articles, given lectures to both lay and professional audiences on issues relating to health and wellness, appeared on numerous television and radio shows, and received many prestigious awards for journalistic excellence. In 1987, she was awarded an honorary doctorate from Princeton University, and she also has honorary doctorates from Hamline University, the State University of New York Downstate Health Sciences University, the University of Minnesota School of Public Health, and Long Island University.[7] Through her contributions as a personal health columnist, providing advice on healthy eating, exercise, and the latest research on staying robust and fit, Brody "has been singularly successful at translating medical and technical jargon into compelling and practical public information."[8]

Certain experiences and individuals helped nurture and encourage Brody's curiosity and passions, which opened the way for her to blaze a trail in the field of science journalism. The events in Brody's childhood and early career provide insights into how she later developed into a health champion. Brody was born in 1941 and raised in Brooklyn, New York, where her father was a lawyer and her mother was an elementary school teacher. She recalls that her father had a big influence on her career path and a healthy lifestyle. Growing up, Brody and her family mainly ate rich Eastern European foods that contained high quantities of fats. However, her father shared with her his knowledge of and appreciation for healthy eating, saying, "fresh fruit in every season; rich, dark bread and oatmeal for breakfast in the winter; shredded wheat for breakfast in the summer."[9]

Brody recollects that from an early age, she has been interested in living things and how they worked. She collected all kinds of creatures, dissecting and studying them. When she was four years old, she told her father she wanted to become a veterinarian, and he mentioned that Cornell University had a great vet program.[10] Afterward, Brody had her heart set on going to Cornell and becoming a veterinarian. Throughout junior high and high school, she always felt encouraged to pursue what she was interested in, and no one ever told her that she could not do something because she was a girl.[11] While in high school, Brody lost her mother to ovarian cancer and her grandmother to cancer.[12] These tragic events opened her eyes to the mechanisms underlying how things work, especially biochemistry—which is what she majored in at Cornell University. Her choice of career changed from veterinary medicine to biochemistry. Although there were quite a number of women at Cornell with this major, very few focused on research.[13]

In her *New York Times* column titled, "To Counter Loneliness, Find Ways to Connect," Brody wrote that during her sophomore year in college, she felt "friendless, unhappy and desperate to get out of there."[14] Her feelings led her to visit a psychologist at the university health clinic. After examining Brody's activities in high school and in her first year in college, the psychologist suggested that she become more integrated into the college community by doing something that would connect her with other students who shared her interests. Although Brody was a biochemistry major with a heavy class load, the psychologist emphasized that she needed to find the time for extracurricular activities, because doing so was crucial for her health and having a successful college experience. Brody joined a monthly student-run magazine, the *Cornell Countryman*, since it was the only activity that fit into her busy schedule. The magazine changed her career trajectory. While working for the magazine, Brody fell in love with interviewing researchers and writing about their work. In addition, she became friends with the magazine's faculty adviser—who, as she wrote in her column, "encouraged me to expand my horizons and follow my heart."[15]

During her first year, while she was still on the path to becoming a chemical research scientist, Brody won a ten-week full-time summer research position with a National Science Foundation project at the New York State Agricultural Experiment Station in Geneva, New York. She conducted biochemical research in a laboratory and realized that this was not something she could see herself doing for the rest of her life. She felt the job of a lab scientist was too solitary and preferred to work alongside others: "After spending the summer between my freshman and sophomore years doing my own research project in a science lab under the auspices of a National Science Foundation Fellowship, I realized that being a lab scientist was too lonely, prolonged, and solitary [an] endeavor for someone who preferred to work in the company of and interacting with other people."[16]

Brody kept her biochemistry major and continued working for the *Cornell Countryman*. During her senior year, she became the magazine's editor and took courses in news reporting and magazine writing.[17] During her time at the magazine, Brody's love of researching and writing flourished. She also enjoyed working with other authors to polish stories. As the editor, she created a summer edition to help incoming students get more acquainted with what would soon be their new home—the university and its city.[18] She graduated from Cornell in 1962 with a bachelor of science degree in biochemistry and a new career trajectory.[19]

Brody's college years were when she found her true passion. Although she arrived at Cornell wanting to pursue a life in the laboratory, she ended up falling in love with communicating health to the general public. Having such experiences and being encouraged to follow her heart, she continued on that path by getting a master's degree in science writing at the University of Wisconsin's School of Journalism (now the School of Journalism and Mass Communication) in 1963, ultimately merging communication and science.[20]

Brody's first job after graduate school was as a general assignment reporter for the *Minneapolis Tribune*, where she wrote articles about the latest research and developments in the health field. At that time, science was focused primarily on treatment rather than prevention. Perhaps led by her personal experiences, Brody started writing an increasing number of stories about understanding the cause of diseases and how to prevent them. Her time in Minnesota affected her personal health. "I wasn't used to Midwestern reticence," she later explained to *Time*. "I felt very isolated and different. So I turned to food." After she reached 140 pounds, reality hit Brody, who is less than five feet tall: "I just woke up in the middle of the night and said, 'I'm killing myself.' . . . From that day on, I started eating regular meals and always carried a healthy snack with me."[21] With this new approach to eating, which later evolved into a lifestyle, Brody saw the pounds fall away. Being short was a disadvantage in maintaining a low body mass index, but Brody took steps to overcome her height, which she often used to her advantage: "In elementary school, I sat in the front of the classroom and stood first in line. Being close to the teacher was much to my academic advantage. In crowds, I could wriggle my way to the front of the pack. Or I could easily hide in the mob if I wanted to hear but not be seen. As a student and then as a professional who wanted to be noticed, I knew I had to be assertive, which strengthened my personality and sharpened my wit."[22]

After two years at the *Minneapolis Tribune*, Brody moved back to New York in 1965 and was hired by the *New York Times* as a full-time specialist in medicine and biology. She continued to focus on prevention in her writing, which she remembers as being very well received.[23] For the next eleven years, Brody continued writing for the *Times*, while getting married and having twin boys along the way. According to an article in the *Harvard Business Review*, when it comes to family responsibilities, "women continue to be the ones who interrupt their careers, take more days off, and work part-time."[24] Brody was not under such pressure. Her husband, Richard Engquist, stayed at home to be the "nurturing parent."[25] In the mid-1960s, it was unusual for fathers to stay at home, and the average number of hours per week spent on child care was ten for mothers and two and a half for fathers.[26] Not only was sharing child care in the home with her husband a key to her balancing work and family, but Brody also maintained a disciplined routine: "Five times a week, though less in winter, she [Brody] plays singles tennis. Every morning she rises at 5 a.m. and makes the family breakfast. After posting the menu matter-of-factly on the inside of the toilet lid, she heads out for a 3 1/2–mile run or ten-mile bike ride; in the evening she takes a half-mile swim."[27]

Data collected in 1971 showed that there were significantly fewer women in journalism compared to men in the United States about 20 percent of journalists in the U.S. news media were women.[28] As Brody recalls, the men in journalism were more focused on new technology and research than on keeping people healthy. The influence of women in health prevention could be because of the lack of male interest: research shows that women tend to write more stories than men do about education and social issues, including health. Data from a national survey of health and medical journalists revealed that female respondents were two and a half times more likely than males to say that educating people to make informed decisions was an important priority in their reporting. Female respondents also said that it is important to develop the health and scientific literacy of audiences and influence health behaviors.[29] According to Brody, "There were no women to compete with to get a job, and any institution that was interested in furthering the cause of women's equality would be happy to latch onto somebody like me who came and said 'this is what I want to do.'"[30]

Brody broke ground with her focus on prevention. Her recognition of the adage "an ounce of prevention is worth a pound of cure" was a strong break from the focus on new technologies and other solutions for medical challenges. In the public domain, Brody was alone in advocating for the prevention of health problems before they occurred. She wanted the public to understand the underlying cause of diseases: "The vast majority of people now realize that's where it's at. Prevention *is* the key to health, not patching people up after they're sick. What you see now—this interest in vitamins, exercise, diet, and all this stuff—boils down to a realization that we have to do what we can to stay as intact and healthy as possible as long as possible."[31] This was a unique viewpoint for the times.[32] Brody explained that prevention was an overlooked topic "because the gee-whiz era was well under way and gee-whiz required new drugs, new surgeries, new something, and not putting into practice what we already knew about how to keep people healthy."[33]

Brody's focus on prevention corresponds to her practical nature. When confronted with a challenge, she assesses it and takes steps to overcome it. For example, when dealing with loneliness in college, she sought professional assistance and then followed recommendations to become better integrated into campus life. When dealing with an increase in her weight, she focused on basic improvements to her diet to become healthier. This practical approach translated well into the advice she delivered in her writing. As noted above, during her time at the *Cornell Countryman*, she developed a special edition focused on helping incoming students become more acquainted and comfortable with the school and its community—which in turn could help prevent some of the isolation and loneliness that she had experienced. This characteristic also helped her develop and deliver advice that was easy to follow.

In the 1970s, under the leadership of Abe Rosenthal, the executive editor of the *New York Times*, the paper was making changes. To attract more readers and revenue, it added advertiser-friendly sections on, for example, the weekend, the home, and living.[34]

In 1976, Brody was asked by her editor if she wanted to start writing a personal health column on a weekly basis. This was the first column of its kind in *The New York Times*.[35] Brody resisted at first, since her passion as a journalist was writing on the biological sciences, living organisms, environments, and how they all worked together. Accepting this offer would mean that she would not be able to write about what she loved. However, her editor insisted that she give it a try, and Brody agreed to do so for three months.

Resolution

After three months of writing for the personal health column, Brody told the editor that she would take on this position officially, only if she was free to write about any subject in the health field that impacts people's well-being. She was asked to write four samples, and in one of them she wrote about impotence. If the *Times* was not willing to let her write on such a topic, she would not do the column. As she recalled, "they swallowed hard and published it."[36] Soon readers encountered topics from the "sensitive (impotence and frigidity) to the humdrum (how to pack a child's lunch)"[37] in the *Times*. *Time* mentions Brody's success, quoting Robert Barnett, an editor of *American Health*, as saying, "She has done more than any other journalist to bring accurate information about nutrition and health to the public."[38] Additionally, Ernst Wynder, a physician and president of the American Health Foundation, said, "When it comes to preventive advice, she is more on target that [sic] most doctors."[39]

Initially, in her new role as the personal health columnist for the *Times*, Brody expected to receive backlash, not support, from the medical professions, given that she was a journalist writing about medical care. To her surprise, doctors loved her columns and wrote her letters with positive feedback. Her columns aided doctors who lacked training on how to effectively communicate medical knowledge in a way that an average patient could easily understand. The column gave Brody a platform from which to educate Americans on various health topics in a way that made sense. She found a bond with doctors outside the mainstream who agreed with Brody's approach to prevention, but had no way to share this information with the wider public.[40] One particular topic that Brody remembers writing about was mitral valve prolapse, which is when the valve between the heart's upper and lower left chambers does not close properly. This creates a leaky valve, causing blood to leak back into the atrium.[41] She recalls that the doctors had a difficult time explaining the phenomenon and found her column to be reassuring and clear. They even made copies of her column to give to their patients.[42] What reinforced Brody's interest in continuing to be a personal health columnist was seeing her work connect with the public and health-care professionals: "I remember walking into the office of a retinologist and finding my three columns on the retina framed and hanging on his wall. It was very interesting to see that kind of reaction, so it reinforced my interest in doing it [the column] because it showed that it was serving a purpose. And of course, I get comments from readers all the time. But it was important to me that the doctors accepted what I was doing and they didn't blast me."[43]

Although not always well regarded by the medical community, journalists like Brody have long played an important role in advancing public health. They are able to bridge the gap between research and the general public. Scientific experts may face several barriers to developing effective communication materials for stakeholders and members of the public. Miscommunications may occur when experts use themselves as model audience members and present the information that they find most important and interesting. Experts in different fields tend to lack good intuition about what nonexperts believe and what they still need to know to make informed decisions. And experts may present needlessly complex information and use jargon that is unfamiliar to or interpreted differently by nonexperts.[44]

The media often have a more rapid impact on public policy decision making compared to scientific research, which progresses slower. The media have an opportunity to reach a broad audience with information, which can catapult an issue to the forefront and as a result drive changes in law and policy. For example, Upton Sinclair's *The Jungle*[45]—which exposed unsafe working conditions and other problems in the meatpacking industry that resulted in food health scares—and led to a federal investigation and the passage of the federal Food and Drug Act of 1906 and the creation of what became the Food and Drug Administration.[46] Similarly, Rachel Carson's *Silent Spring*,[47] which outlined the impact of pesticides on the environment, fueled the expansion of the environmental movement and led to the creation of the Environmental Protection Agency.[48] Journalists are critical to advancing public and individual health by bringing to the masses vital information that can be employed to drive both large-scale and individual change. Journalists also help patients learn about causes and preventive care, and their stories may influence the conversations that patients have with physicians.[49]

Brody was able to react to her readers' concerns and give them actionable information, in addition to serving as a voice for patient empowerment. In 2007, she authored a column titled "The Importance of Knowing What the Doctor Is Talking About," in response to repeatedly hearing from readers that many of them had left a doctor's office not fully understanding what the doctor had told them.[50] In the article, she said that this happens to too many people, no matter what their level of education, and she discussed the importance of understanding the doctor. People may not know that they have the right to understand the doctor and ask questions when they do not. Doctors use medical jargon instead of language adjusted to their patients' understanding.[51] Brody offered tools for readers to help them get more out of doctors' visits. These tools included asking questions, repeating the doctor's instructions back to him or her, asking for demonstrations of new equipment, taking notes, bringing along someone else to the appointment to take notes or record the conversation. The message to readers was that they should not wait for doctors to learn how to communication better. Instead, they needed to take the initiative and serve as their own advocates.[52] This advice was simple, actionable, and important, given that nearly half of all American adults have difficulty understanding and acting upon health information.[53] This gap in communication can have serious health consequences. For example, if a patient does not fully understand how often to take prescribed medications, he or she can prolong or aggravate a condition.[54]

Accepting the position as a personal health columnist was not only a major turn for Brody, but it also allowed her to add something new to the *New York Times*—her personal touch:

> I wrote a column that talked about how I lived because people kept asking me, well, do I follow my own advice? So I said, "Okay. Yes I do. This is what I do." And I wrote a column, a very personal column. That was the first personal column. That was the other thing that was different, [since] the *Times* did not allow personal issues to appear in the news section. So I got permission to write this column on the basis that so many people kept asking me whether I follow my own advice. And that sort of opened Pandora's box and allowed me to slowly increase personal references in my columns and talk about family from my perspective, various habits, and point out that I'm not a paragon of virtue, I don't do everything perfectly, that there's room to slip.[55]

The column was a big hit, and people responded positively to it. The *Times* slowly "loosened up,"[56] as Brody continued to increase the number of personal references in her column.

Many medical professionals from all over the country now know Brody. She has been surprised that people in some of the most far-off places know her because of the *Times*. Not only did she begin to have an impact on the population's health knowledge and behavior, but she also created change in the *Times* by keeping it up to date with public sexual mores and writing her column so her readers could relate to it.

Other writers have criticized Brody for addressing health issues only superficially—failing to present alternative viewpoints and accept alternative nutrition and health views, and instead relying on known experts.[57] Yet Brody played an important role in bringing scientific research and complex data into a public forum. She addressed genetically modified foods in several different columns and advocated that "rather than wholesale rejection, [people should] take some time to learn about how genetic engineering works and the benefits it can offer now and in the future as climate change takes an ever greater toll on food supplies."[58] While Brody urged further research and discussion of this complex issue, her presentation of the pros and cons received some criticism that she does not take a tough enough stance against the food and biotech industries—for example, by not condemning genetically engineered food.[59] Taking on personal health issues in a public forum to advance change can become controversial, and there are many points of view to balance. However, Brody's effort to bring validated scientific expertise into the public domain may be one reason that the medical community continues to see her as a partner.

While Brody's practical style of attempting to bring strategies to improve health into her readers' homes, her comments on weight control, exercise, and self-image have been met with some opposition.[60] She has also been criticized for focusing too much on an individual's physical appearance rather than the state of the person's health.[61] Brody's article on public health experts' concerns about body acceptance leading to overweight and obese people's forgoing a healthier lifestyle to meet weight goals was seen as blaming individuals' choices for obesity.[62] Critics felt that she was not being hard enough on the food industry for creating overly processed options and instead demonizing individuals for not choosing to avoid those foods.[63] Brody talks about increased reliance on fast food, take-out meals, and restaurants and the decrease in home cooking. Although she acknowledges that a change in the food supply is important for population health, she notes that neither the industry nor government regulators are likely to address that issue soon.[64] Brody's message focuses on an individual's health status and whether actions impair that person's ability to live a healthy life. Her critics were in the minority. Brody has consistently addressed issues that do not have settled policy and sparked public debate.

One topic she repeatedly wrote about was the emerging negative effects of cigarette smoking, including effects on nonsmokers. She wrote about her husband's smoking for fifty years, noting that although he quit in 1994, he died of lung cancer in 2010.[65] Brody explained that before May 1, 1999,[66] the *New York Times* accepted advertisements from the tobacco industry, and people wrote her asking how she dared to write such articles while working for that newspaper. Brody responded by asking, "Would you rather there be

no contrary voice in this newspaper?"[67] What she could do was coun-
terbalance the advertisements with the facts, helping people open
their eyes from a public health perspective.

Serving as a health columnist for a newspaper that ranked third
in circulation in the United States gave Brody an incredible platform
from which to educate the public about health. However, with the
growth in alternative news sources, the impact of newspaper journalists appears to be on the decline.[68] Social media sites have sur-
passed print newspapers as a news source for Americans: 16 percent
of adults in the United States say that they often get news via social
media, slightly higher than the share that often does so from print
newspapers.[69] Additionally, more members of the public are searching the internet for health information rather than relying on
newspapers: 26 percent of adult internet users say that in the past
twelve months they have read or watched an item presenting someone else's experience with health or medical issues. And 16 percent
of adult internet users in the United States have gone online in
the past twelve months to find others who share their health
concerns.[70]

Although the format that Brody writes in is waning in popular-
ity, her leadership in the media to bring critical preventive health
information to the public in an easily understandable fashion will
stand out as a powerful method for impacting public health. Given
that the average article in a peer-reviewed academic journal is read
by no more than ten people, journalists still play a vital role in communicating information about scientific and medical advances.[71]
Brody used her position as a personal health columnist to guide
Americans on matters of health, personal growth, and disease prevention. Perhaps it was her boldness, competence, and love for science that led to the success of her column. Or it may have been her
femininity and warmth—the sensitivity and sensibility about the
importance of well-being, her experiences as a mother and grandmother—that made the column well received and easy to relate to.
Brody's experience of never feeling limited because she was a woman
shaped her determination and thinking. She transcended gender
stereotypes when she agreed to become a health columnist for the
New York Times only if she had the authority to choose her topics.

She then began blending personal stories and warmth into her well-researched columns. Although she was offered a position as editor, she did not accept the view that to be successful in the field of journalism, you must rise up in the ranks and become an editor. She found what she loved, and she never looked back.

Notes

1 Jane Brody, telephone interview by Dawn Thomas and Christina Chesnakov, February 13, 2019.

2 Anastasia Toufexis, "Health and Fitness: See Jane Run (and Do Likewise)," *Time*, November 10, 1986, http://content.time.com/time/subscriber/article /0,33009,962818-2,00.html.

3 Daryl F. Mallett, "Brody, Jane E.," Encyclopedia.com, updated February 6, 2021, https://www.encyclopedia.com/arts/news-wires-white-papers-and -books/brody-jane-e.

4 Quoted in ibid.

5 Jane E. Brody, *Jane Brody's Nutrition Book: a Lifetime Guide to Good Eating for Better Health and Weight Control*, (New York: Norton, 1981).

6 Jane E. Brody, *Jane Brody's Good Food Book: Living the High-Carbohydrate Way*, (New York: Norton, 1985).

7 "Jane Brody Bio," Premiere Speakers Bureau, accessed March 25, 2019, http://premierespeakers.com/jane_brody/bio.

8 Kendall Haven and Donna Clark, "Jane Brody, from Test Tube to Sauce Pan," in *100 Most Popular Scientists for Young Adults: Biographical Sketches and Professional Paths* (Englewood, CO: Libraries Unlimited, 1999), 49.

9 Quoted in ibid., 47.

10 Brody, interview.

11 Linda Ocasio, "Noteworthy Graduates: Jane Brody, *New York Times* Health Columnist," United Federation of Teachers, March 26, 2014, https://www.uft .org/news/member-spotlight/noteworthy-graduates-jane-brody-new-york -times-health-columnist.

12 Haven and Clark, "Jane Brody," 47.

13 Jane Brody, email to Dawn Thomas, June 19, 2019.

14 Jane E. Brody, "To Counter Loneliness, Find Ways to Connect," *New York Times*, June 25, 2018, https://www.nytimes.com/2018/06/25/well/to-counter -loneliness-find-ways-to-connect.html?rref=collection/byline/jane-e .-brody&action=click&contentCollection=undefined®ion=stream&module =stream_unit&version=latest&contentPlacement=32&pgtype=collection.

15 Ibid.

16 Brody, email.

17 Haven and Clark, "Jane Brody," 48; Brody, "To Counter Loneliness."

18 Brody, email.

19 Haven and Clark, "Jane Brody," 48.

20 Edwin McDowell, "Behind the Best Sellers; JANE BRODY," *New York Times*, September 20, 1981, https://www.nytimes.com/1981/09/20/books/behind -the-best-sellers-jane-brody.html.

21 Quoted in Toufexis, "Health and Fitness."

22 Jane E. Brody, "Short? No Worries: Just Ask This Texan," *New York Times*, May 10, 2010, https://www.nytimes.com/2010/05/11/health/11brod.html.

23 Brody, interview.

24 Alice Eagly and Linda L. Carli, "Women and the Labyrinth of Leadership," *Harvard Business Review*, September 2007, https://hbr.org/2007/09/women -and-the-labyrinth-of-leadership.

25 Quoted in Toufexis, "Health and Fitness."

26 Kim Parker and Wendy Wang, "Modern Parenthood: Roles of Moms and Dads Converge as They Balance Work and Family," Pew Research Center, March 14, 2013, https://www.pewresearch.org/social-trends/2013/03/14 /modern-parenthood-roles-of-moms-and-dads-converge-as-they-balance -work-and-family/.

27 Toufexis, "Health and Fitness."

28 David H. Weaver, Lars Willnat, and G. Cleveland Wilhoit. "The American Journalist in the Digital Age: Another Look at U.S. News People." *Journalism & Mass Communication Quarterly* 96, no. 1 (2018): 101–30.,https://doi.org/10 .1177/1077699018778242.

29 Michael P. McCauley et al., "The Social Group Influences of US Health Journalists and Their Impact on the Newsmaking Process," *Health Education Research* 28, no. 2 (April 2013): 339–351, DOI: 10.1093/her/cys086.

30 Take Care Staff, "Jane Brody."

31 Quoted in Pat Summers, "Personal Health with, Gulp, Jane Brody," *U.S. 1*, November 4, 1998, https://princetoninfo.com/personal-health-with-gulp -jane-brody/.

32 Brody, interview.

33 Ibid.

34 Gabriel Snyder, "The *New York Times* Claws Its Way into the Future," *Wired*, last modified February 12, 2017, https://www.wired.com/2017/02/new-york -times-digital-journalism/.

35 Brody, interview.

36 Ibid.

37 Toufexis, "Health and Fitness."

38 Quoted in ibid.

39 Quoted in ibid.

40 Brody, interview.

41 "Mitral Valve Prolapse," WebMD, accessed February 24, 2019, https://www .webmd.com/heart/mitral-valve-prolapse-symptoms-causes-and -treatment#1.

42 Brody, interview.

43 Ibid.

44 Wändi Bruine de Bruin and Ann Bostrom, "Assessing What to Address in Science Communication," *Proceedings of the National Academy of Sciences* 110, supplement 3 (August 20, 2013): 14062–14068: DOI: 10.1073/pnas.1212729110.

45 Upton Sinclair, *The Jungle* (New York: Doubleday, Page, 1906; repr., New York: Penguin Books, 1985).

46 Glinda S. Cooper and Rebecca C. Brown, "The Ghost of Public Health Journalism: Past, Present, and Future," *Epidemiology* 21, no. 2 (March 2010): 263–236: DOI: 10.1097/EDE.0b013e3181cb8c3d.

47 Rachel Carson, Lois Darling, and Louis Darling, *Silent Spring*. (Houghton Mifflin: Boston, 1962).

48 Jack Lewis, "The Birth of EPA," *EPA*, November 1985, https://archive.epa.gov /epa/aboutepa/birth-epa.html.

49 McCauley, "The Social Group Influences of US Health Journalists and Their Impact on the Newsmaking Process."

50 Jane E. Brody, "The Importance of Knowing What the Doctor Is Talking About," *New York Times*, January 30, 2007, https://www.nytimes.com/2007 /01/30/health/30brody.html?ex=1175400000&en=3d0bb0cc121ac18b&ei =5070.

51 "The Health-Literacy Crisis: Do You Understand Your Doctor?," *Plain Language at Work Newsletter*, no. 31 (April 2, 2007), http://www.impact -information.com/impactinfo/newsletter/plwork31.htm.

52 Brody, "The Importance of Knowing What the Doctor Is Talking About."

53 Institute of Medicine, *Health Literacy: A Prescription to End Confusion* (Washington: National Academies Press, 2004), https://doi.org/10.17226 /10883.

54 Brian Dakss, "Understanding Doctors' Instructions," CBS News, March 29, 2007, https://www.cbsnews.com/news/understanding-doctors-instructions/.

55 Brody, interview.

56 Ibid.

57 Kevin Lomangino, "When Reporting on Sloppy Science, NY Times 'Well' Section Should Practice What It Preaches," *Health News Review*, November 1, 2018, https://www.healthnewsreview.org/2018/11/when-reporting-on -sloppy-science-ny-times-well-section-should-practice-what-it-preaches/; Steven Novella, "*The New York Times*: Promoting False Hope as Journalism," Science-Based Medicine, May 3, 2017, https://sciencebasedmedicine.org/nyt -promoting-false-hope-as-journalism/.

58 Jane E. Brody, "Are G.M.O. Foods Safe?," *New York Times*, April 23, 2018, https://www.nytimes.com/2018/04/23/well/eat/are-gmo-foods-safe.html.

59 Kristin Wartman, "Jane Brody Gets It (Really)Wrong 'Debunking' Health Myths," *Civil Eats*, January 4, 2013, https://civileats.com/2013/01/04/jane -brody-gets-it-really-wrong-debunking-health-myths/.

60 Zanthe Taylor, "It's How We Eat, Not What We Eat: Changing America's Food Culture by Shifting Our Focus from 'What' to 'How,'" *Psychology Today*,

May 23, 2013, https://www.psychologytoday.com/us/blog/million-meals
/201305/its-how-we-eat-not-what-we-eat.

61 Jane Brody, "The BMI: Myth or Reality? Keynote Address by Jane Brody,"
Institute for Women's Leadership (IWL) Consortium Initiative on Women
and Health Conference at Rutgers University, May 6, 2014, video, https://
www.youtube.com/watch?v=uoPQDUZEMig.

62 Brody, Jane E. "More Fitness, Less Fatness," *New York Times*, February 26,
2018. https://www.nytimes.com/2018/02/26/well/more-fitness-less-fatness
.html.

63 Reina Gattuso, "What the *New York Times* Gets Wrong about Obesity,"
Feministing, accessed October 3, 2019, http://feministing.com/2018/04/11
/what-the-new-york-times-gets-wrong-about-obesity/.

64 Jane E. Brody, "The Growing Toll of Our Ever-Expanding Waistlines,"
New York Times, November 13, 2017, https://www.nytimes.com/2017/11/13
/well/eat/the-growing-toll-of-our-ever-expanding-waistlines.html?action
=click&contentCollection=Well&module=RelatedCoverage&region
=EndOfArticle&pgtype=article.

65 A Fatal Diagnosis, Followed by Goodbyes," *New York Times*, March 15, 2010,
https://well.blogs.nytimes.com/2010/03/15/a-fatal-diagnosis-followed-by
-goodbyes/.

66 Alex Kuczynski, "Tobacco Companies Accused of Still Aiming Ads at Youths,"
New York Times, August 15, 2001, https://www.nytimes.com/2001/08/15
/business/tobacco-companies-accused-of-still-aiming-ads-at-youths.html
?auth=login-email.

67 Brody, interview.

68 Daniel de Vise, "What If the Rankers Ranked Newspapers?," *Washington Post*,
October 4, 2011, https://www.washingtonpost.com/blogs/college-inc/post
/what-if-the-rankers-ranked-newspapers/2011/10/04/gIQAYZl6KL_blog
.html.

69 Ibid.

70 Susannah Fox, "The Social Life of Health Information," Pew Research Center,
January 15, 2014, https://www.pewresearch.org/fact-tank/2014/01/15/the
-social-life-of-health-information/.

71 Kathleen O'Grady and Noralou Roos, "Linking Academic Research with the
Public and Policy-Makers" *Policy Options*, August 1, 2016, https://policyoptions
.irpp.org/magazines/august-2016/linking-academic-research-with-the
-public-and-policy-makers/.

Risa Lavizzo-Mourey. Copyright © 2015 Allan Shoemake. Photo used with permission from the Robert Wood Johnson Foundation.

Risa Lavizzo-Mourey

Leading the Nation to Adopt a Culture of Health

Raquel Mazon Jeffers and Christina Chesnakov

Background

Audre Lorde, an American writer, feminist, womanist, librarian, and civil rights activist, said: "When I dare to be powerful, to use my strength in the service of my vision, then it becomes less important whether or not I am unafraid."[1] It is with courageous and clear vision that Risa Lavizzo-Mourey led and dared to be powerful. She had a vision to give to the nation—a vision of reduced health disparities and improved population health.

In 2003, Lavizzo-Mourey became the first woman and the first Black to serve as the president and CEO of the nation's largest health philanthropic organization, the Robert Wood Johnson Foundation (RWJF).[2] With her leadership, expertise, and insight, Lavizzo-Mourey was able to drive important initiatives to reverse the childhood obesity epidemic, improve access to health care, and help states implement the Affordable Care Act (ACA)—the comprehensive health-care reform law enacted in March 2010 designed to expand health insurance coverage for uninsured Americans and both improve the quality and reduce the cost of health care.

Lavizzo-Mourey achieved these milestones by championing a fundamental reorientation in how the nation steers a course to better health; addressing the social factors that affect health; and encouraging government, business, and civic leaders to consider the health of the public in their decision making.[3] It is this transformative perspective that has—in the words of Daren Walker, president of the Ford Foundation—made her "the most important person in public health philanthropy in a generation."[4]

Lavizzo-Mourey led RWJF to adopt a new mission: promoting a culture of health. This new paradigm emphasizes the link between social issues and health. As Lavizzo-Mourey explained, "By a culture of health . . . I mean making sure that the conditions for people to actually live the healthiest life possible are available in our country, that we have the kind of policies and practices that make it possible for people to choose a healthy lifestyle and [that we] have the supports, the social determinants of health, a good job, a good education, safe communities that influence whether or not you're able to get and stay healthy."[5] She defined this new paradigm as an American movement rooted in social change: "A Culture of Health can look very different to different people—and that's the way it should be. Our nation is splendidly diverse, and a national movement toward better health must reflect our individual beliefs, our family customs, and our community values. RWJF's goal is to weave these many threads of health into the richly textured fabric we call American life."[6]

Lavizzo-Mourey has been a preeminent leader of the movement to build a culture of health, which redefines health as an essential building block for individual self-realization, flourishing communities, equity, and a competitive nation. Her leadership style is described as "soft touch," and she is known for her "keen intellect," "warm heart," and "quiet strength."[7] Speaking about the impact of Lavizzo-Mourey's leadership, Roger Fine, chairman of RWJF's Board of Trustees, stated that "Risa's commitment to improving the health of this nation during her tenure as CEO is simply unparalleled, and she has led this Foundation with an extraordinary sense of purpose and passion."[8]

Perhaps it should come as no surprise that the daughter of the first Black woman pediatrician in Washington State, who was a close friend of Martin Luther King Jr., has made it her mission to merge medicine and social justice to create a national movement toward a culture of health. Lavizzo-Mourey's passion for medicine stemmed from her childhood experiences. Her parents were both physicians (her father was a surgeon), practicing during the time before Medicare in Seattle, Washington, where Lavizzo-Mourey and her brother, Philip, were raised.

The groundbreaking achievements of Lavizzo-Mourey's parents should be seen in their historical context. It is important to recall that in 1945, the American Medical Association did not permit Black doctors to become members, medical schools did not admit Black students, and most hospitals and health clinics segregated Black patients. In light of this discrimination, Black communities created their own health systems. Most Black doctors and nurses trained at one of two Black institutions, Meharry Medical College and Howard University College of Medicine (in Nashville, Tennessee, and Washington, D.C., respectively).[9] In the 1950s Black health-care professionals established their own organizations and fought to end legal segregation of hospitals. This effort converged with the civil rights movement in the 1960s and helped lead to the implementation of Medicare—the first federal health-care system for all elderly Americans.[10] In addition, the Tuskegee Study of Untreated Syphilis in the Negro Male, conducted between 1932 and 1972, contributed to the Black community's mistrust of the medical profession. In this study, Black men with syphilis were not treated with penicillin even after that had become the established standard of care.[11]

In 1950, for Lavizzo-Mourey's father to become board-certified, he needed to get practical experience despite this environment of segregation. With this aim in mind, his residency program at Meharry Medical College sent its surgical residents to Seattle for a year to practice. As Lavizzo-Mourey explained, "they [her parents] went out to Seattle in 1950, and saw a world that was very different than they had experienced in Atlanta, New Orleans, and Nashville, a place that had much less segregation, there was still some segregation in Seattle, but a lot less than they had experienced growing up and [they] thought this would be a good place to move and raise their children."[12]

Blanche Sellers Lavizzo, Lavizzo-Mourey's mother, had a significant impact on her life trajectory. She was a determined woman, Lavizzo-Mourey recalled, and Lavizzo-Mourey's principal life mentor.[13] Historically, women have faced barriers to becoming physicians based on gender discrimination. These barriers were even more significant for women of color, who often confronted financial hardship and racism as well as discrimination against women. Black families lacked resources to spend on medical education, due to generations of slavery and oppression. Black women often had to work to pay their way through medical school or seek funding from supporters of rights for women and members of minority groups. Once they became doctors, women of color often made important contributions by bringing better standards of care to their communities and serving as role models for all women.[14]

It was in this context that Sellers Lavizzo defied cultural stereotypes as well as the men in her family who did not support her aspiration to become a physician. It was controversial for women in general to have a seat in medical school and even more controversial for a Black woman. Under the gender stereotypes of that time, many people perceived that women displaced eligible Black men, who were considered more likely than women to go on to practice medicine and economically support their families.[15] Sellers Lavizzo nonetheless attended Meharry Medical College as one of only five women in her class. The scarcity of Black women physicians persists today. In 2016, only 4.5 percent of physicians in the United States were Black and less than 2.0 percent were Black women.[16]

During her training, Sellers Lavizzo experienced the strain of being a woman in the medical field and being a member of a minority group. However, she went on to set up a pediatric practice in Washington and attended to patients six days a week, including Saturday mornings. These mornings were a special time that Lavizzo-Mourey shared with her mother. They would drive to the office together. Then Lavizzo-Mourey would walk over to the Young Women's Christian Association that was nearby, take a swimming lesson, and walk back to her mother's office. Lavizzo-Mourey would spend the remainder of the morning in the waiting room with her mother's patients, observing how her mother worked. It was this experience that instilled in Lavizzo-Mourey the joy in becoming a physician.[17]

Having physician parents provided Lavizzo-Mourey with a window into the health-care needs of underserved populations, including the uninsured and low-income families.[18] Even at a young age, she began to understand the social and economic issues that impacted health. She recalls that during the recession of 1960–1961, her mother said, "Well we can't send this bill to Mrs. So and So." Out of curiosity Lavizzo-Mourey asked, "Well, why can't you send the bill?" Her mother replied, "If we send this bill, she's not gonna be able to pay it because she's lost her insurance and she's outta work and then she won't come back and she really needs the care, so the best thing to do is just not to send the bill." This situation made Lavizzo-Mourey realize that many factors influence health and the ability to stay healthy.[19]

Social and economic issues continue to impact health outcomes today, making health disparities an important focus of the public health agenda. According to the National Center for Health Statistics, while progress has been made in narrowing the gap in health outcomes, disparities persist.[20] For example, Black people still experience higher rates than whites of chronic disease and premature death. In 2019, Black women were about three times more likely than whites to die from causes related to pregnancy.[21] In 2018, Black women had the highest share of preterm births (14.13 percent) of any racial or ethnic group in the United States.[22] In 2017, infants born to Black mothers experienced the highest rates of infant mortality (10.97 deaths per thousand births).[23] According to a Department of Health and Human Services report from 2016, heart disease and cancer were then the leading causes of death in the United States, and Blacks were 30 percent more likely than whites to die prematurely from heart disease in 2018, while Black men were twice as likely as whites to die prematurely from stroke.[24] Furthermore, "the U.S. Centers for Disease Control and Prevention (CDC) reports that nearly 44 percent of African American men and 48 percent of African American women have some form of cardiovascular disease."[25]

Even long after the abolition of slavery in the United States, Black people continued to suffer from the effects of racism. The fight for equality persisted, giving rise to the civil rights movement of the 1960s.[26] Among those seeking equality and human rights for Blacks was Martin Luther King Jr., who—as noted above—was a good friend of Lavizzo-Mourey's mother. This close family relationship informed Lavizzo-Mourey's commitment to civil rights and social change. As she mentioned in an interview with Larry Crowe in 2016, "Since Martin Luther King was a friend and a very good friend, we were committed to his movement and his assassination meant not only personal grief, but a good deal of soul searching on how do we continue to move forward with what, as I said was a deep commitment in my family, to make sure that the African American community and our people were advancing and that we were fighting discrimination and fighting the larger determinants of the ability for people to achieve all that they could."[27]

The influence of Lavizzo-Mourey's parents, especially her mother, led her to pursue a career in medicine. Her family's social connections to King and the civil rights movement positioned health in the context of social justice and formed the early foundation for Lavizzo-Mourey's vision. She saw that for the majority of Americans, good health is not just about receiving high-quality medical care but is more often determined by an array of societal factors—ranging from the quality of housing to the availability of fresh fruits and vegetables and safe neighborhood parks.

When it came time to attend college, Lavizzo-Mourey was accepted at and planned to attend Yale University. However, her father died the summer before she was to start. Lavizzo-Mourey chose to stay in Seattle. Thus, she began her education at the University of Washington in 1972, where she was the only Black premedical student. That fall the University of Washington had just created the Special Educational Opportunity Program (later known as the Office of Minority Affairs) and the Ethnic Cultural Center/Theater. After spending a year at the University of Washington, Lavizzo-Mourey transferred to Stony Brook University in New York, where she was also part of a small group of Black students.

During college, Lavizzo-Mourey experienced a shift in her thinking. She attributed this to her having met Jack Geiger, a pioneer in the public health field. As she explained, "he became one of the people that illustrated the connection for me between the broader fields of public health and the kind of health care and quality of life that people experience on a day-to-day basis."[28] This encounter helped Lavizzo-Mourey "see the importance of being able to look at patient populations rather than only looking at the patient in front of me."[29]

After completing three years of college, Lavizzo-Mourey and her new husband, Robert Mourey, made an agreement: they were going to alternate cities where they lived so that neither of them got a permanent career advantage. Lavizzo-Mourey had the first choice and wanted to attend Harvard Medical School and train at Brigham and Women's Hospital. So in 1975, she and her husband moved to Boston, where Lavizzo-Mourey began her medical journey.[30]

While at Harvard Medical School, Lavizzo-Mourey found her community. There were approximately twenty Black students in her class. They came from different places and had done various extraordinary things, but they now wanted to do the same thing as Lavizzo-Mourey did: making health and health care better for people. Lavizzo-Mourey said: "I loved Harvard Medical School because it really for me was the first time that I was in an environment where there was a cadre of people, African American people who wanted to do just the same kinds of things that I wanted to do. . . . I felt like I was in my element . . . there were many times we felt we were actively discriminated against, but there was this sense that, we were there with purpose."[31]

From her mother Lavizzo-Mourey had learned that social and economic issues impact health, and these lessons were reinforced during her residency at Brigham and Women's Hospital. She saw the effect of social determinants of health and understood that providing medical care was not enough when she encountered a woman she calls "Patient Ruth."[32] Lavizzo-Mourey recalled that the woman "was a patient who had chronic leg ulcers, also had depression, was homeless and would periodically come to the hospital because her leg ulcers were painful or infected and she was also in need of a warm place to be and a hot meal. So she came to the admitting station on a cold night and it was very clear that what she really needed was mental health services, someone to help her find a home, a social network, but what we did was [we] admitted her to the hospital, gave her some antibiotics, a good meal, a couple of days in the hospital and then sent her right back out to the same problems that she faced every day."[33] It was this case that Lavizzo-Mourey most often refers to when she draws the connection between health and social factors. She has continued to ruminate on the question, "What would it take to prevent Ruth from coming back to the hospital?"[34]

Before joining RWJF, Lavizzo-Mourey was a practicing physician in geriatrics and worked in academic medicine. However, her interest in systems-level improvements led her to pursue expertise in business and health-care policy. Her interdisciplinary training was a key factor in her future achievements, especially her ability to foster partnerships across the health-care, policy, and business sectors.[35]

Lavizzo-Mourey's experiences as a medical student sparked her interest in what she refers to as the "interface between public policy, clinical medicine, and business."[36] After she finished her residency in internal medicine at Brigham and Women's Hospital, it was her husband's turn to choose what city they lived in. He got a faculty position at Philadelphia College of Textiles and Science, in Philadelphia, so the couple moved there. Lavizzo-Mourey became a Robert Wood Johnson Clinical Scholar at the University of Pennsylvania (Penn), joining a three-year post residency program that allows participants to receive a master's degree in the field of their choosing. Although her first choice was to get a degree in public health, in 1984 Penn did not have a school of public health. So instead Lavizzo-Mourey received a master's in business administration with an emphasis on health-care administration and policy at the Wharton School of Business at Penn. This degree equipped her with the knowledge and tools to become an effective consultant on public health policy.[37] The clinical scholars program allowed her to tie together her interests in clinical medicine, academic medicine, and health policy.[38] The program also introduced her to RWJF and the field of philanthropy. In addition to her professional accomplishments after completing medical school, Lavizzo-Mourey gave birth to two children, a daughter, Rel, and a son, Max. She credited her husband for his continuous support saying, "If you don't have a supportive spouse, it will be difficult to take on so many things."[39]

In 1986, Lavizzo-Mourey began the next part of her career, serving "as a professor and administrator at the University of Pennsylvania for fourteen years."[40] During this time, she began developing a relationship with the health policy community in Washington, D.C.[41]

In 1992, Louis Sullivan, who was the head of the Agency for Health Care Policy and Research in the administration of President George H. W. Bush, recruited Lavizzo-Mourey to serve as his deputy.[42] She remained in this role when the administration changed in 1993 to President Bill Clinton. Clinton made universal health insurance coverage one of the first policy initiatives of his administration. While serving in the Clinton administration, Lavizzo-Mourey played a leadership role in the discussions related to health-care reform and "as a member of the White House Task Force on Health Care Reform, she chaired the working group on quality of care" until 1994.[43] As she put it, "I was in a great place for working on health care reform when President Clinton came into his presidency and made affordable, or universal, coverage one of his first policy initiatives."[44] She later explained, "At the time we did not have guaranteed health insurance. There were anywhere from 46 to over 50 million people without health insurance and the Clintons had campaigned on a principle of trying to achieve universal health insurance."[45] Her experience with both the Bush and Clinton administrations increased Lavizzo-Mourey's ability to foster cooperation across different governmental agencies.[46] Her skill in building collaboration across agencies and sectors is an important hallmark of her leadership approach and ultimate success.

Lavizzo-Mourey returned to Penn in 1994, focusing on advancing her career in academic medicine. She served as the associate executive vice president for health policy for the university's health system from 1994 to 2001 and as the Sylvan Eisman Professor of Medicine and Health Care Systems at Penn from 1997 to 2002.[47] Throughout the years, she had considered many leadership positions within academia. However, it soon became clear that her interest lay elsewhere, as she continued to turn down numerous academic leadership opportunities.

In 2001, Steve Schroeder, president and CEO of RWJF, successfully recruited Lavizzo-Mourey to serve as the foundation's senior vice president for health care.[48] According to the RWJF website, "the Foundation was established as a national philanthropy in 1972 with a generous bequest of shares of Johnson & Johnson (J&J) from its chief executive, Robert Wood Johnson."[49] RWJF remains the largest philanthropy dedicated to health in the United States. In 2017, its endowment totaled $11.4 billion, and it annually awarded grants totaling more than $450 million. The foundation's first president, David Rogers, set a course that guided the primary focus of its grant making: to improve health care. In Rogers's words, "The uneven availability of continuing medical care of acceptable quality is one of the most serious problems we face today. We need to better provide health service of the right kind, at the right time, to those who need it. Therefore, in its initial years, the Foundation will try to identify and encourage efforts to expand and improve the delivery of primary, frontline care."[50] Given the complexity of this issue, the foundation's commitment to improving access to and the quality of medical care remained a constant priority for the next three decades.

As RWJF's senior vice president, Lavizzo-Mourey "oversaw all grant making and programs related to the Foundation's goals of assuring that all Americans have access to basic health care at reasonable cost and improving care and support for people with chronic health conditions."[51] During this time, the foundation was transitioning from thinking about itself as a grant maker to thinking of itself as an agent of social change.[52] Lavizzo-Mourey was captivated and driven by the foundation's mission to make a difference in people's lives. In 2003, she became its president and CEO. This was a significant moment in the field of philanthropy, which has been dominated by white men.

Lavizzo-Mourey's rise to this leadership position occurred at a time when more women were assuming managerial and administrative positions in the United States. In 1972, only 18 percent of managerial and administrative positions were held by women. However, by 2002 that percentage had increased to 46 percent.[53] Lavizzo-Mourey was a pioneering female leader not only in the United States, but on the worldwide stage of women leaders in health. Research has demonstrated that global gender "inequity is widespread, especially at the highest levels of management and leadership, for instance, in 2015, only 27% of Ministers of Health were women."[54] In addition, "at the 68th World Health Assembly in

May 2015 of the World Health Organization, only 23% of member state delegations had a woman in the role of chief delegate."[55]

One initial success of Lavizzo-Mourey's early leadership as the CEO of RWJF was her effort to address childhood obesity. She took on this issue when the U.S. health-care system was changing its focus to communities as the cornerstone for good health. The surgeon general's 2001 report, *Call to Action to Prevent and Decrease Obesity and Overweight*, listed five main principles to prevent and treat obesity as a public health goal: to promote awareness of overweight and obesity as major public health problems; make it easier for Americans to eat healthfully and exercise more regularly to maintain a healthy body weight; identify interventions to prevent and treat overweight and obesity; facilitate environmental interventions to prevent overweight and obesity; and support public-private partnerships to enact this vision.[56]

In addition to this landmark report, popular opinion began to influence environmental change. In 2001, Eric Schlosser published a best-selling book called *Fast Food Nation*[57] that informed people about what goes on behind the counter of fast-food restaurants, including meat production and preparation, and how the fast-food industry created poor working conditions for millions of people. Richard Linklater directed a film adapted from the book in 2006.[58] A few years later, Michael Pollan's *The Omnivore's Dilemma*,[59] another best-selling book, examined which food choices are the most ethical, sustainable, and environmentally friendly. By 2006, obesity was competing with tobacco as the nation's leading cause of death.[60] Additionally health policy debates were intensifying in Washington, D.C., health-care costs were increasing, and millions of Americans were uninsured.[61]

Under Lavizzo-Mourey's leadership, in 2007 RWJF launched a $500 million childhood obesity initiative, which has had a significant impact on reversing the nation's obesity epidemic. According to a report published by the CDC, the initiative was partly responsible for the fact that obesity rates among U.S. children ages 2–19 stopped rising and has held steady at 17 percent.[62] Additionally, among the children ages 2–5, the obesity rate decreased from 13.9 percent in 2003–2004 to 8.9 percent in 2011–2014.[63]

In reflecting on her decision to invest the foundation's resources in this area, Lavizzo-Mourey recalled: "As I was preparing my first president's message, I remembered thinking, 'tackling obesity would be perfect as an issue for the Robert Wood Johnson Foundation. It's a big challenge. It's hard. It's messy. And success would really improve the nation's health.'"[64]

RWJF adopted a multipronged effort to impact the obesity epidemic, developing a body of research and cultivating a cadre of researchers who published on the issue; collaborating with other foundations, the government, and the private sector; introducing a wide-ranging communications effort to raise awareness about the epidemic among policy makers and the public; and funding community- and school-based programs focused on transforming the physical environment that was contributing to young people gaining weight.[65]

In achieving this success, Lavizzo-Mourey used a key strategy that continued to be a trademark of her leadership, fostering multisectoral collaboration and unlikely partnerships. This was a task she was well suited for, given her interdisciplinary professional training and skills as well as her childhood in a family that was involved in the nation's civil rights movement. She believes strongly that a key to improving health is to convince other sectors that doing so would also advance their missions.[66]

Lavizzo-Mourey's collaborative leadership approach can be understood in the context of contemporary changes in theories and practices of leadership. In the past, leaders were seen as powerful if they were able to command authority and economic and military power. In postindustrial societies, leaders are more inclined to share power, establish collaborative relationships, and rely on teamwork. As these leadership characteristics are frequently associated with the feminine aspects of Western culture, these changing values may have given female leaders like Lavizzo-Mourey an advantage.[67]

RWJF's "childhood obesity initiative has attracted many high-profile allies, including First Lady Michelle Obama, who adopted the cause through her Let's Move! campaign."[68] An important contribution to the success of this initiative was the cross-sectoral collaboration of Lavizzo-Mourey and the administration of President

Barack Obama, including the Department of Education, with the food and beverage industry.[69] The partnership with the food giants that are at the heart of the problem (and potentially the solution), such as soda makers, to reduce calories in their products was part of an astute strategy. For example, the Olive Garden and Red Lobster restaurant chains swapped in fruits and vegetables for fries on kids' menus, and Walmart cut back on sodium in the foods it sold.[70] Lavizzo-Mourey, the administration of President Obama, and the food and beverage industry also collaborated to guide government nutrition policy and leveraged federal subsidy programs for school lunches that had been filled with pizza and french fries to include more fresh fruits and vegetables.[71]

RWJF convened two consortiums made up of business leaders. The first was called ChildObesity180, a consortium of obesity researchers and executives from the food, insurance, and pharmaceutical industries. The second was the Healthy Weight Commitment Foundation, consisting of the leaders of sixteen packaged-food and beverage companies who pledged to remove 1.5 trillion calories from their products by 2015.[72]

In this effort, Lavizzo-Mourey's quiet but powerful leadership produced results. She partnered with Michelle Obama on childhood obesity. This appeared on the surface to be a light and apolitical issue, since the public face of the obesity campaign portrayed bucolic images of children gardening on the White House lawn. However, winning over the support of food industry CEOs required serious boardroom acumen.

Also, during Lavizzo-Mourey's early tenure at RWJF, the foundation made enormous strides in expanding health insurance coverage and supporting the ACA. Under Lavizzo-Mourey's leadership, RWJF supported efforts to increase enrollment in the health insurance exchanges, with a specific focus on younger and healthier people. This strategy was key to ensuring the success of the ACA. Health coverage was a cornerstone in the RWJF vision of a culture of health.[73]

RWJF made available well over $20 million in grants for public outreach about the ACA and insurance enrollment. It has also provided millions more in grants to evaluate the ACA's effectiveness and impact.[74] Universal coverage is no longer the radical idea it once was. According to the World Health Organization, "Universal health coverage means that all people have access to the health services they need, [prevention, promotion, treatment, rehabilitation and palliative care] when and where they need them, without the risk of financial hardship."[75]

In addition, "good health allows children to learn and adults to earn, helps people escape from poverty, and provides the basis for long-term economic development."[76] That shift, that universal health care is becoming a more established idea, is profound and there is little doubt that Lavizzo-Mourey and RWJF helped bring it about.[77]

Although Lavizzo-Mourey accomplished a great deal in her early years at RWJF, she recognized that more needed to be done to improve the U.S. population's health. Between 1972 and 1990, the foundation focused on improving health care, while from 1991 through 2013, it concentrated on improving both health care and health.[78] Beginning in mid-2012, RWJF went through a process of discovery centered on crafting an entirely new vision. The foundation was interested in building upon its work over its forty-year history and unearthing striking new ways to help make the United States a healthier nation. Initially, RWJF was required to award many millions of dollars of grants quickly. This time pressure led it to support ideas that were quick to fund, noncontroversial, and safe to implement. The pace made it nearly impossible for staff members to invest time in program development and testing new ideas.[79] This process of crafting a new vision took over a year, involved the entire staff, and was overseen by the Board of Trustees, which was chaired by Roger S. Fine, an attorney.[80]

The board had instructed the staff to think broadly and not simply make incremental changes that would reflect the past. Rather, the goal was to create a vision for the future. The board encouraged the staff to not "repeat the mistakes of the eighteenth-century British, who wasted their time building speedier sailing ships just as steam-powered ships were rendering them obsolete."[81]

Thus, Lavizzo-Mourey's challenge was to successfully create a new vision acceptable to the foundation, its staff, and its stakehold-

ers, knowing that it would likely alter the status quo and transform the foundation's grant making and program development.

Resolution

RWJF's strategic planning sessions began with an effort to gather
the information that could help predict what health and health care
might look like in the future. The staff members, led by Lavizzo-
Mourey, sought the counsel of experts and compiled, read, and discussed various well-produced analyses of the future of health and
health care. They held retreats, including an all-staff learning session in which participants were asked to envision how health and
health care were likely to change over the next twenty years and
explore areas that RWJF had traditionally left unquestioned.[82] In
an interview with Alan Weil in 2016, Lavizzo-Mourey stated, "In
exploring this over a series of meetings, we decided that the real
aspect of our daily lives that we needed to address was our culture
and the ways in which our culture makes it more difficult, not less
difficult, to make healthy choices; the ways in which our culture
reinforces policies and practices that are not promoting health; and
the ways in which our culture defines health very narrowly, rather
than broadly, and not in terms of people's overall well-being."[83]

In 2014, Lavizzo-Mourey announced a sweeping reorganization
of RWJF's national activities to support the adoption of a new framework concentrating on the nation's health that culminated in a vision
of a culture of health. She developed this platform after a comprehensive strategic planning effort that was informed by a detailed
review of health data and had invited innovative ideas from thought
leaders across multiple sectors. This not only involved building a
social movement outside RWJF but also required a shift in RWJF's
internal culture. When Lavizzo-Mourey unveiled the platform out-
lining the foundation's commitment to building a culture of health,
she emphasized the urgency for change by illuminating the health
and economic crisis that the country was facing with three surprising facts. She noted that for the first time in U.S. history, the
current generation is living sicker and dying younger than the

previous generation. She pointed out that 75 percent of Americans do not meet the physical fitness criteria necessary to serve in the military. And she highlighted the economic reality that the United States was spending $2.7 trillion on health care and losing $227 billion in lost productivity due to poor health.[84] In a 2017 RWJF blog post, Lavizzo-Mourey summarized the vision.

> What we foresee is a vibrant American culture of health:
> - Where good health flourishes across geographic, demographic, and social sectors.
> - Where being healthy and staying healthy is an esteemed social value.
> - And everyone has access to affordable, quality health care.
>
> In this national culture of health . . .
> - Individuals, businesses, government, and organizations will foster healthy communities and lifestyles.
> - The economy will be less burdened by excessive and unwarranted health care spending.
> - Individuals will be proactive in making choices that lead to a healthy lifestyle.
> - And efficient and equitable health care will deliver optimal patient outcomes.
>
> It will be a given that . . .
> - The health of the population guides public and private decision-making.
> - And, Americans will hold public leaders and policy-makers accountable for the community's health.[85]

In addition to Lavizzo-Mourey's collaborative approach to establishing a new overarching vision for RWJF, she applied a similar ethos to her management of the foundation's operations. She divided program staff members into teams, charging each team with developing an objective with relevant measurements. She also elevated the authority of the team directors to make funding decisions.

Karen Remley, a senior fellow of the de Beaumont Foundation, the first woman CEO of the American Academy of Pediatrics, a physician, and a former commissioner of health for the Commonwealth of Virginia, reflected on Lavizzo-Mourey's leadership during an interview. Remley recalled how many long-term public health professionals initially reacted to Lavizzo-Mourey's efforts to enlist the health care community in convening a broad group of stakeholders to support a culture of health. Many of the core tenants of the culture of health reflected classic public health principles that had been the cornerstone of public health leaders' careers. According to Remley, "Some public health leaders felt as though they had been 'fighting the good fight' for a long time and risked being displaced by health care professionals jumping in at this later stage—especially since many of them wielded more money and power." However, because Lavizzo-Mourey was a good listener and collaborator, she skillfully ensured that both long-standing public health professionals and health-care leaders new to the effort each had a seat at the table. As Remley put it, "Lavizzo-Mourey had a gentle gravitas about her that motivated people to 'lean in' and embrace her clear and consistent mission."[86]

Lavizzo-Mourey began executing her vision to build a culture of health by using her quiet but powerful leadership to create a social movement that relies on a genuine spirit of collaboration. In this way, she started down the long road of change, embracing the wisdom that "change moves at the speed of trust."[87]

Lavizzo-Mourey's career achievements come into full relief when seen against the historical backdrop of the ongoing struggle for health and human rights in the United States. Her leadership draws inspiration from her mother's generation, when three important political and social events took place. In 1945 President Harry Truman campaigned for universal health coverage. At the same time, Black colleges led the fight to desegregate hospitals. In 1964 the Civil Rights Act implemented government-sponsored coverage in the form of Medicare and Medicaid, which ended legal segregation in hospitals. In the 1960s the leading Black medical society, the National Medical Association, coined the slogan, "health care is a human right.'" In retrospect, the credit for these vast changes to the U.S. health-care system can be attributed to the struggle to end inequality.

Nonetheless, millions of Americans who did not meet the age and income eligibility criteria for Medicaid and Medicare remained uninsured. That changed in 2010, when Lavizzo-Mourey's contemporaries picked up from where her mother's generation had left off and worked to ensure that the ACA would bring health insurance to nearly twenty million uninsured adults—the vast majority of whom were people of color.

In 2017 Lavizzo-Mourey stepped down from her position as CEO of RWJF after fourteen years. She is currently serving as the nineteenth Penn Integrates Knowledge (PIK) University Professor and the Robert Wood Johnson Foundation Health and Health Equity Professor at the University of Pennsylvania. The PIK position was created in 2005 to encourage an interdisciplinary approach to knowledge and is aligned with her lifelong commitment to leading by building bridges and connections.[88] Lavizzo-Mourey has been the recipient of numerous awards, including twenty honorary doctorates from institutions like Brown University, the University of Pennsylvania, Tufts University, and the Morehouse School of Medicine. She was on *Forbes*'s list of the most important women in the world eight times and was named as one of *Modern Healthcare*'s hundred most influential people in health care eleven times.[89]

Lavizzo-Mourey did not merely work to expand health insurance coverage, she also went on to lead a movement to promote health equity and build a culture of health as a foundation for American democracy. Her strength served her vision that everyone, regardless of geographic, demographic, and social factors, deserves to live a healthy life. In her words, "health is the bedrock of personal fulfillment. It's the backbone of prosperity. It's what helps our nation stay strong and competitive and compassionate."[90]

Notes

1   "Risa Lavizzo-Mourey Stepping Down as President and CEO of RWJF," Robert Wood Johnson Foundation, September 30, 2016, https://www.rwjf .org/en/library/articles-and-news/2016/09/rlm-stepping-down.html.

2 "Risa Lavizzo-Mourey Stepping Down as President and CEO of RWJF," Robert Wood Johnson Foundation, September 30, 2016, https://www.rwjf .org/en/library/articles-and-news/2016/09/rlm-stepping-down.html.

3 "Risa Lavizzo-Mourey," Tufts Commencement Coverage, accessed March 25, 2019, https://commencement.tufts.edu/coverage/class-2018/honorary -degree/risa-lavizzo-mourey/.

4 Quoted in David Callahan, "So Long, Stay Well; What Did Risa Lavizzo-Mourey Achieve at the Robert Wood Johnson Foundation?," *Inside Philanthropy*, accessed March 27, 2020, https://www.insidephilanthropy.com/home /2017/3/30/so-long-stay-healthy-what-did-risa-lavizzo-mourey-achieve-at -the-robert-wood-johnson-foundation.

5 Dr. Risa Lavizzo-Mourey, interview by Larry Crowe, December 14, 2016, The HistoryMakers Digital Archive, session 1, tape 6, story 6, https://da .thehistorymakers.org/story/522074.

6 Risa Lavizzo-Mourey, "In It Together: Building a Culture of Health," Robert Wood Johnson Foundation, accessed February 13, 2021, https://www.rwjf .org/en/library/annual-reports/presidents-message-2015.html.

7 Peggy McGlone, "Robert Wood Johnson Foundation Chief Combines Drive, Dedication and a Warm Heart," NJ.com, updated March 30, 2019, https:// www.nj.com/business/2013/01/robert_wood_johnson_chief_comb.html.

8 "Risa Lavizzo-Mourey Stepping Down."

9 Jeneen Interlandi, "Why Doesn't the United States Have Universal Health Care? The Answer Has Everything to Do with Race," *New York Times*, August 14, 2019, https://www.nytimes.com/interactive/2019/08/14 /magazine/universal-health-care-racism.html.

10 Ibid.

11 A. K. Agunbiade, "Why Are There So Few Black Men in Medicine?," Medium, February 23, 2018, https://medium.com/@akagunbiade/why-are-there-so -few-black-men-in-medicine-59995fe10837.

12 Lavizzo-Mourey, interview by Crowe, December 14, 2016, session 1, tape 2, story 1, https://da.thehistorymakers.org/story/522024.

13 Risa Lavizzo-Mourey, "Lessons I've Learned about Improving Health in America," lifetime achievement award speech, National Network of Public Health Institutes Annual Conference and Public Health Workforce Forum, New Orleans, LA, May 23, 2018.

14 "Changing the Face of Medicine: Celebrating America's Women Physicians,"American Library Association, September 6, 2011, accessed March 18, 2021, http://www.ala.org/tools/programming/exhibitions /changingface/exhibitiontext.

15 Lavizzo-Mourey, interview by Crowe, December 14, 2016, session 1, tape 1, story 5, https://da.thehistorymakers.org/story/522017.

16 "Black Women in Medicine," American Film Showcase, posted October 17, 2016, accessed October 7, 2019, http://americanfilmshowcase.com/afs-films /black-women-in-medicine/.

17 E. Shostak, "Risa Lavizzo-Mourey Biography," JRank, accessed September 11, 2018, https://biography.jrank.org/pages/2421/Lavizzo-Mourey-Risa .html.

18 Ibid.

19 Lavizzo-Mourey, interview by Crowe, December 14, 2016, session 1, tape 3, story 1, https://da.thehistorymakers.org/story/522035.

20 National Academies of Sciences, Engineering, and Medicine, "The State of Health Disparities in the United States," in *Communities in Action: Pathways to Health Equity* (Washington: National Academies Press, 2017), https://www .ncbi.nlm.nih.gov/books/NBK425844/.

21 Roni Caryn Rabin, "Huge Racial Disparities Found in Deaths Linked to Pregnancy," *New York Times*, May 7, 2019, https://www.nytimes.com/2019/05 /07/health/pregnancy-deaths-.html.

22 Joyce A. Martin, Brady E. Hamilton, Michelle J. K. Osterman, et al. "Births: Final Data for 2018," *National Vital Statistics Reports* 68, no. 13 (2019), https://pubmed.ncbi.nlm.nih.gov/?term=Osterman+MJK&cauthor_id =32501202.

23 Danielle M. Ely and Anne K. Driscoll, "Infant Mortality in the United States, 2017: Data from the Period Linked Birth/Infant Death File," *National Vital Statistics Reports* 68, no. 10 (2019).

24 National Academies of Sciences, "The State of Health Disparities," 60.

25 Ibid.

26 "Civil Rights Movement," History.com updated January 29, 2021, https:// www.history.com/topics/black-history/civil-rights-movement.

27 Lavizzo-Mourey, interview by Crowe, December 14, 2016, session 1, tape 3, story 4., https://da.thehistorymakers.org/story/522038.

28 Mitch Nauffts, "Dr. Risa Lavizzo-Mourey, President/CEO, Robert Wood Johnson Foundation: Philanthropy in the Service of a Healthier America," *Philanthropy News Digest*, last modified May 31, 2005, https:// philanthropynewsdigest.org/newsmakers/dr.-risa-lavizzo-mourey-president -ceo-robert-wood-johnson-foundation-philanthropy-in-the-service-of-a -healthier-america.

29 Ibid.

30 Stephen L. Isaacs, "A Conversation with Risa Lavizzo-Mourey," in *To Improve Health and Health Care, Volume X: The Robert Wood Johnson Foundation Anthology*, ed. David C. Colby, (San Francisco: Jossey-Bass, 2015), 40.

31 Lavizzo-Mourey, interview by Crowe, December 14, 2016, session 1, tape 4, story 1, https://da.thehistorymakers.org/story/522046.

32 Risa Lavizzo-Mourey, "Prescriptions Must Address More than Medicines," LinkedIn, June 12, 2014, https://www.linkedin.com/pulse/20140612112054 -43742182-prescriptions-must-address-more-than-medicines.

33 Lavizzo-Mourey, interview by Crowe, December 14, 2016, session 1, tape 4, story 8, https://da.thehistorymakers.org/story/522053.

34 LDIvideo, "New RWJF Vision: Building a Culture of Health," YouTube, 11:02, October 29. 2014, https://www.youtube.com/watch?v=UKkNFRtYi_A.

35 "Wharton Leader: Dr. Risa Lavizzo-Mourey," *Wharton Magazine*, April 1, 2006, http://whartonmagazine.com/issues/spring-2006/wharton-leader-dr-risa-lavizzo-mourey/#sthash.70Fm7IaQ.dpbs.

36 Quoted in Shostak, "Risa Lavizzo-Mourey Biography."

37 Isaacs "A Conversation with Risa Lavizzo-Mourey," 40.

38 Isaacs, "A Conversation with Risa Lavizzo-Mourey," 41.

39 McGlone, "Robert Wood Johnson Foundation Chief Combines Drive, Dedication and a Warm Heart."

40 "Risa Lavizzo-Mourey."

41 Isaacs, "A Conversation with Risa Lavizzo-Mourey," 41.

42 Lavizzo-Mourey, interview by Crowe, December 14, 2016, session 1, tape 5, story 10, https://da.thehistorymakers.org/story/522066.

43 Shostak, "Risa Lavizzo-Mourey Biography."

44 Lavizzo-Mourey, interview by Crowe, December 14, 2016, session 1, tape 5, story 10, https://da.thehistorymakers.org/story/522066.

45 Lavizzo-Mourey, interview by Crowe, December 14, 2016, session 1, tape 5, story 11, https://da.thehistorymakers.org/story/522067.

46 Shostak, "Risa Lavizzo-Mourey Biography."

47 "Dr. Risa Lavizzo-Mourey: Biography," History Makers, December 14, 2016, https://www.thehistorymakers.org/biography/dr-risa-lavizzo-mourey.

48 Isaacs, "A Conversation with Risa Lavizzo-Mourey," 42.

49 Robert Wood Johnson Foundation: "About RWFJ: Financials," accessed May 29, 2019, https://www.rwjf.org/en/about-rwjf/financials.html.

50 Quoted in Isaacs, introduction to *To Improve Health and Health Care*, 1.

51 "KCMU Members: Risa Lavizzo-Mourey," Henry J. Kaiser Family Foundation, accessed May 29, 2019, https://www.kff.org/person/risa-lavizzo-mourey/.

52 Isaacs, "A Conversation with Risa Lavizzo-Mourey," 44.

53 Alice H. Eagly and Linda L. Carli, "The Female Leadership Advantage: An Evaluation of the Evidence," *Leadership Quarterly* 14, no. 6 (2003): 807–834.

54 Roopa Dhatt et al, "The Role of Women's Leadership and Gender Equity in Leadership and Health System Strengthening," *Global Health, Epidemiology and Genomics* 2 (2017): doi:10.1017/gheg.2016.22.

55 Ibid.

56 Office of the Surgeon General (US); Office of Disease Prevention and Health Promotion (US); Centers for Disease Control and Prevention (US); National Institutes of Health (US), *The Surgeon General's Call To Action to Prevent and Decrease Overweight and Obesity*, (Rockville, MD: Office of the U.S. Surgeon General, 2001), https://www.ncbi.nlm.nih.gov/books/NBK44206/.

57 Eric Schlosser, *Fast Food Nation: The Dark Side of the All-American Meal*, (Boston: Houghton Mifflin, 2001).

58 Richard Linklater, dir., *Fast Food Nation* (Century City, CA: Fox Searchlight Pictures, 2006).

59 Michael Pollan, *The Omnivore's Dilemma: A Natural History of Four Meals* (New York: Penguin, 2006).

60 Danaei Goodarz et al., "Correction: The Preventable Causes of Death in the United States: Comparative Risk Assessment of Dietary, Lifestyle, and Metabolic Risk Factors," *PLoS Medicine* 8, no. 1 (April 28, 2009): doi:10.1371/annotation/0ef47acd-9dcc-4296-a897-872d182cde57.

61 Callahan, "So Long, Stay Well."

62 Cynthia Ogden and Margaret Carroll, "Prevalence of Obesity Among Children and Adolescents: United States, Trends 1963–1965 Through 2007–2008," Centers for Disease Control and Prevention, 2010, https://www.cdc.gov/nchs/data/hestat/obesity_child_07_08/obesity_child_07_08.pdf.

63 "Risa Lavizzo-Mourey Stepping Down."

64 Quoted in Isaacs, "A Conversation with Risa Lavizzo-Mourey," 47.

65 Stephen L. Isaacs, David C. Colby, and Amy Woodrum, "The Robert Wood Johnson Foundation's Efforts to Reduce Childhood Obesity," in *To Improve Health and Health Care*, vol. 16, ed. Stephen L. Isaacs and David C. Colby (San Francisco: Jossey-Bass, 2014), 10.

66 Callahan, "So Long, Stay Well."

67 Carli and Eagly, "The Female Leadership Advantage."

68 "Risa Lavizzo-Mourey Stepping Down."

69 Callahan, "So Long, Stay Well."

70 Helena Bottemiller Evich and Darren Samuelsohn, "The Great FLOTUS Food Fight," Politico, March 17, 2016, https://www.politico.com/agenda/story/2016/03/michelle-obama-healthy-eating-school-lunch-food-policy-000066.

71 Julia Belluz, "How Michelle Obama Quietly Changed What Americans Eat," Vox, October 3, 2016, https://www.vox.com/2016/10/3/12866484/michelle-obama-childhood-obesity-lets-move.

72 Isaacs et al., "The Robert Wood Johnson Foundation's Efforts to Reduce Childhood Obesity," 9.

73 "Dr. Risa Lavizzo-Mourey: Biography."

74 Callahan, "So Long, Stay Well."

75 World Health Organization, "Universal Health Coverage: Overview," accessed February 13, 2021, https://www.who.int/health_financing/universal_coverage_definition/en/.

76 World Health Organization, "Universal Health Coverage: Overview," accessed February 13, 2021, https://www.who.int/health_financing/universal_coverage_definition/en/.

77 Ibid.

78 Risa Lavizzo-Mourey, foreword to *To Improve Health and Health Care*, vol. 16, ed. Stephen L. Isaacs and David C. Colby (San Francisco: Jossey-Bass, 2014), viii.

79 Stephen L. Isaacs, David C. Colby, and Amy Woodrum, "Where Do Ideas Come From? The Robert Wood Johnson Foundation Experience," in *To Improve Health and Health Care*, vol. 16, ed. Stephen L. Isaacs and David C. Colby (San Francisco: Jossey-Bass, 2014), 5.

80 Lavizzo-Mourey, foreword, viii.

81 Quoted in ibid.

82 Ibid.

83 Alan R. Weil, "Building a Culture of Health," *Health Affairs* 35, no. 11 (November 2016): 1953–1958, doi:10.1377/hlthaff.2016.0913.

84 LDIvideo, "New RWJF Vision," 3:06.

85 "About the Culture of Health Blog," *Culture of Health Blog*, February 1, 2017, https://www.rwjf.org/en/blog/2013/05/about_culture_ofhea.html.

86 Karen Remley, telephone interview by Raquel Mazon Jeffers and Christina Chesnakov, July 5, 2019.

87 Stephen M. R. Covey and Rebecca R. Merrill, *The Speed of Trust: The One Thing that Changes Everything* (2006; New York: Free Press, 2018).

88 Callahan, "So Long, Stay Well."

89 "Dr. Risa Lavizzo-Mourey: Biography."

90 LDIvideo, "New RWJF Vision," 0:39.

Marilyn Tavenner. Photo courtesy of Blue Cross Blue Shield of Arizona.

Marilyn Tavenner
From Crashing Patients to Crashing Websites

Heather Howard and Carson Clay

Background

On October 1, 2013, the first comprehensive American health reform in decades faced a critical test: the launch of HealthCare.gov. The website itself was a key provision of the Affordable Care Act (ACA), which was signed into law by President Barack Obama on March 23, 2010. The ACA had already faced a myriad of legal and political challenges, adding tension to an already pivotal moment. The newly confirmed director of the Centers for Medicare and Medicaid Services (CMS), Marilyn Tavenner, oversaw the rollout of HealthCare .gov, which would allow Americans to shop for health insurance plans, take advantage of federal subsidies to make insurance more affordable, and ultimately enroll in a health insurance plan. Everyone—legislators, American citizens, and people around the globe—watched as the website crashed two hours after its launch. Only six people were able to enroll in a plan, out of the millions of users who visited the site on its first day. The fate of Obama's signature domestic achievement was on the line, and Tavenner had important decisions to make on a very public stage.

The ACA was a comprehensive health reform law designed to expand insurance coverage, control health-care costs, invest in public health and prevention programs, and improve the health-care delivery system.[1] For almost a hundred years, U.S. presidents from Theodore Roosevelt and Harry Truman to Richard Nixon and Bill Clinton had tried and failed to enact universal health care. President Lyndon Johnson came closest, with the enactment of Medicare and

Medicaid in 1965—which laid the foundation for the ACA.[2] But by 2010, the health-care system was in crisis, with almost fifty million Americans uninsured, health-care costs skyrocketing, and health disparities widening.[3] The ACA was landmark legislation, and while far from perfect, it promised to improve population health, protect consumers, and begin to address long-standing health inequities.[4] Indeed, as Tavenner would write with Howard Koh in the *American Journal of Public Health*, the ACA provides "an unprecedented opportunity to overcome fragmentation and integrate primary care and public health. Doing so recognizes that health arises not simply from a visit to a doctor's office, but also, more broadly, from where people live, labor, learn, play, and pray."[5]

Even before the crash of HealthCare.gov, the ACA was no stranger to controversy. After Congress narrowly approved the legislation strictly along party lines in early 2010, Republicans were not shy about expressing their disdain for what they termed "Obamacare."[6] House Minority leader, John Boehner, a republican congressman who would become House Speaker in 2011, claimed that "the American people are angry" and that the bill was enacted "against their will."[7] Senator Kit Bond and many other Republicans were quick to predict the "horrific" costs that states would incur because of the law.[8] Indeed, as one commentator noted, "the enactment of the ACA was not the end but rather the beginning of a new chapter in the fight over health care reform."[9]

The political backlash from Republicans ultimately resulted in multiple court cases that challenged the constitutionality of the law, several of which made their way to the U.S. Supreme Court. In *National Federation of Independent Business v. Sebelius*, twenty-six states and the federation challenged two key parts of the ACA: the individual mandate to purchase health insurance and the expansion of eligibility for Medicaid.[10] The Court's decision in 2012, just five months before the presidential election, left the ACA mostly intact but further galvanized Republicans against it. In response, House Majority Leader Eric Cantor called for a vote to repeal the ACA, while Mitt Romney (then governor of Massachusetts) made promises from the presidential campaign trail that if he were elected, he would repeal the ACA on his first day in office. House Speaker Boehner said that the ruling "underscores the urgency of repealing this harmful law in its entirety."[11] A subsequent case, *King v. Burwell*, challenged the constitutionality of the premium subsidies that were designed to make health insurance affordable. That provision, too, was upheld, but the litigation over the ACA was so constant, with the Supreme Court validating its major provisions, that Justice Antonin Scalia wrote, "We should start calling this law SCOTUScare."[12]

The partisan divides surrounding health care extended to the confirmation process for the new director of CMS, the part of the Department of Health and Human Services that operates the Medicare and Medicaid programs and was slated to oversee implementation of the ACA's new insurance rules and HealthCare.gov. Given CMS's central role in implementing the ACA, the nomination of the director was contentious. Perhaps not surprisingly, Donald Berwick, nominated by Obama in 2010, was never confirmed due to intense Republican opposition in the Senate.[13] Senator Orrin Hatch of Utah, the top Republican on the Senate Finance Committee, described Berwick's confirmation as "next to impossible," and suggested that "in the spirit of cooperation, the president should withdraw his nomination and choose a different candidate who has the support and confidence of the American people."[14] And that is what happened: Tavenner, who had served as Berwick's second in command, was nominated to be CMS's director by Obama in 2011, and the Senate confirmed her in early 2013 by a vote of 91 to 7. The surprisingly strong bipartisan support for her nomination reflected the respect she had garnered for her experience in the health-care field and the strong relationships she had developed on Capitol Hill.[15]

In her confirmation hearings, senators repeatedly emphasized the importance of HealthCare.gov's success, foreshadowing its future problems. Senator Max Baucus, chairman of the Committee on Finance, opened the discussion by telling Tavenner: "You will have to make sure these programs are ready to go on, go up, and be working on day one. You need to ensure that the health care law's programs work for the people whom they are intended to serve. There will be a lot of people watching you, myself included."[16]

Indeed, all sides scrutinized the rollout of HealthCare.gov. Democrats, especially Obama, hoped it would highlight their efforts to increase the accessibility and affordability of health insurance for all citizens. Republicans were eager to criticize the implementation of the ACA after their frustration that the Supreme Court had upheld the law.

Tavenner became director of CMS against this volatile political backdrop and under immense pressure. She was confirmed 139 days before the opening of HealthCare.gov, a count that she noted as she started her term "includes weekends and holidays, because we're working all of those."[17]

Born in 1951, Tavenner grew up in Fieldale, a small town in southern Virginia, and received her nursing degree in 1972 from Virginia Commonwealth University, where she also earned a master's degree in 1989. She has three children with her husband, Robert Tavenner, who served as Virginia's director of legislative services for five years after being a state police captain[18] and the state attorney.[19] Two of her children, Matt and Sarah, would follow in her footsteps, earning graduate degrees in health administration from Virginia Commonwealth University and working in health care.[20]

Tavenner started as a nurse in the critical care unit at Johnston-Willis Hospital, in Richmond, Virginia. In only twelve years, she worked her way to the position of CEO of the hospital, earning a master's degree in hospital administration along the way. This speedy ascent is a testament to her strong leadership and decision-making skills. She took advantage of many opportunities to lead and manage other clinicians and departments, including being a nurse supervisor and trainer, running a nursing unit, and later serving as chief nursing officer. Coworkers knew her as the person to turn to for help: "If there was a problem . . . Marilyn would take care of it."[21] This reputation led to her elevation to CEO of the hospital in 1993.

Just as she had moved quickly up the ladder at Johnston-Willis Hospital, Tavenner excelled and ascended the corporate ladder at Hospital Corporation of America (HCA, later known as HCA Health-care), the largest for-profit hospital and health-care facilities system in the United States. She was appointed president of the Richmond division of hospitals for the HCA in 1996 and regional director in 2001, in which capacity she oversaw eighteen hospitals in the central Atlantic region. In her final role at HCA, she served as group president for outpatient services, managing outpatient care for the more than 150 hospitals in HCA.

Asked to describe her leadership style, Tavenner noted that her approach is simple: "I am pretty much what you see is what you get. I am not too big on hierarchy or levels of management."[22] She has always focused on building relationships with her staff, a skill that she acquired during her early clinical work as a nurse. Tavenner explained: "There are some basic skills that I like to think I've kept throughout my career. I still think it's important to build a diverse team, I still think it's important to say you're sorry when you screw up, I still think it's important to get to know people and rely on them."[23] Leadership and gender scholars might describe Tavenner's leadership as "'gender judo'—or combining stereotypically 'feminine' behaviors, like friendliness, humor and empathy, with those behaviors still associated with men, like aggression or ambition."[24] She was proud to speak about her employees from her time as hospital CEO and regional director for HCA: "Not only did I know all my employees, but I knew their families, their children, their good and their bad."[25]

Her clinical roles were also what first exposed her to larger health policy issues that would fuel her career in public service. She was already known as being patient-centered. One colleague said: "What always struck me was her attitude of, how will this help the patient? . . . You better be prepared to talk about that when you meet with Marilyn."[26] It is unsurprising, then, that patient stories are what ultimately pulled her into policy. As a hospital CEO, she said, "I had seen hardworking people who were caught in between jobs and didn't have health care and seeing what that can do to turn your life upside down. That was really how it started . . . over the issue of the uninsured."[27] During her confirmation hearing to be the director of CMS years later, Tavenner reminded the committee that the issue of health insurance is personal for everyone and their loved ones. She spoke of her daughter, Sarah, who was diagnosed with type I diabetes at the age of eleven: "She relies on and needs access to health insurance, no questions asked. . . . It underscores the fact that what we do at CMS directly affects the lives of so many."[28]

Tavenner had the opportunity to pursue her policy interests while still working for HCA. She worked with Tim Kaine, then mayor of Richmond, Virginia, on providing education and health coverage to pregnant women and young children. She partnered with him on health policy issues for several years. When Kaine was elected governor, he made her Virginia's secretary of health and human resources, and she oversaw an annual budget of $9 billion and 18,000 employees.[29]

Tavenner's pragmatism and leadership skills continued to make an impression on everyone around her. Patrick Finnerty, who served as Virginia's Medicaid director under her leadership, explained: "With Marilyn, you present the information, then she makes a decision, and you move on."[30] Kaine said: "As Governor, I gave all of my Cabinet Secretaries problems to solve: 'Marilyn, why are we 10th in the Nation in per capita income and 35th in the Nation in infant mortality? You have to find out the answer to that and help us solve it. What can we do to reduce youth smoking in a State that has a historical connection, and a strong one, to tobacco? Why are we facing shortages among nurses; why are we facing shortages among physicians, and what can we do about it?"[31] Even facing budget cuts during a nationwide recession and a tense political gridlock in the Virginia state legislature, Governor Kaine was proud of her accomplishments for the state, which included expanding eligibility for Medicaid for pregnant women:[32] "There was no one in my cabinet who was more creative and passionate about achieving savings without sacrificing patient care."[33]

An important aspect of Tavenner's success was being a good listener and building respectful working relationships with people on both sides of the aisle. At the state level, she served for four years under a Democratic governor with a Republican-controlled legislature. In that kind of tense political environment, Tavenner stressed the importance of incremental change and compromise, as well as celebrating the small successes.[34] Finnerty explained: "One of the things she's really good at is being respectful, respecting different views and being willing to listen." He also commented that "there are differences of opinion, and she would try to work through those. She's straight with folks but always respectful."[35] When she moved to the federal level in February 2010, first as President Obama's nominee for principal deputy administrator at CMS, it was an opportunity to put her experience and skills to work on a larger stage and wider scale: she helped oversee an annual budget of $820 billion (approximately one-quarter of the federal budget), administering health coverage programs that served a hundred million Americans and shaping development of the Affordable Care Act, which would become the administration's signature domestic policy initiative.[36] She recounted that as deputy administrator, she was in charge of policy development and implementation as well as management and operations, and she would work to quickly solve problems for both Republicans and Democrats alike—which built rapport on both sides of the aisle and would later help her be confirmed as the director of CMS when Obama's previous nominee's confirmation was blocked.[37] Of her bipartisan work, she said, "I think that served me well throughout my career, but it's also the right thing to do."[38] Indeed, she had made such an impression on Hatch that he remarked during consideration of her nomination on the Senate floor: "Overseeing a massive bureaucracy like the one at CMS is not a job for the faint of heart. I will be keeping a close eye on Miss Tavenner as she takes the reins. . . . Thus far, I have reason to believe she will be one of the best leaders we could possibly see in the government."[39] House Majority Leader Cantor, who was a vocal opponent of the ACA and the president, also served as an enthusiastic witness during her confirmation. A Republican from Virginia, Cantor noted his long association with her, dating back to when she was a hospital executive and he a state representative. He testified: "I do not think there is any secret that I differ with the Obama administration on a lot of matters of health care policy. . . . But if there is anyone whom I trust to try to navigate the challenges, it is Marilyn Tavenner. I feel that strongly about her, and that is why I am here."[40]

Tavenner would need to draw on those experiences of working across the aisle, finding solutions to difficult problems, and building relationships with her staff when she faced the difficult month of October 2013. Before 7:00 a.m. on October 1, over a million people visited HealthCare.gov.[41] This was well over what the department had anticipated. Tavenner said: "It never occurred to us that everybody in the world would want to go on this application to see what it was like. People were curious."[42] The website was already complex because it asked users a multitude of questions and ran confirmations at each step, and the additional volume of extra visitors to the site led to a deadly combination that caused the crash.

Headlines rapidly appeared to spread the latest Obamacare scandal, including "The New Obamacare Health Care Exchange Site Has Already Crashed,"[43] "HealthCare.gov Plagued by Crashes on 1st Day,"[44] and "Tech Problems Plague First Day of Health Exchange Rollout."[45] Republican lawmakers were quick to focus on the technical issues. For example, Cantor said: "Americans have seen once again that Obamacare is not ready for prime time. . . . A dysfunctional website is the least of that law's problems."[46]

As the news spread, tensions in her office ran high. All eyes were on Tavenner, who had several options available: For example, she could quit in anticipation of being fired, she could deflect blame to the staff members who had been working on the website longer than she had been director, or she could fire the contracted information technology (IT) firms that had done the bulk of the work.

Resolution

Tavenner remained a confident leader, dedicated to her mission and her staff. She decided to take three immediate actions.

First, she had to boost staff morale and assure her team that she was on their side. She recalls seeing her staff members look at her as if they were wondering: "Are you going to be there for us? Or are we going to get thrown under the bus?"[47] Headlines such as "IT Experts Question Architecture of Obamacare Website"[48] and "Obamacare Site Hits Reset Button on Passwords as Contractors Scramble"[49] caused unrest among the staff. Tavenner drew on her previous strategies that emphasized building up her team and ignoring hierarchy. She noted that the process of firing and replacing the contracted management and IT firms would have taken months and slowed the team down significantly. As Warren Bennis describes in *On Becoming a Leader*, "leadership revolves around vision, ideas, direction, and has more to do with inspiring people as to direction and goals than with day-to-day implementation."[50] Drawing on her early clinical experience, Tavenner inspired her staff to step back from the minute IT details and remember the human-focused mission of the website: "Put the newspapers down. Turn off the television. We don't need to worry about that. There's only one thing we're going to get out of the news media. There's only one way we're going to get off the front page. There's only one way we're going to get off the television. We've got to get the numbers up. As soon as the numbers start to grow, the pressure will come down. That's on each of us."[51] Once she made it clear that she was not going to blame anyone but wanted to work with staff members to fix the problems, "staff morale kind of took care of itself and we started having wins."[52]

Tavenner's second action was to report to the president, Congress, and the secretary of health and human services. President Obama's namesake health-care law, arguably the most influential policy of his presidency, was on the line. Tavenner received daily calls from the White House and had frequent meetings with the president and his staff. It was reported that she was the second most frequent visitor to the White House at one point in the administration, logging over 400 visits.[53] And third, Tavenner knew she had to address the root cause of the problem: the technical malfunctions with the website. She admitted that the inner workings of the website were far beyond her expertise: "It's an area where clinical skills don't really help. Management skills don't really help you. . . . I'm hardly the expert, but we had to figure out how to dissect this problem and fix it quickly. It wasn't just about dissecting it, we had to fix it quickly because people were waiting for health care."[54]

What she lacked in technical background she made up for by stepping back and focusing on the overall goal. She fits the mold of a type of leader that Bennis describes: "Leaders always have faith in themselves, their abilities, their co-workers, and their mutual possibilities."[55] There was political and professional pressure on Tavenner to find solutions quickly, but more importantly, she remembered from early in her career the impact that health insurance can have on individuals and their livelihood.

After the short-term fires were put out and the team was moving forward as steadily as possible, Tavenner had to overcome another leadership challenge. At the end of the month, Congress wanted an explanation for the failures that had led to the crash of HealthCare.gov. They summoned Tavenner to testify to the Ways and Means Committee of the House of Representatives.

As Tavenner prepared her testimony, she remembered thinking that Congress could force Obama to fire her. Even with her career hanging in the balance, she held onto her concept of teamwork and hierarchy: "I didn't point to individuals; we were a group."[56] Thinking back on the testimony, she explained: "I felt like I had to say 'look, this did not go as we intended.'"[57]

Tavenner did not cover up the shockingly low numbers of people enrolled through the website during the first few weeks. Instead, she owned up to the failure in a clear manner: "The initial consumer experience of HealthCare.gov has not lived up to the expectations of the American people and is not acceptable. . . . We know the initial consumer experience at HealthCare.gov has not been adequate."[58] After acknowledging the deficiencies, Tavenner spoke about actionable steps the team was taking: "We are committed to fixing these problems as soon as possible. . . . By enlisting additional technical help, aggressively monitoring errors, testing to prevent new issues from cropping up, and regularly deploying fixes to the site, we are working to ensure [that] consumers' interaction with HealthCare.gov is a positive one, and that the Affordable Care Act fully delivers on its promise."[59] The act did indeed deliver on its promise.[60] Within months, the ACA would insure over twelve million Americans on HealthCare.gov—a total that had increased to twenty million by 2016.[61]

Experts have found that this uptake in coverage has had encouraging results in terms of both the effects on individuals and larger population health outcomes. The ACA increased access to care, and enrollees were significantly more likely to receive medical care and to have a usual place of care than the uninsured.[62] Specifically, the ACA increased access to preventive services and had a greater public health impact, as it "freed up local public health budgets to engage in population health activities."[63] The provisions of the ACA also worked to reduce socioeconomic and racial disparities in health-care access. The gap in insurance coverage between low- and high-income households decreased by 23 percent over four years.[64] Early results from 2014 showed that the uninsurance rate decreased more for minorities than for whites, especially in states that expanded eligibility for Medicaid.[65] In sum, the impact of the ACA on the health of the U.S. population is well documented and far-reaching.

However, results from a 2018 census survey underscore the fact that while the ACA has been remarkably resilient, its benefits can be tenuous and are subject to political forces in its administration. The Census Bureau reported the first increase in the uninsurance rate—from 7.9 percent of the population in 2017 to 8.5 percent in 2018—since the ACA became law.[66] Many experts attribute this increase to the so-called sabotage of the ACA by the administration of President Donald Trump.[67] This includes the administration's cuts in funding for ACA advertising and enrollment assistance, the potentially chilling effect of the public charge rule for immigrants, which tightened restrictions on low-income immigrants seeking U.S. residency and discouraged enrollment in Medicaid, and efforts to encourage states to limit their eligibility requirements for Medicaid.[68]

The ACA has continued to face legal and political challenges. However, it has become a mainstay of the American health system, due in part to the functions of HealthCare.gov and the unwavering commitment to it of political leaders, starting with Tavenner on October 1, 2013. But after spending a decade in the public sector—first at the Virginia Department of Health and Human Resources and later during her ever-dramatic tenure at CMS—Tavenner decided to spend time with her family.[69] In 2015 she moved to the private sector to serve as president and CEO of American Health Insurance Plans, the largest trade association representing health insurance companies and an influential advocacy organization in Washington. She held that position for three years.[70]

The crash of the initial website at its rollout offers many lessons for leaders and decision makers as they face challenges, especially those outside their immediate expertise or beyond their control. First, Tavenner's experiences reinforce the importance of being humble enough to acknowledge mistakes. She was honest about her lack of technological skills and remained diligent about updating Congress and the president on the steps her team was taking toward a solution. In doing so, Tavenner was careful not to assign blame. This decision highlights another lesson from her team-oriented nature: when challenges arise, cultivate and support a cohesive team and a culture of problem solving and critical thinking. She accomplished this by ensuring that no one on her team would be singled out and by helping insulate the team from outside distractions that would undermine their work.

The most important lesson from the dramatic rollout of Health-Care.gov is to never lose sight of the overarching goal. Tavenner recalls the early days when only a dozen people were able to access the site: "You would not believe the type of emails I would get out of the blue from people who had been waiting years for health care. So, if anything, it gave me a stronger sense of purpose that I had to get this done."[71] She shows us that a leader who emphasizes a common goal or vision can create followship as well as leadership, creating a team environment that can overcome unanticipated difficulty. Even when a goal is not as dramatic as providing twenty million Americans with health insurance, we can learn from Tavenner the importance of finding small reminders of the impact of our day-to-day work.

Notes

1   Henry J. Kaiser Family Foundation, "Summary of the Affordable Care Act," April 25, 2013, https://kff.org/health-reform/fact-sheet/summary-of-the -affordable-care-act; Barack Obama, "United States Health Care Reform: Progress to Date and Next Steps," *Journal of the American Medical Association* 316, no. 5 (August 2, 2016): 525–532, https://doi.org/10.1001/jama.2016.9797.

2   Jonathan Oberlander, "Long Time Coming: Why Health Reform Finally Passed," *Health Affairs* 29, no. 6 (June 2010): 1112–1116, https://doi.org/10 .1377/hlthaff.2010.0447; Paul Starr, "Remedy and Reaction: The Peculiar American Struggle over Health Care Reform," *Yale Journal of Biology and Medicine* 85, no. 1 (March 29, 2012): 159–160.

3   Lawrence Jacobs and Theda Skocpol, *Health Care Reform and American Politics: What Everyone Needs to Know* (New York: Oxford University Press, 2010).

4   Obama, "United States Health Care Reform."

5   Howard K. Koh and Marilyn Tavenner, "Connecting Care through the Clinic and Community for a Healthier America," *American Journal of Public Health* 102, supplement 3 (June 2012): S305, https://doi.org/10.2105/AJPH.2012 .300760.

6   Jacobs and Skocpol, *Health Care Reform and American Politics*; Daniel Béland, Philip Rocco, and Alex Waddan, *Obamacare Wars: Federalism, State Politics, and the Affordable Care Act* (Lawrence: University Press of Kansas, 2016)

7   Quoted in Affordable Health California, "Timeline: Affordable Care Act," accessed September 3, 2019, http://affordablehealthca.com/timeline -obamacare/.

8   Jim Meyers, "Kit Bond: Obamacare's Financial Cost to States Will Be 'Horrific,'" Newsmax, March 22, 2010, https://www.newsmax.com/headline /tea-party-rebellion-grows/2010/03/22/id/353528/.

9   Quoted in Béland et al., *Obamacare Wars*, 2.

10 MaryBeth Musumeci and Laurie Sobel, "The Federal Courts' Role in Implementing the Affordable Care Act," Henry J. Kaiser Family Foundation, September 12, 2014, https://kff.org/health-reform/issue-brief/the-federal -courts-role-in-implementing-the-affordable-care-act/.

11 Quoted in Reuters, "Speaker Boehner Renews Vow to Try to Repeal Health Care Law," June 28, 2012. https://www.reuters.com/article/us-usa -healthcare-court-boehner/speaker-boehner-renews-vow-to-try-to-repeal -obama-health-law-idINBRE85R0Y120120628.

12 Quoted in King v. Burwell, 135 S. Ct. 2480 (2015) at 2507.

13 Mary Agnes Carey and Phil Galewitz, "Tavenner to Replace Berwick as Medicare Chief," NPR, November 23, 2011, https://www.npr.org/sections /health-shots/2011/11/23/142715802/tavenner-to-replace-berwick-as -medicare-chief.

14 Quoted in Charles Hoskinson and Brett Coughlin, "W.H. Won't Give up on Berwick," Politico, March 3, 2011, https://www.politico.com/story/2011/03 /wh-wont-give-up-on-berwick-050599.

15 Paige Winfield Cunningham and Jennifer Haberkorn, "Tavenner Approved by Senate," Politico, May 5, 2013, https://www.politico.com/story/2013/05 /marilyn-tavenner-cms-91438.html.

16 "Nomination of Marilyn B. Tavenner," U.S. Senate Committee on Finance hearing, April 9, 2013, https://www.govinfo.gov/content/pkg/CHRG -113shrg86938/pdf/CHRG-113shrg86938.pdf.

17 Quoted in John Reichard, "Newly Confirmed as CMS Administrator, Marilyn Tavenner Eyes a Summer of Change," Commonwealth Fund, May 20, 2013, https://www.commonwealthfund.org/publications/newsletter-article /newly-confirmed-cms-administrator-marilyn-tavenner-eyes-summer.

18 Tavenner, Marilyn," AllGov, accessed September 17, 2019, http://www.allgov .com/officials/tavenner-marilyn?officialid=29523.

19 Ron Shinkman, "Marilyn Tavenner's Troubling Leap from Public to Private Sector," Fierce Healthcare, July 20, 2015, https://www.fiercehealthcare.com /finance/marilyn-tavenner-s-troubling-leap-from-public-to-private-sector.

20 Phil Galewitz, "For Tavenners, It's All in the Family," *Kaiser Health News*, (March 6, 2012, https://khn.org/news/for-tavenners-its-all-in-the-family/.

21 Quoted in Sarah Kliff, "Marilyn Tavenner: Medicare's New Pragmatist-in-Chief?," *Washington Post*, November 25, 2011, https://www.washingtonpost.com/blogs/ezra-klein/post/marilyn-tavenner-medicares-new-pragmatist-in-chief/2011/11/25/gIQADBbgvN_blog.html.

22 Marilyn Tavenner, telephone interview by Heather Howard and Carson Clay, November 27, 2018.

23 Ibid.

24 Jessica Bennett, "What Makes a Leader?" *New York Times*, June 17, 2019, https://www.nytimes.com/2019/06/17/business/women-power-leadership.html.

25 Tavenner interview.

26 Quoted in Kliff, "Marilyn Tavenner."

27 Tavenner interview.

28 "Nomination of Marilyn B. Tavenner."

29 Centers for Medicare and Medicaid Services, "Administrator Tenure Dates and Biographies: 1965–2015," July 2015, https://www.cms.gov/About-CMS/Agency-Information/History/Downloads/Administrator-Tenure-Dates-and-Biographies-1965-%E2%80%94-2015.pdf.

30 Quoted in Kliff, "Marilyn Tavenner."

31 "Nomination of Marilyn B. Tavenner."

32 Tavenner interview.

33 "Warner and Kaine Applaud Confirmation of Marilyn Tavenner," "Tim Kaine: United States Senator from Virginia, May 15, 2013, https://www.kaine.senate.gov/press-releases/warner-and-kaine-applaud-confirmation-of-marilyn-tavenner.

34 Tavenner interview.

35 Quoted in Kliff, "Marilyn Tavenner."

36 Centers for Medicare and Medicaid Services, "CMS Leadership: Administrator: Marilyn Tavenner," accessed February 14, 2021, http://web.archive.org/web/20150113194224/http:/www.cms.gov/About-CMS/leadership.

37 Sarah Kliff, "Medicare Administrator Donald Berwick Resigns in the Face of Republican Opposition," *Washington Post*, November 23, 2011, https://www.washingtonpost.com/national/health-science/medicare-administrator-donald-berwick-resigns-in-the-face-of-republican-opposition/2011/11/23/gIQA5S7mpN_story.html.

38 Tavenner interview.

39 Quoted in Cunningham and Haberkorn, "Tavenner Approved by Senate."

40 "Nomination of Marilyn B. Tavenner."

41 Wyatt Andrews and Anna Werner, "HealthCare.gov Plagued by Crashes on 1st Day," CBS News, October 1, 2013, https://www.cbsnews.com/news/healthcaregov-plagued-by-crashes-on-1st-day/.

42 Tavenner interview.

43 Mandi Woodruff, "The New Obamacare Health Care Exchange Site Has Already Crashed," Business Insider, October 1, 2013, https://www.businessinsider.com /obamacare-health-care-exchange-site-has-crashed-2013-10.

44 Andrews and Werner, "HealthCare.gov Plagued by Crashes on 1st Day."

45 Elise Hu, "Tech Problems Plague First Day of Health Exchange Rollout," NPR, October 2, 2013, https://www.npr.org/sections/alltechconsidered/2013 /10/02/228220325/tech-problems-plague-first-day-of-health-exchange -rollout.

46 Quoted in "Obamacare Website Goes down for Repairs," CBS News, October 4, 2013, https://www.cbsnews.com/news/obamacare-website-goes -down-for-repairs/.

47 Tavenner interview.

48 Sharon Begley, "Analysis: IT Experts Question Architecture of Obamacare Website," *Reuters*, October 5, 2013, https://www.reuters.com/article/us-usa -healthcare-technology-analysis/analysis-it-experts-question-architecture -of-obamacare-website-idUSBRE99407T20131005.

49 Sean Gallagher, "Obamacare Site Hits Reset Button on Passwords as Contractors Scramble," Ars Technica, October 8, 2013, https://arstechnica .com/information-technology/2013/10/obamacare-site-hits-reset-button-on -passwords-as-contractors-scramble/.

50 Warren Bennis, *On Becoming a Leader* (Cambridge, MA: Perseus, 2009), 130.

51 Tavenner interview.

52 Ibid.

53 Jason Howerton, "Here Are the 25 People Who Have Visited the Obama White House the Most—No. 3 Is Apparently Shrouded in Mystery," *Blaze*, February 8, 2016, https://www.theblaze.com/news/2016/02/08/here-are-the -25-people-who-have-visited-the-obama-white-house-the-most-no-3-is -apparently-shrouded-in-mystery.

54 Tavenner interview.

55 Bennis, *On Becoming a Leader*, 131.

56 Tavenner interview.

57 Ibid.

58 Marilyn Tavenner, "Statement of Marilyn Tavenner, Administrator, Centers for Medicare and Medicaid Services, on Affordable Care Act Implementation before the U.S. House Committee on Ways and Means," October 29, 2013, https://docs.house.gov/meetings/WM/WM00/20131029/101439/HHRG-113 -WM00-Wstate-TavennerM-20131029.pdf.

59 Ibid.

60 Obama, "United States Health Care Reform."

61 Ibid.

62 Sherry Glied, Stephanie Ma, and Anaïs Borja, "Effect of the Affordable Care Act on Health Care Access," Commonwealth Fund, May 8, 2017, https://www .commonwealthfund.org/publications/issue-briefs/2017/may/effect -affordable-care-act-health-care-access.

63 Nadia Chait and Sherry Glied, "Promoting Prevention under the Affordable Care Act," *Annual Review of Public Health* 39 (2018): 507.

64 Kevin Griffith, Leigh Evans, and Jacob Bor, "The Affordable Care Act Reduced Socioeconomic Disparities in Health Care Access," *Health Affairs* 36, no. 8 (August 1, 2017): 1503–1510, https://doi.org/10.1377/hlthaff.2017.0083.

65 Thomas C. Buchmueller et al., "Effect of the Affordable Care Act on Racial and Ethnic Disparities in Health Insurance Coverage." *American Journal of Public Health* 106, no. 8 (August 2016): 1416–1421, https://doi.org/10.2105/AJPH.2016.303155.

66 Ben Casselman, Margot Sanger-Katz, and Jeanna Smialek, "Share of Americans with Health Insurance Declined in 2018," *New York Times*, September 10, 2019, https://www.nytimes.com/2019/09/10/business/economy/health-insurance-poverty-rate-census.html.

67 Jasmine Kim, "Rate of Uninsured Americans Rises for the First Time since Obamacare Took Effect in 2014," CNBC, September 10, 2019, https://www.cnbc.com/2019/09/10/rate-of-insured-americans-decreases-for-the-first-time-since-obamacare.html.

68 Ibid.; Casselman et al., "Share of Americans with Health Insurance Declined in 2018."

69 Cathryn Domrose, "Up Close with Marilyn Tavenner, MHA, RN," Nurse.com, March 26, 2015, https://www.nurse.com/blog/2015/03/26/looking-back-moving-forward/.

70 Susan Morse, "AHIP Names Matt Eyles CEO to Replace Marilyn Tavenner," Healthcare Finance, March 14, 2018, https://www.healthcarefinancenews.com/news/ahip-names-matt-eyles-ceo-replace-marilyn-tavenner.

71 Tavenner, interview.

Ruth Williams-Brinkley. Photo courtesy of Kaiser Permanente.

Ruth Williams-Brinkley

Facing Opportunities and Challenges at the Intersection of Community and Health Care

**Elizabeth A. Ryan, Ruth Charbonneau,
and Alexander M. Bartke**

Background

Ruth Williams-Brinkley has risen to a premier job in health care, president of Kaiser Foundation Health Plan of the Mid-Atlantic States, which includes Washington, D.C., Maryland, and Virginia. She is responsible for all of Kaiser's care delivery and health plan operations in this region which includes oversight of 34 medical office buildings and has 768,154 members. Kaiser Permanente is the nation's largest nonprofit, integrated delivery health system.[1] As a Black woman in health care leadership, she has a unique perspective. Williams-Brinkley was named one of the ten most admired CEOs in health care in 2014 by *Becker's Hospital Report* and recognized as one of the 100 Most Influential People, one of the top twenty-five women in health care, and one of the top twenty-five minority executives in health care in 2020, 2017, and 2016, respectively, by *Modern Healthcare*.[2] She identifies three major factors as having shaped her career: a family role model in her grandmother, who urged her to pursue nursing as a career; her willingness to be mobile and accept new and difficult assignments; and her husband's unexpected death, which increased her already strong commitment to the health care industry.

Williams-Brinkley's grandparents had adopted four children from their families (three from the grandfather's side of the family and one from the grandmother's). Williams-Brinkley's mother was attending college when she became pregnant. Because of the social stigma of a pregnancy out of wedlock, Williams-Brinkley's grandmother and grandfather raised her on their family farm in Girard, Georgia. She became their fifth adopted child, and one of the youngest. Her memories of growing up consist primarily of her grandmother and her aunt, who was eight years her senior. Williams-Brinkley's grandfather passed away when she was just four or five years old, but her grandmother kept the farm going. The farm has been in her family for over a hundred years.

Her grandmother had attended college, but she left before graduating when her family ran out of money. Still, she was able to teach. Her grandmother emphasized the importance of education and attending college, and many of her family members became teachers. Williams-Brinkley describes her school as "the heartbeat of our community. It was a place to learn, grow, explore, and feel safe."[3] All the other children in the house were encouraged to finish high school, and Williams-Brinkley's mother and uncle also attained college degrees.[4] This emphasis on education is noteworthy, considering that "disparities in educational attainment among women were significant . . . in Alabama, Georgia, and Mississippi. . . . Black women were as much as three times less likely than white women to complete high school or its equivalency, and nearly two times less likely to hold a bachelor's degree or above than their white counterparts."[5]

Growing up in the segregated South influenced Williams-Brinkley in ways that would manifest themselves later in life. Her family's farm was in a rural location, with a town of approximately five thousand people being the closest place to go for provisions. The farm was largely self-sustaining, providing food for the family. However, like many people at the time, her relatives bought sundries in town and ordered clothing through the mail from Sears and Roebuck.

Williams-Brinkley recalls trips into town with her grandmother to conduct farm business. She was aware of segregation because of the "white and colored drinking fountains and restrooms."[6] She remembers that the restroom she had to use was not clean, smelled bad, and was unwelcoming. But when she passed the white restrooms, she noticed that they were clean and smelled fresh. Even the drinking fountains she had to use were dirtier than those for whites. Because she and her relatives left the house so early in the morning, they did not have a chance to eat anything before setting out, so Williams-Brinkley and her aunt were usually hungry by the time her grandmother completed her errands. There were only one or two restaurants in town, and Williams-Brinkley's grandmother had to go to the back of any of them and buy a box of food that the family would eat in the car.

Williams-Brinkley did not fully understood those trips into town until she went away to college in Illinois, when she realized that white people could enter and sit down in the restaurant, while her family could not. Because her grandmother took pains to make the excursions pleasant for Williams-Brinkley and her aunt, they felt that eating the box of food in the car with her was a treat.[7] Williams-Brinkley realized that her grandmother had been protecting her from the waning days of enforced Jim Crow laws, which mandated "the separation of the races in practically every aspect of public life. . . . Water fountains, restaurants, theaters, restrooms, stores, buses, trains, workplaces, and other public facilities were typically designated with 'White Only' and 'Colored' signs."[8] Her grandmother had protected her from the racial inequalities surrounding them as much as she could, while still encouraging her to pursue all things academic that would lead her to college and opportunities beyond rural Georgia.

Williams-Brinkley describes her grandmother as "one of the strongest women I've ever known."[9] She raised five children from the extended family as her own, had a teaching career, ran the family farm after her husband passed away, and found ways to help her community. Williams-Brinkley learned about the importance of helping people from her grandmother: "We would take clothes, and we would take food from our farm to the people in the community. She was always just very generous."[10] Her grandmother "was 4-foot-11 and not even 100 pounds soaking wet. I was 5-foot-6 by the time I was in sixth grade, but I thought she was a giant. I had great respect for her."[11]

Her grandmother did everything she could to encourage Williams-Brinkley to attend college and also encouraged her to consider a career in nursing: "She taught me my worth as a woman and as a woman leader. I'm sure there were times when she must have been afraid and alone, but I never saw her flinch."[12] Her grandmother taught her many leadership lessons, the foremost of which was courage.[13]

Williams-Brinkley attended the University of Chicago and wanted to earn a bachelor of arts degree in psychology: "When I went to college, I wasn't really sure what I wanted to be. My grandmother had told me to be a nurse . . . and of course, I rebelled against that choice."[14] She admitted that in her transition to an urban college environment, she was a little unfocused. At one point, she resolved to take some time off and looked for a job. She recalls one eye-opening interview with a company that had advertised a job in the *Chicago Tribune*—an interview that convinced her she didn't have the qualifications to get that job or many others. She decided to return to college and give nursing a chance.

Because the University of Chicago did not have a nursing program, Williams-Brinkley transferred to Michael Reese Hospital in Chicago, where she earned her diploma in nursing. While in school, Williams-Brinkley married and had two children. Her marriage ultimately ended in divorce. She went on to earn a bachelor of science degree in nursing with high honors from De Paul University. Her grandmother, who had encouraged her to become a nurse, lived to see her earn a master of science degree with distinction in nursing: "She was so proud at my graduation, and I was proud to have her there."[15]

Williams-Brinkley held a variety of nursing positions in Chicago beginning in 1975: postanesthesia nurse, evening supervisor, and eventually chief nurse and chief operating officer at St. Anne's Hospital (which closed in 1988).[16] In reflecting on her nursing career, she commented: "Almost all of my nurse colleagues, as well as a few of my physician anesthesia and surgery colleagues, were women. We formed a strong bond around our mutual care and concern for patients navigating the journey through the perioperative care delivery process. As a young nurse, I was truly grounded by that experience, and over the years, I continued to see how much value women contribute to the health care delivery system and leadership teams."[17] It was at St. Anne's that she first experienced the relationship between health care and the community, which would be a major influence throughout her career.

Williams-Brinkley moved to St. Louis to work at De Paul Hospital as chief nurse. While in St. Louis, she met and married Kenneth Brinkley. Soon, a job opportunity as associate executive director, chief nurse executive, and associate dean for clinical practice arose at the University of Alabama, in Birmingham (UAB), and she agreed to take that leadership position and relocate. Her husband worked in management at the United Parcel Service and was not able to transfer to Alabama. He lived and worked in St. Louis while Williams-Brinkley worked at UAB, and they commuted between the two cities. Williams-Brinkley loved the academic setting and her work at UAB, but her marriage suffered. She needed to decide between the marriage and her career, and her choice to keep her family together led to another pivotal point in her career.

Williams-Brinkley left her leadership position at UAB to return to St. Louis and her family. She could not find a job as a chief nurse or any leadership position in hospital operations, so in 1994, determined to challenge herself, she took a consulting job with American Practice Management (acquired by Computer Sciences Corporation [CSC] Healthcare in 1996). As described in CSC's 1997 annual report, "American Practice Management, the largest independent strategic consulting company in North America serving the health care industry, joined CSC. Its knowledge of the health care industry's needs, together with CSC's related capabilities in management consulting and systems integration, position [CSC] very strongly" to compete in this market.[18]

Before Williams-Brinkley accepted the position, her most senior management job had been as chief nursing officer. She did not know how to get to the next level or "what the next level might be because back then, most CEOs weren't nurses"[19] or women from any background. She had no mentor or coach to consult. Williams-Brinkley was not unique in her desire to advance and her wondering how to make that move. A 2011 McKinsey report stated that "the reasons why women choose to remain at their current level or move on to another organization—despite their unflagging confidence and desire to advance—include: lack of role models, exclusion from the informal networks, not having a sponsor in upper management to create opportunities."[20] According to a 2019 report, "more than 80 percent of the decision-makers in the U.S. healthcare workforce are women—and 65 percent of women in C-suite healthcare positions fill technical or influencer roles—yet only 13 percent make it to CEO."[21]

By entering a career in consulting, Williams-Brinkley stated, "not only did I learn a lot about general hospital management but also how to deal with troubled organizations. . . . It also gave me a different way to show up professionally."[22] She entered the consulting field as the number of hospital mergers peaked in 1996: there were 152 mergers in that year but only 18 in 2000. Consolidations from hospital acquisitions by systems far outnumbered hospital mergers. The number of mergers and acquisitions combined peaked at 310 in 1997 and remained relatively high in 2000, at 132.[23]

After several years at CSC of giving hospitals in financial or clinical trouble strategic advice to turn them around, Williams-Brinkley began to receive calls from recruiters for CEO positions. The consulting experience changed her career trajectory. She believes that her experience as a nurse drives her leadership style, which focuses on providing care to the patients and their communities. She believes "that the movement from clinical provider to organizational/enterprise leader is best done progressively, adding additional education and experiences along the way."[24] People saw her in a different light, given her consulting experience with turning troubled hospitals around. Her success as a consultant strengthened her credentials within the health care industry, as suggested by one report: "despite their best efforts, women are often evaluated for promotions primarily on performance, while men are often promoted on potential."[25]

In 1998, Williams-Brinkley was recruited by Catholic Health Initiatives (CHI) to be a regional vice president. One of the country's largest faith-based health care systems, CHI maintains a physical presence in over fifteen states. Williams-Brinkley's husband had retired and was going to seminary. He was able to accompany Williams-Brinkley to Louisville, and then to her placement in Denver. Six months after being hired by CHI, she was asked to lead the system's national operational turnaround. Over three years, she achieved a $200 million turnaround in financial improvement. With the turnaround completed, in 2001 she was asked to take the interim CEO position at Memorial Healthcare System in Chattanooga, Tennessee. One of CHI's hospital systems, Memorial was an integrated delivery system with two hospitals and several ambulatory surgery, primary care, and specialty practices. Williams-Brinkley was interim CEO for a few months and then was asked to serve as president and CEO on a permanent basis.

Williams-Brinkley and her husband served as sources of support for each other and their children. While in Chattanooga, Williams-Brinkley's husband completed his bachelor's, master's and doctoral programs in ministry and pastoral studies and earned a doctoral degree in theology. He founded the Chattanooga-based Transforming Faith Baptist Church in June 2005. From 2002 to 2008, Williams-Brinkley served as CEO of Memorial Healthcare System. She created centers of excellence in cancer, cardiovascular care, and orthopedics that were supported by strong hospital-physician alignment and integration.

In 2008, Williams-Brinkley was offered a position that would expand her role and provide her with an opportunity to integrate her management work with community services. She accepted the position, becoming president and CEO at Ascension Health Carondelet Health Network, in Tucson, Arizona. Here she was able to operate an expanded role as West Ministry Market Leader for Ascension, supervising the faith-based missions of hospitals in several western states. In 2010, her husband unexpectedly died. Williams-Brinkley was determined to continue working despite her grief. She thought of her grandmother, who could have abandoned the family farm when her husband died. Yet though she had little to no experience in farming, her grandmother had found a way to complete the harvest and run the farm successfully.

CHI recruited Williams-Brinkley back as senior vice president of operations. Williams-Brinkley brought her experience in mergers and acquisitions, academic medical centers, community hospitals, and health systems to CHI and was involved in the effort to merge three health systems: Lexington-based St. Joseph Health System,

Louisville-based Jewish Hospital and St. Mary's HealthCare, and the University of Louisville Hospital. The proposed merger was complex due to the number of institutions involved, faith-based missions, complexity of academic medicine, expansion of eligibility for Medicaid and Medicare and its impact on each hospital, and University of Louisville's status as a state institution. Ultimately the private Catholic and Jewish systems merged to become KentuckyOne in Louisville, Kentucky, and a partnership, instead of a merger, was developed with the public University of Louisville Hospital. CHI named Ruth Williams-Brinkley as CEO/President of KentuckyOne in 2012. "Integrating these organizations into a statewide system was a great vision; it was laudable," said Williams-Brinkley. But "at the end of the day, the university wanted to go in a different direction."[26] The partnership with the university was established after the proposed merger was rejected in late 2011 by former Kentucky Governor Steve Beshear. He argued that it would mean losing control over a state asset, and he and others feared that the university facilities would have to abide by the ethical and religious directives of the Roman Catholic Church. After the proposed merger with the University of Louisville failed, KentuckyOne entered into a joint operating agreement with the University of Louisville. Williams-Brinkley was responsible for overseeing a successful implementation of the transfer of operations and the postmerger systems integration of the acquired assets under the management of KentuckyOne[27] to establish a statewide health system with an emphasis on increasing access to health care. In 2016, there was a decision to "redesign [the] partnership with a vision to better support health and wellness" and create "a framework for future partnerships."[28]

In 2017, CHI announced that it was seeking to divest Jewish Hospital, the Frazier Rehab Institute, St. Mary's and St. Elizabeth, and Jewish Hospital Shelbyville following financial troubles. In May 2017, Williams-Brinkley announced her resignation as CEO. Richard Schultz, chair of KentuckyOne Health's Board of Directors, credited her with "develop[ing] the statewide structure for a complex organization and establish[ing] the vision and purpose for our path forward."[29]

After putting so much time and effort into effectuating the agreement between KentuckyOne and the University of Louisville, which ultimately failed, Williams-Brinkley describes feeling burned out and needing time to find herself. She thought that she could work through her husband's death and her grief,[30] but she never gave herself the time to heal. After leaving KentuckyOne, Williams-Brinkley moved back to the house she had shared with her husband in Chattanooga, which held the memories associated with their twenty-one-year marriage. She was holding onto the house they had built during her first CEO job, to which they thought they would retire. She reflected: "Time is a great healer and work is a great healer, if you use it correctly. But I will also tell you that we all eventually have to pay the debt of grief. I like to say that grief can be delayed, but it won't be denied. The work gave me something to focus on, but we each have to go back and deal with the issues we need to deal with, and I did that as well."[31]

A month or so after Williams-Brinkley announced that she was leaving KentuckyOne, she received a call from a recruiter about a leadership position at Kaiser Permanente. She decided to speak to the recruiter, thinking that if she decided to return to work in the future, this person might help find her next position. After she left KentuckyOne, she had determined to "continue my professional life through mentoring and developing leaders" and "supporting organizations . . . as a health care executive and as a board member."[32]

Williams-Brinkley had long admired the Kaiser Permanente model of integrated health care delivery. She also respected the Kaiser Permanente mission, to care for the communities the organization serves and to improve health care in America. She considered accepting the position in a system that valued leadership, diversity, and community. However, she thought she needed time to rest, recover, and reflect before taking any new position and a possible move (in this case, to Portland, Oregon). As Warren Bennis notes, "Because reflection is vital at every level in every organization and because burnout is a very real threat in today's hectic atmosphere all executives should practice the new three R's—retreat, renewal, and return."[33]

For several months, Williams-Brinkley rested and reflected. Her professional experiences as a nurse and consultant had allowed her to build and sustain her career as a health care leader, and a personal experience now allowed her to recommit to health care. She said: "what really recommitted me to health care was the loss of a family member, who was misdiagnosed and eventually passed away in a hospital. I spent countless hours in that hospital and saw the best of our health care system. But most of all, I saw people dedicated to caring for my family member—and me. During that intense time, things came full circle for me. Ultimately, it was a nurse who was the angel that I needed. She was compassionate, honest, and truthful without taking away hope."[34]

Resolution

In November 2017, Williams-Brinkley recommitted to leadership with renewed drive as she began working as president of Kaiser Permanente Health Plan and Hospitals of the Northwest in Portland. In this role she oversaw health care for the regions' more than 620,000 members and its hospitals, medical offices and other medical services. Kaiser Permanente was able to convince Williams-Brinkley to move across the country because of its belief that "strong leadership is not a function of gender; however, leadership performance is greatly enhanced when teams are equitable, inclusive and diverse. The strongest companies understand the need for diversity at all levels of leadership—particularly at the top."[35] Recent studies show that "diversity brings many advantages to an organization: increased profitability and creativity, stronger governance and better problem-solving abilities. Employees with diverse backgrounds bring to bear their own perspectives, ideas and experiences, helping to create organizations that are resilient and effective, and which outperform organisations [sic] that do not invest in diversity."[36] Diverse leadership will benefit patients because "it's so important for our patients to have people in leadership who look like them and can relate to them."[37]

Williams-Brinkley supports Kaiser Permanente's efforts to build up the community it serves. Health care providers and systems must understand the communities they serve and the social determinants of health, such as the factors that influence health—good nutrition, safe housing, and childhood trauma. Williams-Brinkley notes the changing demographics of the United States, recognizing that disparities and diversity in health care are more important than ever before: "We have to understand each other better, especially in the helping and the healing professions like health care. We have to understand our customers, who are changing. The demographics also are changing. . . ."[38] In June 2020, Williams-Brinkley made another move when she took on the role of president of Kaiser Foundation Health Plan of the Mid-Atlantic States. Kim Horn, a Kaiser executive, said that, "Ruth's deep experience in integrated and non-profit health care systems and the significant accomplishments of the Northwest Region under her leadership make her uniquely qualified to assume the role of regional president, Mid-Atlantic States. On a personal note, this opportunity allows Ruth to move closer to family."[39]

Her experience growing up in rural Georgia, along with a career trajectory that has taken her all over the country, has taught Williams-Brinkley how U.S. health-care systems operate with regard to disparities and diversity. She has "never forgotten what it was like to grow up in a rural area with less than ideal—much less than ideal—access to health care. . . . When people are in rural areas, often they don't have insurance. And even if they have insurance, they've got to [schedule a doctor's visit] on a day they have to do their farm work, so people put things off."[40] She believes that it is her responsibility to speak up for people who do not always have a voice or the necessary contacts or support systems.

When Williams-Brinkley reflects on her leadership style, she considers herself "a servant leader . . . here to steward this organization along with those who are here with me. . . . So [I am] helping the organization be successful in such a way that we pass on a successful organization to the next generation on behalf of the community we serve."[41] She advocates for women in leadership positions and the development of an equitable, inclusive, and diverse workforce. She wants to see that women have a seat at the table and are recognized for their contributions. She recognizes how much value women contribute to the health-care delivery system and leadership teams: "Leadership as a function of growth is also, then, the process of building confidence, not so that others will follow, but also so that others will attempt leadership themselves. . . . It is especially important that leadership be considered a form of stewardship."[42]

Williams-Brinkley recently shared her thoughts, based on her personal experiences, on how women can build their careers and thrive in today's competitive business environment:

- Run your career as you would a business that you own and lead—no one is going to care more about your career than you.
- Create your own board of directors—surround yourself with people who will help you carry out your vision.
- Take advantage of mentors and sponsors who can help you along the way.
- Be fearless in order to manage and advance your career—for me, that meant being mobile and willing to take on difficult assignments.[43]

From a small town in segregated rural Georgia, Williams-Brinkley has journeyed a long way: to Chicago, St. Louis, Alabama, Tennessee, Arizona, Louisville, Portland, and Maryland. She now roams the C-suite of one of our nation's premier integrated health care delivery systems. But the influence of her grandmother still looms large. Williams-Brinkley wrote a children's book called *Grandma Said* with Irma Williams, to pass on the wisdom her grandmother imparted all those years ago.[44] "She was always a very strong and independent woman. And so I think I learned that from her," said Williams-Brinkley.[45]

She recalls the lessons of supporting the community and those who have less that she learned from her grandmother and others: "Dr. Martin Luther King Jr. once said, 'Life's most persistent and urgent question is, "What are you doing for others?"'"[46] Williams-

Brinkley is answering this question every day as leader, clinician, mentor, coach, advocate, parent, and grandmother, working to improve access to high-quality health care for her community. She leads with the belief "that we are on a mission in life to help others. Personally, I'm focused on building others up at all levels—whether it's mentoring the next generation of health care workers or fostering diversity and inclusion at the highest leadership levels in large organizations."[47] In many ways, she found her own path to this point, but her legacy will be in helping others find their way.

Notes

1 According to Austin Frakt, "integrated delivery systems (IDSs) are vertically integrated health service networks that include physicians, hospitals, post-acute services, and sometimes offer health insurance. In short, within a single organization, they provide a broad spectrum of coordinated inpatient and outpatient care. Kaiser Permanente is the quintessential example, but there are many other IDSs" ("The Performance of Integrated Delivery Systems," Academy Health, July 20, 2016, https://www.academyhealth.org/node/2151).

2 Tamara Rosin and Lindsey Dunn, "The 10 Most Admired CEOs in Healthcare," Becker's Hospital Review, December 23, 2014, https://www.beckershospitalreview.com/healthcare-blog/the-10-best-ceos-in-healthcare.html; Kaiser Permanente Insider, "Ruth Williams-Brinkley named one of Modern Healthcare's 100 Most Influential People of 2020," accessed March 24, 2021, https://insider.kaiserpermanente.org/ruth-williams-brinkley-named-one-of-modern-healthcares-100-most-influential-people-of-2020; Modern Healthcare, "Top 25 Women in Healthcare—2017," accessed March 20, 2021, https://www.modernhealthcare.com/awards/top-25-women-healthcare-2017; Modern Healthcare, "Top 25 Minority Executives in Healthcare for 2016 (text list)," accessed February 13, 2016, https://www.modernhealthcare.com/article/20160213/MAGAZINE/302139955/top-25-minority-executives-in-healthcare-for-2016-text-list.

3 Ruth Williams-Brinkley, "A Community Refreshed: Honoring Dr. King's Vision," LinkedIn, January 24, 2019, https://www.linkedin.com/pulse/community-refreshed-honoring-dr-kings-vision-ruth-williams-brinkley/.

4 Ruth Williams-Brinkley, telephone interview by Elizabeth A. Ryan and Alexander Bartke, January 10, 2019.

5 C. Nicole Mason, "Unequal Lives: The State of Black Women and Families in the Rural South" (Jackson, MS: Southern Rural Black Women's Initiative, 7, accessed February 15, 2021, http://srbwi.org/images/uploads/45553_Report_Final-LR.pdf.

6 Williams-Brinkley, interview.

7   Ibid.
8   Library of Congress: Exhibitions, "The Civil Rights Act of 1964: A Long Struggle for Freedom: The Segregation Era (1900–1939)," accessed February 15, 2021, http://www.loc.gov/exhibits/civil-rights-act/segregation-era .html#obj024.
9   Williams-Brinkley, interview.
10 Ibid.
11 Furst Group, "What Healthcare Leaders Need to Know Now," C-Suite Conversations, September 29, 2017, https://www.furstgroup.com/blog/2017 /09/ruth-brinkley.
12 Ibid.
13 Ibid.
14 Williams-Brinkley, interview.
15 Ibid.
16 Ibid.
17 Ibid.
18 Computer Sciences Corporation, "1997 Annual Report," accessed February 15, 2021, http://www.annualreports.com/HostedData/AnnualReportArchive/c /NYSE_CSC_1997.pdf.
19 Williams-Brinkley, interview.
20 Joanna Barsh and Lareina Yee, "Unlocking the Full Potential of Women in the US Economy," McKinsey & Company, April 1, 2011, https://www .mckinsey.com/business-functions/organization/our-insights/unlocking -the-full-potential-of-women.
21 Diana Manos, "Lack of Women CEOs Is a Problem for Healthcare, Oliver Wyman says," *HealthCare IT News*, January 8, 2019, https://www .healthcareitnews.com/news/lack-women-ceos-problem-healthcare-oliver -wyman-says.
22 Williams-Brinkley, interview.
23 Allison Evers Cueller and Paul J. Gertler, "Trends in Hospital Consolidation: The Formation of Local Systems," *Health Affairs* 22, no. 6 (November–December 2003): 77–87, https://doi.org/10.1377/hlthaff.22.6.77.
24 Furst Group, "Healthcare Executive Ruth Brinkley: 'I'm Not Retiring,'" C-Suite Conversations, September 29, 2017, https://www.furstgroup.com /resources/tag/ruth-brinkley.
25 Barsh and Yee, "Unlocking the Full Potential of Women in the US Economy."
26 Furst Group, "Healthcare Executive Ruth Brinkley."
27 Boris Ladwig, "Jewish Hospital Was Once Profitable. Then It Joined Forces with UofL," Insider Louisville, January 15, 2019, https://insiderlouisville .com/archived-news/jewish-hospital-was-once-profitable-then-it-joined -forces-with-uofl/.
28 "University of Louisville/KentuckyOne Relationship to Enter Next Phase," University of Louisville School of Medicine, accessed September 1, 2019, https://louisville.edu/medicine/news/university-of-louisville-kentuckyone -health-relationship-to-enter-next-phase.

29 Dave Barkholz, "Brinkley Resigns as CEO of KentuckyOne," *Modern Healthcare*, May 19, 2017, https://www.modernhealthcare.com/article /20170519/NEWS/170519833/brinkley-resigns-as-ceo-of-kentuckyone.

30 Williams-Brinkley, interview.

31 Furst Group, "2016 Top 25 Minority Executives in Healthcare," C-Suite Conversations, November 28, 2016, https://www.furtstgroup.com/resources /tag/ruth-brinkley.

32 Chris Otts, "Ruth Brinkley to Resign as CEO of KentuckyOne Health," WDRB.com. May 19, 2017, https://www.wdrb.com/news/business/ruth -brinkley-to-resign-as-ceo-of-kentuckyone-health/article_5c54fff6-d11d -5bef-8c9f-b3ff951154ce.html.

33 Warren Bennis, *On Becoming a Leader* (New York: Basic, 2003), 181.

34 Christina D. Warner, "Lessons with Leadership with Ruth Williams-Brinkley, President of Kaiser Foundation Health Plan and Hospitals of the Northwest," Thrive Global, April 25, 2019, https://thriveglobal.com/stories /lessons-with-leadership-with-ruth-williams-brinkley-president-of-kaiser -foundation-health-plan-hospitals-of-the-northwest/.

35 "Ruth Williams-Brinkley, President, Kaiser Foundation Health Plan and Hospitals of the Northwest, and Imelda Dacones, MD, President and CEO, Northwest Permanente, P.C.," *Portland Monthly*, May 1, 2018, https://www .pdxmonthly.com/sponsored/2018/05/ruth-williams-brinkley-president -kaiser-foundation-health-plan-and-hospitals-of-the-northwest-imelda -dacones-md-prseident-and-ceo-northwest-permanente-p-c.

36 Vijay Eswaran, "The Business Case for Diversity in the Workplace Is Now Overwhelming," World Economic Forum, April 29, 2019, https://www .weforum.org/agenda/2019/04/business-case-for-diversity-in-the-workplace/.

37 Furst Group, "2016 Top 25 Minority Executives in Healthcare," C-Suite Conversations, November 28, 2016, https://www.furtstgroup.com/resources /tag/ruth-brinkley.

38 American College of Healthcare Executives Archives, Cambridge Management Group, July10, 2015, https:cmg625.com/tag/American-college-of -healthcare-executives./

39 Ibid.

40 Ibid.

41 Williams-Brinkley, interview.

42 Srilatha Batliwala, "Feminist Leadership for Social Transformation: Clearing the Conceptual Cloud," *Quest: A Feminist Quarterly II* 4: 60–66,(CREA: New Dehli, 2011), 23, https://www.uc.edu/content/da/uc/ucwc/docs/CREA.pdf.

43 Ruth Williams-Brinkley, "Women and Leadership: Becoming the CEO of Your Own Career," LinkedIn, June 12, 2019, https://www.linkedin.com/pulse/women -leadership-becoming-ceo-your-own-career-ruth-williams-brinkley/.

44 Williams-Brinkley, interview.

45 Williams-Brinkley, interview.

46 Williams-Brinkley, "A Community Refreshed."

47 Warner, "Lessons with Leadership with Ruth Williams-Brinkley."

Suerie Moon. Photo courtesy of Lukas Schramm-DNDi.

Suerie Moon

Shaping the Governance of a Complex Global Health System to Achieve Equity

Alexander M. Bartke and Ann Marie Hill

Background

On March 11, 2020, the World Health Organization (WHO) declared that COVID-19, a disease caused by a newly discovered coronavirus, was a pandemic and noted their concerns related to the level of disease spread and severity. Two days later, a national emergency was declared in the United States. A year later, on March 20, 2021, WHO's dashboard reported nearly 122 million confirmed cases and 2.7 million deaths world-wide with sustained transmission ongoing.[1] The complexity and intensity of the pandemic demonstrates the need for a collective international response to curb the devastating consequences of COVID-19.

Suerie Moon, codirector of the Global Health Centre at the Graduate Institute of International and Development Studies in Geneva, Switzerland, has spent her professional life unraveling the complex challenges and gaps in national and international public health responses posed by conditions generated by an interconnected society. Unfortunately, the early months of the COVID-19 pandemic highlighted weaknesses in the global health system examined in her work. Her commitment to addressing the neglect of basic human needs at a global level—combined with her academic career at Princeton and Harvard Universities, where she developed innovative thinking on global governance—has positioned Moon to be both a premier thought leader and a fierce advocate for fundamental health rights that are essential in a multifaceted and integrated world, where economic, social, and political forces impact global health in unexpected ways and often create inequality and disparities.

Moon's work focuses on the importance of global health governance, and she defines the global health system as including a range of actors—such as nations, communities, and international organizations—that work together to develop health policies, regulations, and agreements to provide a new type of governing authority. This concept goes beyond the boundaries of national sovereignty and instead focuses on the complex ways in which communities, cultures, or organizations work together to establish the shared beliefs and common agendas that Moon refers to as informal norms.[2] An example of how Moon uses this thinking was demonstrated during a panel discussion sponsored by the Center for Strategic and International Studies, when she called for all governments to give WHO more tools, authority, and funding if they want to create a truly transparent and effective global organization.[3] She also advocates for equitable access to all the scientific advancements such as those developed with COVID-19 funding, including vaccines and new treatments. Finally, she argues that national politicized agendas "can really get in the way of having a science-based, public-health-based approach"[4] to threats, opportunities, and the ability to mobilize political will and leadership to develop systems and reforms.[5] Moon suggests setting priorities and looking to progress accomplished at the international and domestic level "to protect and promote public health worldwide.[6] She notes that changes made at WHO in recent years makes it more prepared and better positioned to lead the fight against global outbreaks such as COVID-19.

While Moon's thinking on global governance is relatively new, she has been successful in applying it to a range of other global health issues—including access to medicines in developing countries; the West African Ebola crisis; and, more recently, the international debate on health care as a human right. Countries no longer have the kind of power or resources sufficient to control wide-ranging health threats like viral outbreaks. Pharmaceutical companies cannot limit access to drugs and technology to rich countries, while ignoring the needs of people in developing countries. Rather, we must rely upon a network of various players that can significantly impact health policy across sovereign borders. It is recognizing the informal but powerful nature of this kind of global health system, and understanding both its possibilities and governance gaps, that Moon feels will help us deal with some of the world's most daunting health problems.[7] How she reached this conclusion is a journey worth exploring.

It was not uncommon for Moon's elementary school to invite outside guest speakers who often shared films on various subjects like science, geography, and history. One day, students in Moon's second grade class saw a film about living conditions in developing countries that showed the limited access to clean water, sanitation, and food there. Moon recalled that "I was living in a fairly privileged setting in Chicago, and the fact that some people on the planet could live with a shockingly small amount of resources deeply moved me."[8] For Moon, this film prompted a recognition of global inequality that would stay with her.

Moon's parents, Ineon and Youjae Moon, immigrated to the United States from South Korea in 1969, and Moon was born five years later in Chicago, Illinois. Her memories from childhood paint a picture of hardworking parents who were struggling to raise a family while adjusting to a new country. Both of her parents were acupuncturists, so health and wellness were a part of growing up for Moon. From an early age, she was able to watch how her parents navigated and adjusted to American culture, working to make a good life for their daughters. After pushing her to study hard throughout her childhood, Moon's parents seemed somewhat confused when she chose a career in academia rather than in medicine, law, or engineering. However, they did not object too strongly and ultimately supported her. "Looking back," she said, "I can see, more and more clearly, how their values, work ethic, and my immigrant upbringing have shaped the way I see the world."[9] She enjoyed the benefits of growing up in a family of five, living in Chicago and later Southern California, although she never forgot that others were not as fortunate and maintained her interest in global inequities and the developing world.

Moon's interest in inequality and lack of access to resources led her to an academic career that started at Yale University, where she earned a bachelor's degree in history in 1996. After working for several years on immigrant rights and services in Oakland, California, followed by stints with the Peace Corps and Doctors without Borders, she attended the School of Public and International Affairs at Princeton University, where she obtained a master's degree in public affairs with a focus on development and international relations. In 2010 Moon earned a PhD in public policy from Harvard University's John F. Kennedy School of Government. She has become a leader in the global health governance arena.

Although the work of her parents helped shape Moon's perceptions of public health, her early professional interest was to make a difference in the global front. This interest led her to join the Peace Corps in 1999 and accept a posting in rural South Africa. This experience was her first lengthy exposure to conditions leading to health disparities that are typical in many developing countries. Moon's host family consisted of a single mother who was raising three children on her own. This woman was a well-known educator and a highly respected community member. While Moon was living with the family, her host mother developed symptoms of multidrug-resistant tuberculosis and died suddenly in the hospital. Her death deeply affected her family and community, as well as Moon. It opened Moon's eyes to how devastating poverty and the lack of access to health care could be in the developing world and left her with a renewed drive to address such social injustice. For Moon, the overall experience "made it very real . . . , very human—what was happening more broadly in sub-Saharan Africa at the time."[10]

However, during her posting, Moon was almost sexually assaulted in what was a very frightening experience for her. Moon notes, "The [Peace Corps] staff knew that crime and rape were serious issues in South Africa, but I was totally not expecting it." The risks were never explained to her before her departure from the United States. She said that the Peace Corps "didn't find daily harassment to be a sufficient reason to change their plans. It became a steady stream of drop-outs—I was one of them."[11] (Years after her experience, in 2011, the Kate Puzey Peace Corps Volunteer Protection Act required the Peace Corps to provide comprehensive sexual assault risk reduction and undertake other related efforts to enhance volunteers' safety and security and the organization's response to victims of sexual assault.)

After deciding to leave the Peace Corps, Moon found herself grappling with what she wanted to do next in her life. She moved to New York City and obtained an entry-level position as a communications assistant with a nonprofit organization called Médecins sans Frontières (MSF). Also known today as Doctors without Borders, MSF provides medical assistance to regions and communities throughout the world that are affected by conflict, poverty, natural disasters, epidemics, and lack of health resources. Its mission is "providing lifesaving medical humanitarian care, and speaking out about what we see."[12] This was a perfect setting for someone committed to making a difference on a larger scale, and it opened Moon's eyes afresh to the importance of advocacy as a tool to address larger public health agendas. She also met "a number of mentors who set examples for how you can really change global affairs."[13] Moon's time at MSF provided just the right experiences for her to develop her self-confidence and mature as a talented professional.

The HIV/AIDS crisis in Africa became one of the most important responses in demonstrating the need for a coordinated global health response. In 1999, WHO announced that AIDS had become the fourth most common cause of death worldwide and the leading cause of death in Africa. Since the start of the epidemic, over seventy-five million people globally have become infected with HIV, and over thirty-two million have died from AIDS-related illnesses.[14]

The intellectual property (IP) rights held by transnational pharmaceutical companies prevented people living with HIV in developing countries from obtaining lifesaving antiretroviral drugs due to their extremely high costs. In turn, this situation contributed to a growing global public crisis that over time stimulated widespread international cooperation to tackle these issues. MSF joined this effort with vigor and commitment.

Having gained international recognition after being awarded the 1999 Nobel Peace Prize, MSF significantly expanded its role in health advocacy and became involved in securing access to lifesaving HIV/AIDS medicines in developing countries. That year, MSF launched an international campaign for access to essential medicines, which sought to "bring down barriers that keep people from getting the treatment they need to stay alive and healthy."[15] One example of the solidarity that MSF was able to generate in advocating for access to essential medicines is evident in the media and the public attention it mobilized to influence a landmark South African lawsuit. Pharmaceutical corporations had sued the government of South Africa in 1998 for trying to lower the cost of medicine. Collaborating with national and international organizations, MSF built an extensive network of informal relationships that generated enough negative public attention toward the pharmaceutical companies to persuade them to drop their lawsuit in 2001.[16]

Moon initially worked on the campaign from the MSF offices in New York, but she relocated to the campaign headquarters in Geneva. There she conducted policy research and wrote and edited campaign reports. She commented that she "would have to say it was my experience from 2000 to 2001—when the big debates were happening around intellectual property rights and access to HIV medicines, and we saw the most significant policy change—that had the biggest influence on me."[17] Her understanding of how influential informal norms could be in changing policy and national agendas matured and expanded. Public media attention, court cases in Africa, and the World Trade Organization's Doha Declaration on the TRIPS [Trade-Related Aspects of Intellectual Property Rights] Agreement and Public Health,[18] all played a collective role in creating change. Moon noted that, "I saw how dramatically policy could change, how you can change thinking in society at the highest levels of business in the pharmaceutical industry and the government. I thought it was, depending on your perspective, either a perfect storm or a beautiful coincidence that all these factors came together. That really stayed with me as an example of how dramatically change can happen to the course of events, sometimes in ways that you would never predict."[19]

Moon next worked for MSF in developing countries out of a desire to increase her understanding of on-the-ground realities and how global policies played out in people's lives. During her first placement, in the Democratic Republic of Congo in Central Africa, Moon was immersed in the realities of an insecure post-conflict setting and worked on a cost analysis for MSF's HIV treatment. This field-work opened her eyes to the challenges of delivering high-quality HIV treatment in an insecure and severely resource-poor setting, but she saw that doing so was possible despite significant hurdles. The fieldwork also started to shape her understanding of how governance and policy could impact the everyday lives of thousands of people.

Moon was next assigned to advocate for more health-sensitive IP rights policies in the People's Republic of China (in a way, to push for implementation of the Doha Declaration on a national level), to improve access to medical treatment for people living with HIV in that country. From the start, Moon faced problems as an advocate in a country ruled by the communist party, where strict controls over public criticism and demonstrations existed. At this time, GlaxoSmithKline (GSK) was trying to protect its HIV drug market in China by influencing government officials to ban the import of a generic drug that would cut sales of GSK's drug.[20] Moon prepared an evidence-based economic analysis on how a lack of access to generic drugs and the high prices for patented drugs prevented many Chinese from receiving adequate treatment. Armed with facts and success stories from other countries, she argued her case tenaciously across all levels of the Chinese government. Moon noted: "It really did make a difference to go to the Ministry of Health and present them with clear evidence that limiting access to drugs meant people were suffering or dying needlessly. Presenting them with success-ful policy initiatives from other countries and citing evidence from highly ranked peer-reviewed journals could sometimes act as a counterweight to money and other forms of political influence."[21]

A small but significant victory came to MSF and Moon when the Chinese government ultimately changed its position and authorized the import of a generic drug. This decision represented a significant shift in thinking by Chinese health officials on IP rights during a time when there had been no exceptions to those rights for public health reasons. This experience offered Moon new insights into how to use her reasoning and critical thinking to forge new policy. It showed her that formidable ideas supported by evidence have the power to influence thinking and change policy on a large scale. This lesson would stay with her as she moved on to engage even more deeply in the debate about access to medicines.

Moon was now intrigued by the role that research had played in her small success in China, and she decided to pursue a PhD in public policy at Harvard's Kennedy School of Government. She was trying to decide whether running programs, doing direct service, or engaging in policy was the best path to follow.

Eventually, she notes, "in my heart, it became more and more clear to me that I was going to be more useful in the policy arena."[22] She credits her dissertation advisor—John Ruggie, the Berthold Professor of Human Rights and International Affairs at the Kennedy School—with "help[ing] me to see that this specific issue of HIV and IP and trade agreements represented a case that could be used to build theory, and this really helped me to see beyond the specific to the much more generalizable."[23] With the help of her Harvard mentors, including Professor Bill Clark,[24] and her natural talent for integrating complex issues into rational models, Moon was able to link global governance debates together. Her dissertation, "Embedding Neoliberalism Global Health and the Evolution of the Global Intellectual Property Regime," focused on how neoliberal forces situated IP rights for private-sector benefit often at great cost to poorer, developing countries but showed that space for policies that stress health and human rights could be carved out through strategic action.

With this intellectual understanding of the evolution of the property rights regime, Moon was poised to move systematically into a much more expansive theory of global governance. This theory centers on the influence of informal norms—those shared beliefs that can exist at all levels of social organizations and that can become pervasive and indirectly hold power for change. She would later collaborate with Wolfgang Hein to articulate the concept as, "There is no formal [legal] obligation to comply with informal norms, but social sanctions against non-compliance can be severe, such as exclusion from important social groups or access to material or political resources."[25] They argued that networks form when various stakeholders, often with diverse perspectives, engage in an iterative process that can eventually lead to the development of informal norms within a particular network, giving it influence and, in turn, helping shape public health policy. Moon cited the example of transnational pharmaceutical corporations to show that the well-established IP rights policy in developing countries such as Brazil, Thailand, and South Africa can shift significantly. These shifts occur if networks press hard enough for alternative solutions, such as providing broader access to medicines for the common good. This novel concept offers an approach to global governance that is far different from the legalism or state-based thinking that has dominated the field in the past.[26]

After Moon's graduation from the Kennedy School, she joined the faculty of Harvard's School of Public Health (HSPH). She began working with Julio Frenk, a former minister of health of Mexico who was dean of HSPH. Frenk would become an important long-time mentor for Moon and exemplified the kind of hybrid academic and policy practitioner that she sought to become.[27] "We collaborated extensively as professional colleagues. I was impressed with [Moon's] intelligence, mastery of the substantive context of global health, and outstanding skills to organize," commented Frenk.[28] Throughout their friendship, he helped Moon see health and global governance as two fields that needed to interact more. Moon was presented with an intellectual juncture in determining how to integrate health and global governance in her academic and policy work. This decision would lead to the development of a new area of scholarship, in which she drew on prior experiences and was influenced by collaboration with her mentor.

Resolution

Moon's emphasis on the translation of research into actionable items was further advanced by her publishing a series of articles in *PLOS Medicine*, a journal that serves as "an influential venue for research and commentary on the major challenges to human health worldwide."[29] The most notable of these, "The Global Health

System: Lessons for a Stronger Institutional Framework," focused on the concept and functions of a global health system and, while recognizing that such a system lacked predictability and structure, asked what it must do to function.[30] This question was designed to spark the dialogue necessary to advance this concept and move theory toward practice.

In 2013, Frenk and Moon published a landmark report in the *New England Journal of Medicine* titled "Governance Challenges in Global Health," which integrated these two fields into a new way of thinking about global health governance. It became the most widely cited academic publication in the field. In this pioneering paper, Frenk and Moon argued persuasively that the current challenges facing global health stem from a lack of leadership at the global level, and that we must create what the authors call a "global health system" by working multilaterally across networks and sharing ideas to improve the governance of health systems around the globe.[31] The authors conceptualized the global health system at an even higher level by using the language of systems theory to start to understand what was happening beyond the national level. This forward-looking article represented a critical leap for Moon, as her ideas now took center stage in global health governance.

She and Frenk developed a course on global health governance for HSPH students that incorporated her belief that powerful change can come from small ideas by turning her classroom into a think tank where her students could experiment with new concepts of global governance that pushed the envelope and stimulated excitement. She equipped her students with the discipline to think, an understanding of advocacy, and the motivation to face tough challenges without giving up.

Moon also began to publish extensively in academic journals on the conflict over access to medicines as a problem for securing the public good at the international level.[32] Her concept of global health equity developed rapidly as a combination of her scholarly thinking with a call for activism. For Moon, it was not enough to develop rational arguments and generalized theories. Her experience of working in the field taught her that it was equally important for her beliefs to be used to find real-world solutions through engagement and advocacy. She pointed out that "articles have been the way in which I have gotten my ideas out."[33]

In 2009, she published another big-idea paper, "Medicines as Global Public Goods: The Governance of Technological Innovation in the New Era of Global Health."[34] Here she argued that the costs and benefits of developing new technologies should be shared on a global level by transcending institutional hierarchies that rely upon patent protections to control access to new technologies and protect proprietary profits.[35] This article used the debate about access to medicines to shift the paradigm away from national innovation systems and toward a broader understanding of research and discovery as an investment in global public goods.[36]

In 2010, at the annual meeting of the International Studies Association in New Orleans, Louisiana, Moon met Hein, who was also studying global governance and the HIV/AIDS crisis. The meeting sparked a working relationship that would deepen over time and culminate in the coauthorship of a book titled *Informal Norms in Global Governance*, an in-depth analysis of the development of the access-to-medicine movement. Shortly thereafter, Moon and her coauthors published a paper titled "Innovation and Access to Medicines for Neglected Populations," which built on her earlier theoretical analysis and argued for the creation of some type of global treaty or platform to address the current failings of the pharmaceutical system, and the rules and incentives that result in poor outcomes for the overall system. Again, she argued that discovery and knowledge should be not seen as proprietary but as a public good, and that the slowing down of information transfer due to IP rights delayed the advancement of new drugs resulting in a focus on profit over scientific advancement.

Moon's ideas called attention to the fact that in the absence of financial support, the pharmaceutical industry has no incentive to invest in neglected diseases. She attributes this situation to a lack of global regulation and leadership that would encourage innovation and research and development, such as motivating companies to routinely share their knowledge to help in the development of new drugs. Moon also took issue with the way that financial incentives, rather than health needs, primarily drive private research and development investments. She asserted that the creation of a formal agreement among multinational stakeholders that is designed to shift the profit motive for pharmaceutical companies toward shared knowledge and drug development and that, in turn, would have the potential to form governance policies to ensure that the public health interest—not financial gain—is the force that drives scientific discovery.[37]

Moon believes that "the problem is not industry but rather the combination of rules, incentives, and actors (including industry) that results in poor outcomes."[38] With ever-increasing insistence, Moon continued to put pressure on the pharmaceutical companies to consider alternative business models. In 2012, she took her message to a higher level when she testified before the Subcommittee on Primary Health and Aging (of the U.S. Senate Committee on Health, Education, Labor, and Pensions), chaired by Senator Bernie Sanders of Vermont, on the cost of HIV/AIDS medications and monopolies created in the HIV/AIDS drugs market.[39] To this end, she called for a global system in which the contributions from all transnational actors could lead to a more stable and global administrative arrangement. In the final analysis, this would enable underserved communities to gain a forceful voice in creating conditions where they have a real say in policy decisions that affect their health.

In April 2016, GSK's CEO Andrew Witty unveiled new patent policies that could make it easier for people in the world's poorest countries to access drugs, a shift that reflected the impact that these pressures were having on the pharmaceutical industry. "[T]he London-based company's plan to stop filing for patents in least developed and low-income (LDCS and LICs), countries such as Afghanistan and Zambia," making "it easier for other manufacturers to supply generic versions of GSK's drugs in those countries. . . .[40]

Moon moved quickly to take her ideas on the road and answer "questions on her specific research initiatives that brings evidence to bear on what was still a rather polarized debate at the time."[41] This strategic approach demonstrates that Moon values the shared perspectives and transparency she espouses in her theories and engages in the kind of interpersonal connections needed to create informal norms and build a community of shared interest around her thinking. With over a dozen academic publications on informal norms in global governance and a wide network of key stakeholders supporting her, Moon's innovative thinking on the subject cemented her position as a leader in the field of global governance and access to medicines.

Because of the efforts of Moon, among others, the pharmaceutical industry has become more open to providing broader access to critically needed medicines and more focused on neglected diseases. Developing countries have expanded access to lifesaving drugs using many of the policies Moon has advanced. Most importantly, Moon was able to fully develop her ideas on health and global governance as an access issue and disseminate the information into the global health community, where it was received positively by leaders and experts alike. In 2010, critics were saying that a governing system did not exist. Moon clarifies this view: "The system does not necessarily work well, but there is a system of actors who are engaged and influence each other, and they are all interdependent. . . . I think intellectually that was the important stepping-stone to then begin thinking about how well the system is working, and what should the system try to do?"[42]

Moon's work on providing access to medicine for developing countries comes from her core belief that we need a plurality of views to generate innovative ideas that can be shared on a global scale to transcend national boundaries—and, in this case, secure the right to health care. Her foundational work to improve access to medicine goes well beyond bringing lifesaving medicine to people in desperate need in developing countries. It also brings forward a fundamentally different way of thinking about global health governance, one that may have large-scale implications across developing countries as well as high- and middle-income countries.

Moon's innovative thinking was demonstrated in 2014, when the West African Ebola outbreak caused widespread suffering and damaged fragile public health systems as it struck the nations of Guinea, Liberia, and Sierra Leone. It was the deadliest Ebola outbreak in history, with more than ten thousand lives lost.[43] In 2015 in response to this devastation, Moon was selected to be the study director for the report of the Harvard-LSHTM [London School of Hygiene and Tropical Medicine] Independent Panel on the Global Response to Ebola. This study, the product of twenty independent experts from civil society organizations, think tanks, and academia, examined the weaknesses in the global health system and made recommendations for improvement. Moon and her coauthors explained, "We gathered world-class experts and asked, how can we bolster the dangerously fragile global system for outbreak response?"[44] They focused on four essential functions of any global health governance system—namely, the production of public goods, sharing of information, mobilization of global solidarity, and assurance of stewardship. They carefully crafted evidenced-based discussions about these functions, relying upon research findings, transparency, and accountability across all proceedings.

It was clear that the devastation wrought by Ebola was largely due to weak national and global health systems. However, Moon's ideas on global governance and the use of informal norms to break down boundaries have helped move closer to achieving a more effective international global health infrastructure. The panel recommended more robust enforcement of rules for government responses during a health crisis, such as not closing borders or shipping passages and allowing for an efficient means of communication to dispense aid. Moon emphasized that "a contribution the panel made in the area of outbreaks, [was] in emphasizing the need for a global accountability mechanism."[45] This call for accountability led to the creation of the Global Preparedness Monitoring Board, which met for the first time in September 2018. The charge of the board is to act as a global accountability mechanism and respond to outbreaks of infectious disease. As Moon pointed out, "The creation of this monitoring mechanism and accountability . . . would not have happened had we and others not continued to argue and push for the importance of accountability at the global level on outbreak and response."[46] She added that the "impact at the end of the day and in the people's lives is an extremely long causal chain."[47]

The board identified actions and priorities for attention moving forward, including empowering community engagement and participation in preventing, preparing for, and responding to an outbreak, engaging multiple sectors of society, and strengthening governance and coordination.[48] It issued its first report in September 2019, which focused on several components to improve preparedness for outbreaks. They include the heads of governments working together, countries leading by example and preparing for the worst, and the United Nations' strengthening its coordination mechanisms.[49]

The board's second report was issued in September 2020 and prioritized a call for urgent actions to strengthen the current response to COVID-19 and better prepare the world for future pandemics, as well as to bring order out of catastrophe and chaos. The 2020 report highlights the importance of national leaders and leaders of international organizations in taking early decisive action based on "science, evidence, and best practice when confronted with health emergencies." Citizens need to demand accountability from their governments for responding to emergencies, "which requires that governments empower their citizens and strengthen civil society."[50]

Moon argues strongly that WHO is the right organization to bring key players together to deal with the COVID-19 pandemic. She argues that a global health system that unites states, communities, and international organizations around a common agenda to deal with the pandemic is needed. For Moon, "global health is not only about the needs of the world's poorest countries, but about how to manage the health interdependence that comes with globalization."[51]

The response to COVID-19 is increasing public awareness of the many important government and international organizations' agendas, but addressing WHO's funding vulnerabilities, Moon argues, was not among them. However, she remains optimistic and sees the public health responses to the COVID-19 pandemic as, "very powerful- the unified voice that then gives political leaders the backing to push through some reforms that might not have been so easy to do otherwise."[52]

The COVID-19 outbreak highlights the many weaknesses in the global health system that Moon examines in her work. For example, arrangements at the international level are weak to nonexistent for ensuring that drugs and vaccines reach the people who need them most. Wealthier countries, with the United States in the lead, are rushing to buy up available drug and vaccine supplies in a surge of nationalism that has disastrous implications at the international level. Moon points out that "Many countries found it nearly impossible to procure diagnostics and masks on the global market in the first months of the pandemic, as larger, wealthier countries outbid them for scarce supplies. Developing countries are deeply concerned they will be last in line for medicines too."[53] Moon says further: "Covid-19 posed a tough choice for the [multinational pharmaceutical] industry: to rehabilitate its public reputation by delivering much-needed innovation at an affordable price worldwide, or to go for windfall earnings, as the financial markets expect, raising accusations of pandemic profiteering. Leaders of several large firms have tried to walk a fine line between the two. The heads of GlaxoSmithKline, Johnson & Johnson, Pfizer and Sanofi, for example, have committed to making vaccines available at cost while the pandemic persists. But they have not agreed (nor have Chinese firms) to transfer technology or patents to enable the large-scale manufacturing needed to meet global demand, nor to share their data and scientific findings to accelerate overall scientific progress, both of which have been called for by the WHO technology pool."[54]

Moon continues to develop her ideas on public health as a human right transnationally and to call for new strategies to build an innovative global health system that works for everyone during a time of rising nationalism. Her leadership position also provides a bully pulpit from which she can use her unique perspective as a woman who understands how important rational and evidence-based advocacy is to ensure that global health systems are inclusive and equitable.

At an early age, Moon had a deep concern for others, and she came to understand something unseen by her predecessors, which marks her contribution as a pioneer in global health governance. Specifically, the world can often be changed when groups of interested players unite around powerful ideas and speak in a common voice for a greater good.[55] According to Moon, "It's an important function that academics play, to put ideas into words in a way that helps us make sense of an extremely complex reality. Their ways of articulating ideas, defining concepts, and trying to be rigorous in the way you do that sets the boundaries to guide the global health system."[56]

She has now positioned herself to play an even greater role in the global health arena. As Roopa Dhatt, the cofounder and executive director of Women in Global Health, has shown in recent studies on women's leadership and gender equality that "increasing women's leadership within global health is an opportunity to further health system resilience and system responsiveness."[57] The study also finds that women make up the vast majority of those working in the field of global health; however, they are underrepresented within top institutions, in global policy and governance forums, in thought leadership panels, and across decision-making structures in the public and private sectors."[58] Moon has proven herself to be an innovator who deploys evidence strategically, with the realization that the power of informal norms can be used to create governance, growth, and change. This is in many ways a very modest description of a dedicated and passionate woman who brings an ability to observe a world with significant and complex public health needs and then applies deep critical thinking and logic to find innovative solutions to address those needs. As she tells her students, "there are lots of examples that are surprising in the sense that organizations or actors who would not assume they had the power to change things, do, in fact, end up doing that."[59] Moon is a clear example of a leader who has that very power.

Notes

1 World Health Organization, "WHO Coronavirus (COVID-19) Dashboard," https://covid19.who.int/.

2 Wolfgang Hein and Suerie Moon, *Informal Norms in Global Governance: Human Rights, Intellectual Property Rules and Access to Medicines* (Farnham, UK: Ashgate, 2013).

3 Center for Strategic and International Studies, "Online Event: Establishing a Bipartisan Covid-19 Commission," May 4, 2020, https://www.csis.org /analysis/online-event-establishing-bipartisan-covid-19-commission.

4 Ibid.

5 Ibid.

6 Julio Frenk, Octavio Gómez-Dantés, and Suerie Moon, "From Sovereignty to Solidarity: A Renewed Concept of Global Health for an Era of Complex

Interdependence," *The Lancet* 383 no. 9911(2014): 94–97, https://doi.org/10 .1016/S0140-6736(13)62561-1.

7 Suerie Moon, email correspondence with Alexander M. Bartke and Ann Marie Hill, October 4, 2019.

8 Suerie Moon, interview by Alexander M. Bartke and Ann Marie Hill, November 5, 2018.

9 Ibid.

10 Suerie Moon, interview by Alexander M. Bartke and Ann Marie Hill, May 16, 2019.

11 Ibid.

12 Médecins Sans Frontières, "What We Do," accessed September 8, 2019, https://www.doctorswithoutborders.org/what-we-do.

13 Moon, interview, November 5, 2018.

14 UNAIDS, "Global HIV and AIDS Statistics—2020 Fact Sheet," accessed February 16, 2021, https://www.unaids.org/en/resources/fact-sheet.

15 Médecins sans Frontières, "Access Campaign," accessed January 2019, https://msfaccess.org/about-us.

16 Médecins sans Frontières, "MSF Demands Pharmaceutical Industry Stop Obstructing Access to Medicines in South Africa," February 28, 2001,https:// www.doctorswithoutborders.org/what-we-do/news-stories/news/msf -demands-pharmaceutical-industry-stop-obstructing-access-medicines.

17 Moon, interview, May 16, 2019.

18 The DOHA Declaration states that "WTO members affirmed that the TRIPS Agreement should be interpreted and implemented in a manner supportive of WTO members' right to protect public health and, in particular, to promote access to medicines for all and that TRIPS should not prevent members from taking measures to protect public health" *World Trade Organization*, November 20, 2001, https://www.wto.org/english/thewto_e /minist_e/min01_e/mindec1_trips_e.htm.

19 Moon, interview, May 16, 2019.

20 Ibid.

21 Ibid.

22 Ibid.

23 Ibid.

24 Moon, email correspondence.

25 Hein and Moon, *Informal Norms in Global Governance*, 3.

26 Ibid.

27 Moon, email correspondence.

28 Julio Frenk, interview by Alexander M. Bartke and Ann Marie Hill, October 22, 2018.

29 *PLOS Medicine,* "Who we are," PLOS, accessed March 25, 2021, https:// https://journals.plos.org/plosmedicine/s/journal-information.

30 Suerie Moon et al., "The Global Health System: Lessons for a Stronger Institutional Framework," *PLOS Medicine* 7 no.1:e1000193 (2010), https://doi .org/10.1371/journal.pmed.1000193.

31 Julio Frenk and Suerie Moon, "Governance Challenges in Global Health," *New England Journal of Medicine* 368, no. 10 (March 7, 2013): 936–942, www.nejm.org/doi/full/10.1056/nejmra1109339.

32 "A public good has two critical properties: nonrivalrous consumption—the consumption of one individual does not detract from that of another—and nonexcludability—it is difficult if not impossible to exclude an individual from enjoying the good," according to Frederick M. Abbott, Thomas Cottier, and Francis Gurry (*International Intellectual Property in an Integrated World Economy*, 4th ed. [New York: Wolters Kluwer, 2019], 113).

33 Moon, interview, May 16, 2019.

34 Suerie Moon, "Medicines as Global Public Goods: The Governance of Technological Innovations in the New Era of Global Health," *Global Health Governance* 2, no. 2 (2009), http://www.ghgj.org/moon2.2medecinespublicgood.htm.

35 The term *institutional hierarchies* refers to "institutional interplay—interactions as mutually influencing relations between two or more actors or entities" (Hein and Moon, *Informal Norms in Global Governance*, 36.

36 Suerie Moon, John-Arne Røttingen, and Julio Frenk, "Global Public Goods for Health: Weaknesses and Opportunities in the Global Health System," *Health Economics, Policy and Law* 12, no. 2 (2017): 195–205, www.ssrn.com/abstract=3188050.

37 Suerie Moon, Jorge Bermudez, and Ellen 't Hoen, "Innovation and Access to Medicines for Neglected Populations: Could a Treaty Address a Broken Pharmaceutical R&D System?," *PLOS Medicine*, May 15, 2012, journals.plos.org/plosmedicine/article?id=10.1371/journal.pmed.1001218.

38 Moon, email correspondence.

39 "Costs of HIV Medicines," C-SPAN, May 15, 2012, https://www.c-span.org/video/?306014-1/costs-hivaids-medicines.

40 Asher Mullard, "What New GSK Patent Policy Means for the Developing World," *Nature*, April 5, 2016, https://www.nature.com/news/what-new-gsk-patent-policy-means-for-the-developing-world-1.19695.

41 Moon, interview, May 16, 2019.

42 Ibid.

43 Centers for Disease Control and Prevention, "2014–2016 Ebola Outbreak in West Africa," accessed February 16, 2021, www.cdc.gov/vhf/ebola/history/2014-2016-outbreak/index.html.

44 University of California, San Francisco (UCSF) Institute For Global Health Sciences, "GHS's Eric Goosby and Other Global Experts Call for Critical Reforms to Prevent Future Pandemics," November 23, 2015, https://globalhealthsciences.ucsf.edu/news/ghs's-eric-goosby-and-other-global-experts-call-critical-reforms-prevent-future-pandemics.

45 Moon, interview, May 16, 2019.

46 Ibid.

47 Ibid.

48 Global Preparedness Monitoring Board, GPMB, "Our Work," World Health Organization, https://apps.who.int/gpmb/work.html.

49 Global Preparedness Monitoring Board, "A World at Risk: Annual Report on Global Preparedness for Health Emergencies," September, 2019, http://apps.who.int/gpmb/assets/annual_report/GPMB_annualreport_2019.pdf.

50 Global Preparedness Monitoring Board, "A World in Disorder: Global Preparedness Monitoring Board Annual Report 2020," September , 2020, https://apps.who.int/gpmb/assets/annualreport/GPMB_AR2020.pdf, 7.

51 Frenk, Gomez-Dantes, and Moon, "From Sovereignty to Solidarity."

52 Covid-19 Commission," May 4, 2020, https://csis-website-prod.s3.amazonaws.com/s3fs-public/publication/200504_COVID_Commission.pdf.

53 Suerie Moon, "The Vaccine Race: Will Public Health Prevail over Geopolitics?," Graduate Institute of International and Development Studies, July 11, 2020, https://www.graduateinstitute.ch/communications/news/vaccine-race-will-public-health-prevail-over-geopolitics.

54 Ibid.

55 Moon, interview, May 16, 2019.

56 Ibid.

57 Roopa Dhatt et al., "The Role of Women's Leadership and Gender Equity in Leadership and Health System Strengthening," *Global Health, Epidemiology and Genomics*, May 17, 2017, https://www.cambridge.org/core/journals/global-health-epidemiology-and-genomics/article/role-of-womens-leadership-and-gender-equity-in-leadership-and-health-system-strengthening/A6AEB63AFE17295E0EF9E40741A2EC5B.

58 Ibid.

59 Moon, interview, May 16, 2019.

Acknowledgments

We are extraordinarily grateful to the late Alison R. Bernstein, director of Rutgers Institute for Women's Leadership (IWL), and Lisa Hetfield, associate director and director of development, for choosing us to serve as co-editors. As we noted in the preface to this volume, this project was beyond the scope of anything we had done in the past. Because of our professional backgrounds, we were able to appreciate the complexities of the junctures our case subjects faced and the tremendous contributions they made in health care and public health. We also recognize the benefits of sharing their stories so that others can learn from them and continue to build upon their work.

Mary Trigg, associate professor, Women's Gender, and Sexuality Studies, and faculty director for the leadership scholars certificate program, was so gracious in spending time walking us through the process from beginning to end—acting as mentor, reviewer, and advisor. Emily Haran, administrative director and communications coordinator at IWL, gracefully responded to our many requests for assistance in the early stages of our work.

We want to thank Kimberly Guinta and Jasper Chang at Rutgers University Press, who helped to move this volume forward and kept us on schedule. And all those at Westchester Publishing Services, especially Jeanne Ferris and Sherry Gerstein, who spent their time editing this work, which clarified and strengthened each chapter.

We are grateful to the women who are subjects of the case studies for taking the time to speak with our authors either through telephone conversations, emails, or reviewing drafts of the chapter. We learned so much from getting to know them through the course of this project and gained an appreciation for the ways in which they approached life, leadership, and decision making. Our contributing authors were also working, going to school and taking care of their families while they completed this volume of case studies with us. We admire all of them for their hard work, perseverance, and contributions to improving health.

We are very thankful to all of our individual and shared mentors, colleagues, friends, families, and teachers who have helped us along our personal and professional journeys; their guidance has led to the privilege of writing this book.

We want to acknowledge and recognize the many health care, public health and essential workers who have responded with great courage and perseverance during the COVID-19 pandemic while we were in the final stages of writing this volume.

Ruth Charbonneau dedicates this effort to her mother and wishes she could have read it. Ruth thanks her friends for their patience, encouragement, and patience (again).

Mary E. O'Dowd sends her love and gratitude to husband Kevin and to their three sons, Patrick, Jack, Kevin, who have taught her so much and inspire her every day. She thanks her parents Maureen and Anthony Marchetta who have loved, supported, encouraged, inspired, and challenged her as their first of six children.

Contributors

AKANKSHA ARYA, MD, MBA, is an internal medicine resident at Thomas Jefferson University Hospital. She graduated from Rutgers University with a BA in cell biology and neuroscience, and she also has a certificate in women's leadership and an MD from Robert Wood Johnson Medical School, Rutgers University and an MBA from the Kellogg School of Management at Northwestern University. She has worked as a public health associate at the Centers for Disease Control and Prevention and the New York State Department of Health.

ALEXANDER M. BARTKE, BS, is a research assistant at the Edward J. Bloustein School of Planning and Public Policy at Rutgers University, where he earned his degree in public health. His upbringing by a single mother in the suburbs of Bergen County, New Jersey, exposed him to the unique challenges women face from a young age that affect health. He plans to attend medical school and specialize in maternal-fetal medicine.

COLLEEN BLAKE, MPH, is the senior population health and risk management coordinator for Sun River Health, a federally qualified health center that provides patient-centered care to the underserved populations of New York. She graduated from Pennsylvania State University and earned her MPH from Rutgers University. Blake lives in Lyndhurst, New Jersey, where she spends her free time baking for friends and family members.

RUTH CHARBONNEAU, RN, JD, is the associate director of the Lambert Center for the Study of Medicinal Cannabis and Hemp at Thomas Jefferson University. She served in the executive leadership team of several commissioners for the New Jersey Department of Health and was chief of staff for the department. She served as a New Jersey

Governor's Fellow and has held various management and oversight posts within state government. She received an RN from Faulkner Hospital School of Nursing, a BA from Clark University, and a JD from Case Western Reserve University School of Law.

CHRISTINA CHESNAKOV, MPH, is a public health fellow at the Nicholson Foundation. She conducts background research on the foundation's strategic focus areas as well as assisting in managing grants related to adverse childhood experiences. She earned a master's degree in public health at Columbia University in 2018, with a certificate in child, youth, and family health.

CARSON CLAY graduated in 2019 from Princeton University with a BA from the School of Public and International Affairs and a certificate in global health and policy. She has worked on a variety of international and domestic health policy issues, including injury prevention in South Africa, Medicaid expansion, and rural hospital closures.

PATRICIA A. FINDLEY, DRPH, MSW, LCSW, is an associate professor and the director of the Master of Social Work Program in the School of Social Work at Rutgers University. She also serves as the special assistant to the dean for interprofessional health initiatives. Her research focuses on health care, particularly on the interaction of mental and physical illness in patient care. She is a coinvestigator on a number of Health Services Research Administration grants as a collaborating member in interdisciplinary clinical teams across Rutgers University to promote and research interprofessional health care.

ANN MARIE HILL, MBA, is an associate professor of practice in health administration and public health at the Edward J. Bloustein School of Planning and Public Policy at Rutgers University and also serves as lead internship coordinator for the experiential learning program. She teaches courses in leadership, health care marketing, and professional practice. Previously, she was the executive director of the New Jersey Department of Health's Commission on Cancer Research. Her research interests include research diffusion, health disparities, and emerging leadership theories.

ELIZABETH HOOVER, MA, PHD, is an associate professor of environmental science and policy management at the University of California, Berkeley. She publishes books and articles about environmental reproductive justice in Native American communities, the cultural impact of fish advisories on Native American communities, Native American food sovereignty and seed rematriation, and tribal citizen science. She received her BA from Williams College; MA from Brown University in anthropology and museum studies; and PhD from Brown University in anthropology, with a focus on environmental and medical anthropology as it applies to Native American communities responding to environmental contamination.

HEATHER HOWARD, JD, is a lecturer at Princeton University's School of Public and International Affairs. She has extensive federal and state government service, including as New Jersey's commissioner of health and senior services and the associate director of the White House domestic policy council in the administration of President Clinton, and at the U.S. Department of Justice. She received her BA from Duke University and her JD from New York University School of Law.

JACQUELINE HUNTERTON-ANDERSON BSN, BHS, RN-BC, received a doctor of nursing practice degree in psychiatric and mental health nursing from Rutgers University. Board-certified as a psychiatric and mental health registered nurse, she works in psychiatric emergency services as a behavioral health screener. During her undergraduate studies, she was a research assistant and served as president of the Bloomfield College Nursing Association and vice president of the New Jersey Student Nurses Association.

GRACE IBITAMUNO is an MD and PhD candidate at Rutgers University's Robert Wood Johnson Medical School and School of Public Health. She completed the Leadership Education in Neurodevelopmental Disabilities fellowship and is a maternal child health graduate fellow in New Jersey's Department of Health. She has published a novel on human trafficking and is a TEDx speaker on the topic of resilience. She lives in New Jersey with her husband and their son.

RAQUEL MAZON JEFFERS, MPH, MIA, is a senior program officer at the Nicholson Foundation, leading its work on telehealth, population health, and the intersection of health and early childhood. She has many years of experience in public health and health care. She previously worked at the New Jersey Department of Human Services, where she served in various capacities. Her final position in the department was deputy director of the Division of Mental Health and Addiction Services.

MARY E. O'DOWD, MPH, currently works in population health at Rutgers University. She led the New Jersey Department of Health as commissioner, after serving as its deputy commissioner and chief of staff. She has held positions in hospital finance at New York University Medical Center and in health policy at the New Jersey Hospital Association and the New Jersey General Assembly. She is a graduate of Douglass College and the Institute for Women's Leadership Scholars Program, and she earned her MPH from Columbia University. She has served on numerous governing and advisory boards including the Institute for Women's Leadership; University Hospital, in Newark, New Jersey; and Association of State and Territorial Health Officials. She lives in New Jersey with her husband and three sons.

ERICA REED, MA, works in the dean's office of the School of Graduate Studies at Rutgers University and is a part-time lecturer in the university's department of Women's and Gender Studies, where she is a PhD candidate. Her research focuses on motherhood studies, with an emphasis on maternal grief. She is a graduate of Susquehanna University, and earned her MA from Rutgers University in 2016.

DENISE V. RODGERS, MD, is vice chancellor for interprofessional education at Rutgers Biomedical and Health Sciences. She is also a professor in the Department of Family Medicine and Community

Health at Rutgers University's Robert Wood Johnson Medical School. Throughout her career she has held a number of administrative positions in academic health centers while also maintaining her commitment to serving poor, minority, and underserved families and communities.

ELIZABETH A. RYAN, JD, is a faculty member in the Edward J. Bloustein School of Planning and Public Policy at Rutgers University. She was the first woman president and CEO of the New Jersey Hospital Association. She served in the administration of Governor Jim Florio of New Jersey and the transition teams for President Bill Clinton and New Jersey Governors Jon Corzine and James McGreevey. She earned a JD from Seton Hall University and a BA with honors from Rutgers University.

CHRISTINA TAN, MD, MPH, FACP, is the state epidemiologist and assistant commissioner of the Division of Epidemiology, Environmental and Occupational Health at the New Jersey Department of Health. A Princeton University graduate, Tan earned her MD from Mount Sinai's School of Medicine and her MPH from Johns Hopkins University's Bloomberg School of Public Health. She completed an applied epidemiology fellowship with the Epidemic Intelligence Service of the Centers for Disease Control and Prevention and a residency in internal medicine and primary care at New York University Medical Center. Board-certified in internal medicine, she is an adjunct associate professor at the Rutgers School of Public Health.

DAWN THOMAS, MPP, serves as deputy director of communications at the New Jersey Department of Health. With more than twenty years of writing experience, she has written for leaders in both the legislative and executive branches of New Jersey's state government. She received her bachelor's degree and master's degree in public policy from Rutgers University. She lives in New Jersey with her husband, Dennis, and their dog, Jax.

MARY WACHTER, MS, RN, is director of state government affairs for Genentech, Inc. Her previous positions include chief strategy officer for a large, nonprofit visiting nurse association, chief of staff for the New Jersey Department of Health, deputy director for the New Jersey State Nurses Association, and bedside critical care nurse at Cooper University Hospital. She holds a BS in nursing from Rutgers University and a dual MS in health policy and community / public health nursing from University of Maryland. She lives with her daughter in the pinelands of Burlington County, New Jersey.

SUZANNE WILLARD, PHD, APNC, FAAN, is a clinical professor at the School of Nursing at Rutgers University. She has over thirty years of experience in providing care to people living with HIV/AIDS. Early in the epidemic she became keenly aware of the need for team-based care to support people and their families facing a terminal illness. She is grateful for nursing leaders like Florence Wald, who provided a path for her and her patients.

Index

Hughes, Marilyn, 132. *See also* Gaston, Marilyn Hughes

Hughes, Myron, 132

humidity, and food safety, 78, 81

Hurley Medical Center, 32, 33, 34

Hussein, Saddam, 24, 25

hydroelectric dams on Saint Lawrence River, 2, 3

hypertension, 141, 143

ice box, use of term, 79

ice cream vendors, food safety practices of, 70

ice refrigeration, 78–84

immunizations. *See* vaccines

Indigenous communities, xx, 1–22; birthing practices in, 1, 2, 12, 15; community-based participatory research in, xx, 5–15; empowerment of women in, 7, 15; health care disparities for, 136; Legacy Leader Fellowship Awards in, 13; Mohawk (*See* Mohawk Tribe)

Industrial Workers of the World (Wobblies), 89

infant mortality rate, 44; Apgar approach to reduction of, 117; in food safety issues, 69; in infants of Black mothers, 171; in obstetric anesthesia, xxii, 116, 117; racial disparities in, 111, 136; in sickle cell disease, 136; trends in, 110–111

infants. *See* children and infants

influenza virus pandemic (1918), 89

Informal Norms in Global Governance (Hein and Moon), 235

informal norms in global health system, 226, 230, 232–233, 235, 236–237, 238, 241

Institute for Women's Leadership, ix, xi, xiii

Institute of American Poultry, Pennington at, 84

institutional review board approval, 57; of lead exposure research, 32, 34

insulation: of ice refrigerators, 82, 83; of refrigerated railroad cars, 78

integrated delivery health systems, 209, 215, 221n1; Kaiser Permanente as, 209, 217, 220, 221n1

intellectual property rights, 232; in China, 231; Doha Declaration on, 230, 231, 242n18; on drugs, 229, 230, 231–232, 233, 235, 242n18; and informal norms, 233

interdisciplinary approach, xvii, 94; in birth defect prevention, 124; in hospice care, xxii, 98, 99, 100, 102, 103; of Lavizzo-Mourey, 178; in obstetrics, xxii, 116–117

Interdisciplinary Study of the Patient and His Family (1968–1971) (Wald), 99

International Anesthesia Research Society, 112

International Woman Suffrage Alliance, 49–50

internet as source of health information, 160

intestinal abnormalities in PCB exposure, 4

Inventors Hall of Fame, Pennington in, 84

Iran-Iraq War, 25

Iraq, Hanna family emigration from, 24, 25

Is My Baby All Right? (Apgar), xxix, 123–124

James, Stanley, 118

Jane Brody's Good Food Book (Brody), 149

Jane Brody's Nutrition Book (Brody), 149

Jayne, Horace, 67

Jim Crow laws, 211

Johnson, Lyndon B., 134, 191

Johnson, Robert Wood, 176

Johnson & Johnson COVID-19 vaccine, 240

Johnston-Willis Hospital, Tavenner at, 194

journalism: of Brody in NYT (*See New York Times* columns of Brody); gender roles in, 153–154

Jungle, The (Sinclair), 72, 156–157

Kaine, Tim, 196

Kaiser Permanente: as integrated delivery system, 209, 217, 220, 221n1; Williams-Brinkley at, xxvi, 209, 217–219

Kanonkwe Council, 14

Keith, H. J., 75

Keith Company eggs, safety of, 75–77

Kelly, Sharon Pratt, 142

Kennedy, Edward, 142

Kennedy School of Government, Moon attending, 228, 232, 233

KentuckyOne, Williams-Brinkley at, 216–217

Keohane, Nannerl O., viii

King v. Burwell, 192

King, Martin Luther, Jr., xxiv, 168, 171–172, 220

Kingsley, Margaret H., 82

Koh, Howard, xxv, 192

Kübler-Ross, Elisabeth, 96

LaChance, Jenny, 32, 34

Lauzon, Trudy, 8–9

Lavizzo-Mourey, Risa, xxiv–xxv, 167–189; awards and honorary doctorates of, 184; birth of, xix; childhood and family of, 168–171; in childhood obesity initiative, 177–179; and culture of health, 168, 181–184; education of, xxviii, 172–174; leadership of, 167, 168, 175, 176, 178, 179, 183; mentor of, xxviii; photo of, 166; at Robert Wood Johnson Foundation, xxiv–xxv, 167, 168, 175–184

leadership, vii–x, xii–xiii; of Apgar, 125; and career advancement of women, 213–214, 220; collaborative, 178; diversity in, 218; followship,

202; of Gaston, 134, 140; gender inequity in, 176–177; gender stereotypes in, 195; in global health system, 234, 241; of Hanna-Attisha, 36–37; of Lavizzo-Mourey, 167, 168, 175, 176, 178, 179, 183; of McCormick, 50–51; of Moon, 241; servant, xv, xx, xxiii, 37, 219; stewardship, 220, 238; of Tavenner, 194, 195, 196, 198–200, 202; of Wald, 95, 100, 102; of Williams-Brinkley, 214, 219–220

lead exposure: blood levels of lead in, 31, 32; as environmental injustice, 28, 37; in Flint, xx, 23, 27–37; impact of, 23, 27–28, 30, 31; from paint and dust, 31–32; prevention of, 23; symptoms of, 23, 27–28; in Washington, D.C., 29, 30–31

Leading the Way Award, Wald as recipient of, 101

Legacy Leader Fellowship Awards, 13

Lennon, John, 135

Let's Move! campaign, 178

Levine, Pete, 34

life expectancy in the United States, 181–182

Lincoln Heights Health Center, 134, 139

Lindsay, Dolores, 134

Linklater, Richard, 177

Lishinski, Karen, 32

Lorde, Audre, 167

Malone, Thomas E., 136

March of Dimes: Apgar at, xxii–xxiii, xxix, 120–124; polio vaccine work, 120

Massachusetts Institute of Technology, 34; McCormick at, 46, 48, 59; number of women attending, 46, 59

maternal and child health, vi, xxii, 12, 109, 125

maternal mortality rate, 119; decrease in transition to hospital births, 113; in obstetric anesthesia, xxii, 116,